The Dance and Opera Stage Manager's Toolkit

The Dance and Opera Stage Manager's Toolkit details unique perspectives and approaches to support stage managers beginning to navigate the fields of dance and opera stage management in live performance.

This book demystifies the genre-specific protocols and vocabularies for stage managers who might be unfamiliar with these fields and discusses common practices. Filled with valuable industry-tested tools, templates, and practical information, *The Dance and Opera Stage Manager's Toolkit* is designed to assist stage managers interested in pursuing these performance genres. The book also includes interviews and contributions from a range of professional stage managers working in dance and opera.

From the student stage manager studying in Theatrical Design and Production university programs to the experienced stage manager wanting to broaden their skill set, this book provides resources and advice for a successful transition into these worlds.

The Dance and Opera Stage Manager's Toolkit includes access to an online repository of resources and paperwork examples to help jumpstart the reader's journey into dance and opera stage management. To access these resources, visit www.routledge.com/9780367566579.

Susan Fenty Studham has been stage managing professionally in many genres of theatre for almost four decades. She has stage managed at major performing arts venues including on Broadway, at Lincoln Center, Carnegie Hall, and the Sydney Opera House. Sue began working with dance companies in New York City in 1986 and toured extensively before relocating to Australia, where she was resident stage manager with West Australian Ballet for ten years. During her four-year tenure as Head of the BFA Stage Management Program at DePaul University in Chicago, Sue created a curriculum that introduced students to the unique world of dance stage management. Sue holds a PhD from Edith Cowan University, Australia, and a BFA from Adelphi University, New York. She is a pioneer in doctoral studies in the field of stage management and a published author on topics that explore brave spaces, intimacy and violence protocols in performing arts, supporting language revitalization in performance, and stage managing intercultural theatre.

Michele Kay has been stage managing for over 30 years across all genres, musicals, plays, opera, and dance, in a variety of environments including New York, Chicago, and regionally across the US. She spent several years stage managing opera regionally, including two and a half years as the resident production stage manager at the Virginia Opera. She is an Associate Professor of Stage Management at the University of Cincinnati's College-Conservatory of Music (CCM) where she has translated her practical opera knowledge into a curriculum for BFA and MFA stage management students, many of whom have graduated to work at prestigious opera companies across the country. Michele holds a MS in Organizational Leadership and a BA in Theatre from Miami University of Ohio. She is a member of Actors Equity Association, American Guild of Musical Artists, Stage Managers' Association, and USITT. Most recently, Michele authored the essay "Already Calm, I'm the Stage Manager" for *Off Headset: Essays on Stage Management Work, Life, and Career* edited by Rafael Jean and Christopher Sadler (Routledge, 2022).

The Focal Press Toolkit Series

Regardless of your profession, whether you're a Stage Manager or Stagehand, The Focal Press Toolkit Series has you covered. With all the insider secrets, paperwork, and day-to-day details that you could ever need for your chosen profession or specialty, these books provide you with a one-stop-shop to ensure a smooth production process.

The Assistant Lighting Designer's Toolkit, 2nd edition
Anne E. McMills

The Projection Designer's Toolkit
Jeromy Hopgood

The Scenic Charge Artist's Toolkit
Tips, Templates, and Techniques for Planning and Running a Successful Paint Shop in the Theatre and Performing Arts
Jennifer Rose Ivey

The Costume Designer's Toolkit
The Process of Creating Effective Design
Holly Poe Durbin

The Literary Manager's Toolkit
A Practical Guide for the Theatre
Sue Healy

The Production Manager's Toolkit, 2nd edition
Successful Production Management in Theatre and Performing Arts
Cary Gillett and Jay Sheehan

The Voice Coach's Toolkit
Pamela Prather

The Dance and Opera Stage Manager's Toolkit
Protocols, Practical Considerations, and Templates
Susan Fenty Studham and Michele Kay

For more information about this series, please visit: https://www.routledge.com/The-Focal-Press-Toolkit-Series/book-series/TFPTS

The Dance and Opera Stage Manager's Toolkit

Protocols, Practical Considerations, and Templates

Susan Fenty Studham and Michele Kay

Routledge
Taylor & Francis Group

NEW YORK AND LONDON

Designed cover image: Stage Manager's calling desk *The Nutcracker*. Photo by Hugo Aguilar Lopez. With permission from West Australian Ballet.

First published 2025
by Routledge
605 Third Avenue, New York, NY 10158

and by Routledge
4 Park Square, Milton Park, Abingdon, Oxon, OX14 4RN

Routledge is an imprint of the Taylor & Francis Group, an informa business

© 2025 Susan Fenty Studham and Michele Kay

The right of Susan Fenty Studham and Michele Kay to be identified as authors of this work has been asserted in accordance with sections 77 and 78 of the Copyright, Designs and Patents Act 1988.

All rights reserved. No part of this book may be reprinted or reproduced or utilised in any form or by any electronic, mechanical, or other means, now known or hereafter invented, including photocopying and recording, or in any information storage or retrieval system, without permission in writing from the publishers.

Trademark notice: Product or corporate names may be trademarks or registered trademarks, and are used only for identification and explanation without intent to infringe.

Library of Congress Cataloging-in-Publication Data
Names: Fenty Studham, Susan, author. | Kay, Michele (Stage manager), author.
Title: The dance and opera stage manager's toolkit: protocols, practical considerations, and templates / Susan Fenty Studham and Michele Kay.
Description: New York: Routledge, 2025. |
Series: The Focal Press toolkit series | Includes index.
Identifiers: LCCN 2024018302 (print) | LCCN 2024018303 (ebook) |
ISBN 9780367566555 (hbk) | ISBN 9780367566579 (pbk) | ISBN 9781003098812 (ebk)
Subjects: LCSH: Stage management. | Theater–Production and direction. | Opera–Production and direction. | Theaters–Stage-setting and scenery.
Classification: LCC PN2085 .F36 2025 (print) | LCC PN2085 (ebook) | DDC 792.02/32–dc23/eng/20240710
LC record available at https://lccn.loc.gov/2024018302
LC ebook record available at https://lccn.loc.gov/2024018303

ISBN: 978-0-367-56655-5 (hbk)
ISBN: 978-0-367-56657-9 (pbk)
ISBN: 978-1-003-09881-2 (ebk)

DOI: 10.4324/9781003098812

Typeset in Times NR MT Std
by Deanta Global Publishing Services, Chennai, India

Access the Support Material: www.routledge.com/9780367566579

For those who went before us, those who shaped us,
Those who we learned from and collaborated with

For our parents and families, and ever-supporting partners

For those who will continue to evolve this field

Contents

Foreword	xiii
Preface	xv
Acknowledgments	xix
Online Resources	xxi

Chapter 1	An Introduction to Dance and Opera for Stage Managers	1
	Perspective	2
	A Very Brief History of Opera	2
	A Snapshot of the History of Dance	7
	Expectations of the Stage Manager	18
	Acknowledgments	19
	Notes	19
Chapter 2	Organizational Structures, Personnel, and Communication	21
	Organizational Structures	22
	Unions, Unions, Unions	29
	Communication	30
	Final Thoughts	32
	Note	32
Chapter 3	Pre-Production	33
	Meeting the Team	33
	Getting Started	35
	Building a Working Score	36
	Creating the Stage Manager's Score	40
	Opera-Specific Paperwork	42
	Dance-Specific Documents, Blocking, and Tasks	49
	Opera Blocking	58
	Preparing the Rehearsal Venue for the Company	60

	Opera Scheduling	65
	Final Thoughts	70
	Online Templates	70
	Note	70
Chapter 4	**Studio Rehearsals**	**71**
	Dance Rehearsals	71
	Opera Rehearsals	84
	Final Thoughts	93
	Notes	94
Chapter 5	**Technical Rehearsals**	**95**
	Opera Technical and Dress Rehearsals	95
	Dance Technical Rehearsals	116
	Variations to the Process	136
	Final Thoughts	136
Chapter 6	**Opening and Running the Show**	**137**
	Final Dress Rehearsal and Previews	137
	Preparing for the Opening	139
	Paperwork!	140
	Opening Night Schedule and Formalities	141
	Stage-Related Opening Night Protocols	142
	Maintaining the Show	144
	Tracking Information and Archiving the Production	146
	Show Stops	147
	Final Thoughts	151
Chapter 7	**Repertoire, Repertory Companies, Co-Productions, and Touring**	**153**
	Terminology	153
	Opera Repertoire	154
	Dance Repertoire	154
	Touring Dance	155
	Opera Co-Productions or Transfers	161
	Final Thoughts	162

Chapter 8	Specialist Shows, Unique Companies, and Changing Landscapes	167
	Isabel Martinez Rivera, Associate Director, Les Ballets Trockadero de Monte Carlo	167
	Nykol DeDreu, Stage Manager, Kinetic Light	169
	Nancy Pittelman, Stage Manager, Radio City Music Hall, 2005–2023	171
	Lillian Hannah U, Stage Manager, Bangarra Dance Theatre (Australia), 2018–2020	174
	Betsy Ayer, Stage Manager, Susan Marshall & Company	176
	Erin Joy Swank, Stage Manager, Freelance	179
Chapter 9	Employment in Dance and Opera	183
	Networking	183
	Resumes	184
	Cover Letters and Interviews	186
	Final Thoughts	187
Glossary		189
Appendices		195
Index		201

Foreword

As a lifelong fan of the arts and a career theatrical stage manager, the opera and dance worlds have not only intrigued me as a patron, but they have left me curious as a professional. With my focus being in theatre, I have always yearned for the chance to learn more about the inner workings of opera and dance. These are worlds steeped in tradition and great history. As a stage manager, it is imperative not only to know the nuts and bolts of management of these genres, it is also imperative to know and understand the specificity involved in these long-standing traditions. In their text, my colleagues and friends, Ms. Kay and Ms. Fenty, have provided us with this and so much more. Their book provides anyone with a working knowledge of stage management – from students to seasoned professionals – a plethora of information to add to their existing toolbox. It is excellent at drawing the similarities between not only opera, dance, and other performing arts genres, it also provides specific, on-point information about each discipline. It is a wonderful addition to any curriculum, program, and bookshelf. The stage management community has been longing for a text like this for so many years and at last it has arrived!

– Christy Ney, Stage Manager

Preface

SUE'S STORY

I didn't grow up with dance, I wasn't a kid who took dance classes or anything. I came up through the ranks of crew, a 'techie' who was offered a stage management position on a play in 1980. It wasn't until my third year at university in New York that I formally stage managed a dance show. The dance captured my imagination. I could see how the technical elements layered into the production helped convey the story. As a stage manager, I would be part of the delivery of that story by responding to the dancers, the dance, the music, the design, and the audience on a daily basis. By being focused and engaged in each moment, I would be able to determine the careful placement of each cue point, placing me within a team of storytellers.

Later that year, I stage managed the first of many *Nutcracker* tours in my life. In the mid-1980s, the companies I worked with were generally New York-based and toured the US, Asia, the Middle East, and Europe. How I perceived performance, dance, and what my role was within this world shifted with every production. It was a space that had fewer restrictions than traditional theatre, and a little less financial stability as well, but a great deal of adventure as we travelled the world. These early tours would shape my trajectory and personal evolution as a stage manager. Some of the main learnings were that performance can encompass many things and that there is more than one way to stage manage a show. I realized if I was open to possibilities my life would be enriched by these experiences.

In 2019, I attended the United States Institute for Theatre Technology (USITT) conference as a mentor for the SMMP: The Stage Management Mentor Project. It was held in Louisville, Kentucky, where I had 'cut my teeth' as a professional stage manager at Actors' Theatre of Louisville (ATL). As I wandered through the preview of the exhibition floor at the Convention Centre with fellow stage managers, we came to the Routledge book tables. I mentioned that there was no Dance Stage Manager's Toolkit book, to which author Jay Sheehan responded: "You should write one." That's how it started.

As dance stage managers, many of us didn't have formal training in the specific genre, we learned as we went, adapting our foundational stage management skills to fit the situation; experiential learning. Because of this, each of our processes developed in their own way. So, there are many approaches to stage managing dance, and a plethora of paperwork samples. In this book, I am sharing mine. I have also invited others to comment, share, and have a voice in this book.

When I spoke with Routledge's senior editor about the book, she was interested in combining it with opera. Serendipity led the way here, in Louisville. At ATL, way back in the early '90s, I met Michele Kay, who was an intern stage manager there. We share the same mentors, Debra Aquavella and Lori M. Doyle, and have quite similar training. After our early shows, I went back to New York City to continue in dance and new developments, touring extensively. Michele went to New York and Chicago, specializing in plays and musicals, and then eventually in opera. After decades, which included my relocation to Australia (later returning to the US to teach in Chicago), it was as if the stars aligned in 2019 that we were in Louisville together again for the USITT conference when this book project first developed. My most sincere thanks to Michele for joining me on this adventure. I can't imagine embarking on this path of writing, collaborating, debating, and tag-team editing across continents with anyone else.

MICHELE'S STORY

As Sue mentioned, I was an intern at Actors Theatre of Louisville and then returned a few years later where I reconnected with Sue launching a friendship that has spanned three decades and two continents. I continued stage managing traditional theatrical productions, plays and musicals, until several years later when I moved to Chicago and found myself at a membership meeting at Actors Equity Association. In a brief conversation with the front desk receptionist, I mentioned being new to Chicago and she said she wanted to introduce me to her friend 'Bula' who stage managed operas. Being new to town, I was willing to accept any professional introductions.

I worked with Bula that summer on two productions as an assistant stage manager. Other than cueing singers onstage, assistant stage managing wasn't all that different than what I had experienced in theatre until one rehearsal when I learned how different opera singers were from actors. We were rehearsing in a warehouse owned by a board member of the company. One day during rehearsal, a supernumerary knocked a florescent bulb out of a fixture with a spear or pole and rehearsal ground to a halt. That part was "normal," I cleaned up the mess, but that's where the "normal" stopped. Rehearsal didn't resume once the mess was cleaned-up. One of the lead performers left the room and refused to return. The stage manager and AGMA rep convened with the staging director, a discussion ensued, and it was decided that the singer would not be returning to rehearsal for three days due to the toxicity of the contents of the florescent bulb. At the time I was stunned; I could not imagine that happening in a theatre production. Now I realize how smart that singer was, and that they were protecting their very fragile instrument, their health and their voice.

After that summer, I didn't do another opera for several years. Then fate brought me to the tech table of a musical I was stage managing where the lighting designer leaned over and asked me if I did opera. I said, and this makes me chuckle now, "I do musicals; how different could they be." And with that, I stepped into the opera circuit for several years, eventually landing at the University of Cincinnati where I now teach stage management and mentor stage managers through opera, dance, musical theatre, and plays. I realize that when I teach stage management, I mostly frame everything through the lens of stage managing an opera with the caveat that to stage manage the other genres you cut back from the scale of an opera production. I had no idea that opera could be a part of my career. When I graduated from college it never occurred to me to add opera or dance to my skill set. Now, I couldn't imagine letting my own students graduate without having an opportunity in either or both genres.

I love the genre. I love its scale and its structure. I love the formality and the tradition. And I love that, like Shakespeare, modern opera directors take a lot of risks conceptualizing new productions of very old pieces. In 2019 I saw a production of *Romeo and Juliet* at the Cincinnati Opera. I found myself in tears as the young lovers came to their tragic demise. The staging and music were so beautiful they carried a story I've seen a dozen times over to a place that could still touch my heartstrings. That's opera.

When Sue asked me to join her as a co-author, I'd like to say that I jumped at the chance, but really, I was scared. Then she suggested that we start with Chapter 3: Pre-production, and it was like putting on my favorite sweater. I hope you come to love these art forms as we have and that our shared experience, along with Pro Tips and examples from friends and colleagues, gives you the confidence to try something that may seem scary to you as well. I'd like to thank Sue for inviting me along this journey, being extremely patient along the way, and nudging when necessary to get across the finish line.

Now we share with you the work of several years of writing and more than seven decades of industry credits between us. We hope that our experiences and musings guide you in your paths as you enter these performance genres. We look forward to seeing where you will take this industry, and how stage management and its processes will continue to evolve as you continue on this journey, responding to its ever-changing discussions and technology.

Figure 0.1 Author Photo: Michele Kay and Sue Fenty.
Source: Photo by Michele Kay.

Acknowledgments

Sue thanks her husband, Ian Studham, parents Rita and Ron Fenty, and extended family who have supported not only this book, but her whole unpredictable career path and traveling shenanigans.

Michele would like to thank her husband, Karl Siemsen, and their children, Karl and Parker, without whose support she would get nothing done.

Together we thank our teachers and mentors, our editors, and the many people who have inspired, contributed to, and previewed these pages – and the curious who will read them.

We gratefully acknowledge:

Lucia Accorsi	Ivan King AO
Deb Aquavella	Randy Klein
Betsy Ayer	Hugo Aguilar Lopez
Christine A. Binder	Sarah Lozoff
Daryl Brandwood	Craig Lord-Sole
Fiona Boundy	Jonathan W. Marshall
Rosie Burns Pavlik	David McAllister AC
Jon Buswell	Danielle Micich
Lawrie Cullen-Tait	Kyle J. Morrison
Phil R. Daniels	Samantha Murray
Nykol DeDreu	Christy Ney
Maria Fenty Denison	Megan Parker
Lori M. Doyle	Chrissie Parrott AO
John Flak	Nancy Pittelman
Kristina Fluty	Jenny Poh
Susan Giles	Jo Pollitt
Cary Gillett	Isabel Martinez Rivera
Laura E. Glover	Deborah Robertson
Connie Grubbs	Rowan Rozzi
Robin Guarino	Lorraine Sanders
Hannah Holthaus	Jay Sheehan
Sandra Kaufmann	Neil Sheriff

Karl Siemsen
Ian Studham
Erin Joy Swank
Angela Swift
Stacy Taylor
Amy C. Thompson
Molly Tipping
Shona Treadgold

Lillian Hannah U
Nancy Uffner
Stacey Walker
Shauna Weeks
Meagan Welsh
Evangeline Rose Whitlock
Bugs Bunny

Arts and Culture Trust of Western Australia

Dance Kaleidoscope

His Majesty's Theatre, Perth Australia

The Museum of Performing Arts, Perth Australia

West Australian Ballet

The student and alumni stage managers at the University of Cincinnati, College-Conservatory of Music (CCM)

The University of Cincinnati, College-Conservatory of Music Opera and Theatre Design and Production programs

United States Institute of Theatre Technology

Upstage Designs

USITT Stage Management Mentor Project

The production staff of the Virginia Opera from 2001–2003

The students, mentees, and colleagues who have explored dance stage management in workshops, 'Stage Management Variations,' and master classes in Australia, Indonesia, and the United States

Online Resources

We have included resources on Routledge.com, so be sure to check in for templates, samples, and interesting online links for further information.
URL: www.routledge.com/9780367566579.

CHAPTER 1

An Introduction to Dance and Opera for Stage Managers

Welcome stage managers! We are delighted that you are interested in stage management for dance and opera. There are many reasons for transitioning into these genres and a variety of ways to acquire the information needed to be successful. Not sure where to start? Well, you are not alone. Let's face it, every dance or opera stage manager out there once experienced their 'first time stage managing' these shows. They may not have been sure of what to expect, but they wanted to be part of these genres. Here, with this book, we hope to set you on your path to success in these fields. Within these chapters are tools that you will need in your toolkit to be well on your way to a fulfilling career in dance and opera stage management.

There is an old saying: you don't know what you don't know. Our goal is to introduce you to the differences between stage managing a play or musical and stage managing dance or opera so that you know what to expect and are not caught off-guard by these variations. In the past, it was not unusual to be hired as the stage manager in any one of these genres without prior management experience or training as so many stage managers either came to the position from being a performer in the genre or learned the ropes of the business on the job. However, in today's industry, if you are interviewing for the job, there will be a presumption that you do in fact know the ins and outs of these performing genres. With that in mind, we decided to put our ideas, experiences, and approaches on paper to give you an understanding of what the stage management role encompasses and prepare you for a discussion of company expectations as you step into this world of music and movement. No matter what your current situation or your reason for seeking this information, we are glad you are here! So, let's get started!

We have written this book to demystify stage management for dance and opera. In doing so, we'll share a brief history of the development of the genre with you to help you place your role within it. Then we move on to your collaborators, organizational structures, and unions before diving into the procedural chapters. We'll also look at terminology, operational processes, approaches to the rehearsal room, technical rehearsals, and so on! Once we've taken you through to closing the show, you will hear from industry professionals about variations to the processes we've

DOI: 10.4324/9781003098812-1

expanded on. They will also add tips throughout the book as we include: Pro Tips, Green Tips (environmentally friendly), and anecdotes throughout. The glossary at the back will help you navigate unfamiliar terms.

PERSPECTIVE

In the following chapters, we specifically look at histories, practices, and traditions that developed in Europe and the United States. For clarity, our perspective is grounded in our experiences and foundational training in North America, although we have worked throughout the world. As such, the data centers on a Western approach with a US emphasis but strives to be inclusive of other protocols. Therefore, you will hear from guest contributors, sharing documentation from regions that have similar approaches to performance management, including Australia and Europe. This book is placed at an intermediate level of stage management, which assumes the reader has basic foundational knowledge of stage management. The chapters share tools, terminology, and etiquette as an entry point to dance and opera. We offer ways to hone your skills and practice genre-specific styles of paperwork. We invite readers to explore these areas of live performance and engage in the work. Our intention is to create an awareness of not only how, but also why we approach the management of these genres in this way, and how some of the protocols developed.

Both dance and opera are steeped in tradition. The contemporary, Western approach that we share here derives from a European lineage. We will begin by sharing a brief overview of the specific history that leads to our current professional protocols, while also acknowledging there are many traditions (written and unwritten) for the telling of stories through both movement and song. One might speculate, as well, on the undocumented existence of stage managers in the early years of human existence, as Larry Fazio suggested in 2017, or the development of the artist organizer who prepared or assisted with reenacting a pivotal moment in history through drama, festivals, religious rites, ceremonies, or celebrations in the distant past.[1]

A VERY BRIEF HISTORY OF OPERA

What follows is a very brief, very broad overview of the history of Western opera as researched and told from a stage manager's perspective. We present this not as a comprehensive education in opera history, but rather to give context to some of the core components of opera that influence how we stage manage. As you move into the field of opera, you may discover that you are able to adapt your paperwork and rehearsal/performance practices quickly to the traditions expected in the genre, but what may surprise you is how knowledgeable everyone in the room is about the history of opera and how deeply that history influences what is happening in the rehearsal or performance now. The following history addresses many of the most significant twists, turns, key players, and standard opera repertory that you'll find on the season schedule of many US opera companies. As we'll discuss in Chapter 9:

Employment in Dance and Opera, before you walk into an interview, or start your prep work on a production, be sure to research the opera and its significance in the historical timeline.

Western opera began about four hundred years ago with recitative, speech declamation set to music as in *Dafne* (1598) by Jacopo Peri and Ottavio Rinuccini which was probably the first opera although only the libretto survives.[2] As such, Claudio Monteverdi's *Orfeo* (1607) is often recognized as being the earliest surviving Baroque opera. Operas from the Baroque period span from around 1600 to 1740 and regularly retold the stories of Greek and Roman mythology through music and dramatic text. These operas often have a small accompaniment of instrumentalists or sometimes only a harpsichord. The art form began at the favor of the wealthy and privileged classes, for example, Francesca Caccini's *La liberazione di Ruggiero dall'isola d'Alcina* (1625) was composed and performed for Prince Władyslaw of Poland's visit to Cosimo Il de'Medici's court during Carnival, the liturgical season between St. Michael's Feast and Lent when staged works were performed; however, by the late 1600s, opera began to spread in popularity across Italy.[3] Audiences began to prefer longer songs and showed a preference for voices from the higher range, particularly the male **castrato** singers, who sang at a higher tone of voice. At this time, we also saw the rise of the star performer, later to be coined the **diva**.[4]

Under the patronage of Ferdinando de'Medici, Baroque composer Alessandro Scarlatti rose in favor, and is later credited as transitioning the genre from Baroque to Classical.[5] His contributions to the discipline included the **Da capo aria**, which is an aria in three parts, ABA (or ABA1), with the first (A) and second parts (B) differing in theme or mood, and the third part (A1, sometimes called "A prime") returning to the first part, and largely improvised by the singer. The term "da capo" means "from the top" or "from the head," so the singer is going back to the beginning and repeating the top, but with some vocal ornamentation. Scarlatti is also credited for inventing the Italian overture, a three-movement orchestral piece which opened an opera.[6] These later led to the birth of the **sinfonia, a.k.a. symphony**, orchestral pieces scored with string sections, brass, woodwind, and percussion. This added complexity in the orchestration is why it is helpful for an opera stage manager to understand a musical score.

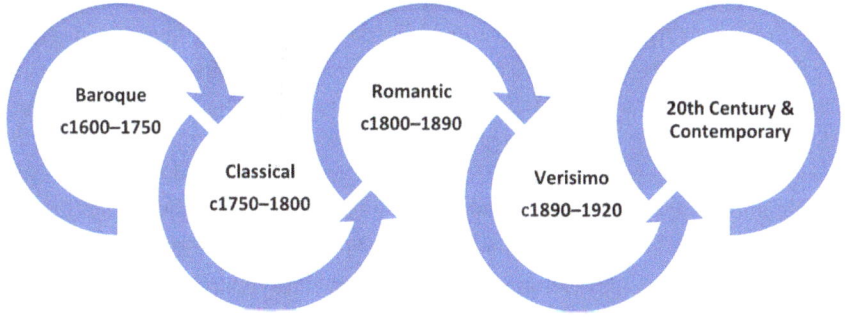

Figure 1.1 Opera timeline.

In France during the early part of the 18th century, compositions tended toward simple plot lines and composers preferred the use of **recitative** over arias, these being dialogue which was spoken over music, but not sung, per se. Later, in the mid-1700s as Classical opera emerged, we saw the rise of the Italian style **opera buffa**, or comic opera which was written for and depicted everyday people with everyday problems. This was also a response to **opera seria**, which was written for and depicted the lives of kings and nobility. Where the aristocracy identified with opera seria, opera buffa had a broader, more populist appeal. Another notable difference between the two is that opera seria, which tells tales of gods and ancient heroes, is often performed in three acts, whereas opera buffa is performed in two acts and uses lower register voices, excluding castrati.[7] One of the most important opera composers to emerge following the turn of the century was Gioacchino Rossini who dominated the Italian opera buffa style; his most famous opera, and one of few operas to be canonized in cartoon history by Warner Brothers' Bugs Bunny, was *Il Barbiere di Siviglia / The Barber of Seville* (1815). Rossini and his Italian contemporaries, Vincenzo Bellini (*Norma*) and Gaetano Donizetti (*Lucia di Lammermor* and *La fille du regiment*) represented the bel canto style of opera. **Bel canto**, meaning, "beautiful singing," demanded vocal dexterity, technique, and beauty. Soprano roles from bel canto operas can be recognized by very fast vocal embellishments in the higher register called **coloratura**.

Meanwhile, in Germany, Frederick Handel was leading the way in the German Baroque movement. In the early 1700s he spent several years in Italy at the invitation of Ferdinando de Medici and later moved to London in 1712, where he brought both the grand choral traditions of Germany along with Italian opera to the English nobility.[8] Handel started three opera companies including the Queen's Theatre at Haymarket and opera at Covent Garden Theatre which later became the Royal Opera House, home to The Royal Opera and The Royal Ballet. Many of his operas were written to be performed at Covent Garden including *Ariodante* and *Alcina*. Handel suffered a stroke and eventually turned toward choral works, including the **oratorio**, *Messiah* in 1742. In 1756, Wolfgang Amadeus Mozart was born in Austria, and by the age of twelve, he had composed his first opera among many other music pieces. In his short 35 years, Mozart made a profound impact on the art form, and on contemporary and future composers alike. He wrote prolifically in opera seria, *Idomeneo* (1781) and *La Clemenza di Tito* (1791), opera buffa, *Le Nozze di Figaro / The Marriage of Figaro* (1786) and *Cosi fan tutte* (1789), and the German **singspiel**, *Die Zauberflote / The Magic Flute* (1786). The singspiel interspersed spoken dialogue with song, much like a modern musical, eliminating the harpsichord for recitative.[9] For Mozart and others such as Joseph Bologne, Chevalier de Saint-George (*L'amant anonyme*, 1780), opera buffa provided a popular medium to extol the ideals of the Enlightenment, a rejection of the traditional and an embrace of rationalism through comic expression.[10] And again, it had great appeal to society's lower classes.

At the end of the 18th century, the French Revolution arrived followed by the rise of Romanticism with its strong emotions. The social impact of the French Revolution followed by the Napoleonic era gave rise to an era of epic opera in France with larger choruses and orchestras, and storylines that extolled military rhythms and patriotic sentiment.[11] Then, in the first half of the 19th century, we see the birth of "**grand opera**" at the Paris Opéra. These productions bore the markings of grand opera as we often think of it today with large casts and choruses, elaborate scenery and costumes, significant orchestras, and even the addition of ballet. These operas were fully sung without recitation, and often four or five acts long. The works of Giacomo Meyerbeer, the German-born composer, were particularly appealing to the French audiences' taste for grandeur and spectacle; however, although he greatly influenced the likes of Giuseppe Verdi and Richard Wagner, Meyerbeer's works fell out of favor following his dominance of the French opera scene for over 50 years due to their critique.[12] However, the latter half of the century was filled with passionate, lyric operas including Ambroise Thomas's *Mignon* (1866), Léo Delibes' *Lakmé* (1883), and George Bizet's incomparable *Carmen* (1875), as well as Jules Massenet's *Manon* (1884) and *Werther* (1892).

The Romantic period in Italy was dominated by Giuseppe Verdi whose abhorrence of absolute power and promotion of humanity can be seen throughout his work.[13] He wrote an allegory for the freedom from Italy's oppressors, France and Austria, through the tale of *Nabucco* (1841) and his name became synonymous with Italian unification. In his later period, he turned toward subject matter of psychological depth and human emotion as seen in *Rigoletto* (1851), *Il Trovatore* (1853), *La Traviata* (1853), *Un Ballo in Maschera* (1859), *Aida* (1871), *Otello* (1887), and *Falstaff* (1893) among others; operas which endure in opera house repertory today.[14] Verdi shifted Italian opera from bel canto to one that deeply links the drama to the music.[15]

Likewise, in Germany, we see this intrinsic link between the drama and the music in the works of Richard Wagner whose effective use of the **Leitmotiv**, the use of music to demonstrate the thoughts and feelings of the character, underscored the deep emotional states of his characters. While the early works of Wagner, including *Lohengrin* (1848) and *Tannhäuser* (1845) are linked to the bel canto style, the opera *Tristan and Isolde* (1859) introduces a discordant tonality, paving the way for modern opera.[16] In this opera, Wagner introduces what will come to be known as the **Tristan Chord**, a musical chord that creates tension through lack of resolution. At the time, the music of *Tristan and Isolde* was considered so controversial that after more than fifty rehearsals, the production was abandoned and did not premiere for another six years.[17] Of considerable fame is Wagner's epic, four-opera "Ring Cycle" *Der Ring des Nibelungen* (1848) which includes *Das Rheingold* (1869), *Die Walküre* (1870), *Siegfried* (1871), and *Götterdämmerung* (1874) and represented Wagner's view of opera as a complete artwork including music, acting, poetry, and scenery known as "**Gesamtkuntswerk**."[18] Incidentally, *Die Walküre* is also canonized by Bugs Bunny. The first full Ring Cycle premiered at the Bayreuth Festival in 1876, a full 26 years after the first opera of the cycle was written. Many opera houses have produced all or portions of the Ring Cycle; the Metropolitan Opera's (New York City) famed production under the direction of Robert Lepage boasts of a 40-ton structure of 24 identical sloping, rotating aluminum planks affectionately known as "The Machine." The set was designed by Carl Fillion and built at both the Met and Scène Éthique in Montreal.[19] There are several articles on the Machine on The Met's website; we recommend that you check them out.[20]

Before we move into modern opera, we'd be remiss not to introduce Giacomo Puccini, a veritable superstar of Italian opera of the post-Romantic period. This period with its tales that represented real-life was opera's step into Realism, or **verismo**.[21] At a young age, Puccini was lured to the Casa Ricordi publishing house where Giulio Ricordi matched Puccini with poets and dramatists as librettists to write the sentimental tales we've come to associate with this composer: *Manon Lescaut* (1893), *La Bohème* (1896), *Tosca* (1900), *Madame Butterfly* (1904), *La Fanciulla del West* (1910), *La Rondine* (1917), and three one-act operas, *Suor Angelica*, *Gianni Schicchi*, and *Il Tabarro* (1918).[22] *Turandot* was completed posthumously by Franco Alfano (1926).[23] The one-act operas are regularly paired with each other or Pietro Mascagni's *Cavalleria Rusticana* or Ruggero Leoncavallo's *Il Pagliacci* to make full opera productions. Fun fact: *La Bohème* provided the inspiration for Jonathan Larson's musical *Rent* (1996).

Although there are many more key 20th-century European composers: Dame Ethel Smyth (*The Wreckers*, 1902), Clause Debussy (*Pelléas et Mélisande*, 1902); Richard Strauss (*Salome*, 1905, *Elektra*, 1909, *Der Rosenkavalier*, 1911, and *Ariadne auf Naxos*, 1916); Czechoslovakian composer Leon Janácek (*Jeunfa*, 1916 and *The Cunning Little Vixen*, 1924); Igor Stravinsky (*The Rake's Progress*, 1951); the considerable canon of British composer, Benjamin Britten (*Peter Grimes*, 1945, *The Rape of Lucretia*, 1946, *Albert Herring*, 1947, *Billy Budd*, 1951, *Turn of the Screw*, 1954, and *A Midsummer Night's Dream*, 1960), and Scottish composer Thea Musgrave (*A Christmas Carol*, 1975, *Mary Queen of Scots*, 1977, and *Simon Bolivar*, 1992), we'd like to turn to the Americans for a glimpse at 20th-century opera.

What we see in the United States in the 20th century and today spans the gamut of styles and storytelling. American stories were being told through the medium of opera. Scott Joplin is known to have written two operas, (*A Guest of Honor*, 1903 and *Treemonisha*, 1911), though the first has been lost to time and the second was not fully produced until 1972. Joplin was posthumously awarded the Pulitzer Prize in 1976 for *Treemonisha*'s music.[24] In Aaron Copland's *The Tenderland* (1954) we see the story of a Midwest farm family's struggles during the 1930s. Likewise, George Gershwin's *Porgy and Bess* (1935) tells a tragic tale of the black inhabitants of Catfish Row, albeit from the white vantage of the composers and librettist. The opera has both been heralded as the first opera to feature a nearly all-black cast, paving the way for access to the stage for many black performers in the time of Jim Crow, and yet, also rightfully criticized for perpetuating negative stereotypes and tropes surrounding black communities, hypersexualized gender roles, and minstrelsy.[25] For a very interesting critical analysis of the opera, check out Naomi André's *Black Opera: History, Power, Engagement*.[26]

Contemporary of Gershwin, African American composer William Grant Still's opera *Troubled Island*, which premiered at the New York City Opera in 1949, was initially a collaboration with Langston Hughes, but the libretto was completed by Still's wife Verna Arvey. This piece is significant as it is widely recognized as the first grand opera to be composed and produced by an African American composer in a major opera company. And yet, although the opera received high acclaim from audiences, it is believed that the New York critics collaborated to pan the opera.[27]

Further tales of the American experience were drawn from popular novels and dramas: Libby Laron's *A Wrinkle in Time* (1962, 1991); Carlyle Floyd's *Of Mice and Men* (1969) and *The Great Gatsby* (1999); Mark Adamo's *Little Women* (1998); William Bolcom's *A View from the Bridge* (1999); Jack Heggie's *Dead Man Walking* (2000) and *Moby Dick* (2010), among many others; and Jennifer Higdon's *Cold Mountain* (2015).

By the mid-20th century, American opera took a minimalist turn with Philip Glass, whose works include *Einstein on the Beach* (1975), a collaboration with theatre producer Robert Wilson; *Satyagraha* (1979); *Akhnaten* (*1983*); *Galileo Galilei* (2002), a collaboration with theatre director Mary Zimmerman. Similarly, John Adams collaborated with theatrical director Peter Sellars on several operas including *Nixon in China* (1987), *The Death of Klinghoffer* (1991), *Dr. Atomic* (2005), and *Girl of the Golden West* (2017).

Opera continues to flourish in the United States with new works being commissioned by opera companies and through other incubators including Opera Fusion: New Works, a collaboration between the Cincinnati Opera and the University of Cincinnati's College-Conservatory of Music. Commissions have included *Doubt* (2013) by composer Douglas Cuomo and librettist John Patrick Shanley, *Champion* (2013) by composer Terence Blanchard and librettist Michael Christofer, *Fellow Travelers* (2013) by composer Gregory Spears and librettist Greg Pierce, *Morning Star* (2015) by composer Ricky Ian Gordon and librettist William Hoffman, and *Intimate Apparel* (2016) by Gordon and librettist Lynn Nottage, among many others. The turn in contemporary American opera can be seen in the content that reflects the human condition as we see it today. What we're also beginning to see is a shift toward the intentional support and promotion of operas written by people of color, women, and LGBTQ+ composers, and the diversification of offerings produced by major opera companies. We can only hope that in 100 years when writers reflect upon this time in opera history, they see a representational body of composers and stories.

APPLICATION TO THE OPERA STAGE MANAGER

We recognize that this may have been a lot of information to take in, but we felt it was crucial to share as your opera colleagues will know this inside and out. That does not mean you must have opera history memorized, but maybe when someone mentions a curious term or references something related to a specific period in opera, a little memory will fire about what you learned here. Hopefully, you found the brief tour through opera history fascinating and want to know more. Much has been written about the history of opera, including many fantastic online resources. The online companion to this book will have a place to jumpstart your research.

A SNAPSHOT OF THE HISTORY OF DANCE

Dance predates modern documentation. This book does not attempt to claim knowledge or expertise on the dances of the First Peoples around the world, nor to hazard a guess on how those dances were potentially managed. While there is research in this area, it does not fall within the scope of this book. Nor do we explore practices around the many cultural, regional, and specific national approaches to performance over the course of recorded history. If you are interested in finding out more about this, we encourage you to engage with the work of these communities and the current published research.

American dance history, for the purposes that have been shared, will begin in this context with the 17th century, Europe and the Americas, with a brief overview that only skims the surface of this rich and abundant art form. Dance could be experienced at this time in social contexts. As the colonies formed into a nation, the United States encapsulated a diverse mix of customs and traditions from many lands. The colonization of North America initially promoted European traditions, with a base in English and French techniques, which held fast for some time. Alongside this, the cultural dances of Africa, the United Kingdom, and France led to emergent styles including clog, tap, shuffle, variations of folk dances, and square dance. The form and styles crossed genres, borrowing or appropriating from the many cultural groups now living in the United States. As the country developed and matured, the trend eventually moved away from dances of the royal courts and became more innovative, celebrating the individual as well as the group performance and creating hybrid variations that may have been deemed less sophisticated by their contemporaries than the European models. Nevertheless, dance continued to gain momentum. Even as the prohibition and bans threatened to destroy the art form, it persisted, growing in popularity at a rapid pace. Ballroom waltz took the high ground in social dance, but the music halls brought burlesque and vaudeville shows. In the 1900s, ballroom styles that had their origins in waltzes gave way to speedier forms such as polka, Charleston, swing dance, quickstep, and country western influences. We also saw the popularity of Latin dances with complex rhythms including salsa, tango, rumba, and cha cha as contemporary movements continued to 'hit the floor' for the next century with popular dance. Ballet would become prominent in the US during the 20th century, nurtured by Russian dancers and choreographers. The lineage of dance is vast and complex, so here we concentrate on specific forms, companies and elements that directly informed the development of stage management in this genre.

BALLET

The roots of ballet began in the Italian Renaissance of the 15th century, where nobility were taught steps and performed as social entertainment. Dance as social entertainment continued for two centuries.

Louis XIV's infamous court dances in the 17th century were a notable influence on the trajectory of the genre. Bringing with it an elitism of wealth and social class. During this classical period, in 1661, the first ballet school was founded in Paris: Academie Royale de Danse, later to become the Paris Opéra Ballet, which sought to turn ballet into an art form. Under Jean-Baptiste Lully's direction, dancers transitioned from courtiers to professional artists. Court dances turned from proscribed moves to narratives with expressive movement. And the first **pointe shoe** was created, altering the history of ballet (see Figure 1.2). Professional companies formed in the 18th century throughout Europe.

The 19th century brought the Romantic era of ballet, where performances were marked by expressive emotion, and costumes no longer reflected upper-class fashion, but transformed into a vehicle to serve the technique of the dance with the introduction of the **Romantic tutu.** The focus during this period was on the female ballerina as she transformed into an ethereal being, lifted and moved around the stage. Popular ballets of this era such as *Giselle* (Adolphe Adam 1842), *Coppélia* (Léo Delibes, 1870), and the Tchaikovsky ballets *Swan Lake* (1876), *The Sleeping Beauty* (1889), and *The Nutcracker* (1892, a veritable rite of passage for most ballet stage managers), are still performed today.

It was also in this period that Raoul Auger Feuillet developed ***Choreographie***, a publication for dance execution and notation. This was specifically for the teaching of dance as a popular pastime ... not for anything such as stage management. However, it is the precursor of how we record blocking for a show as described later in this chapter.

It wasn't until the Ballet Russes led by Diaghilev in the early 20th century that male dancers stepped into their own light as soloists with performers such as Vaslav Nijinsky leading the way. This led into the Neoclassical era around 1920.

COSTUMES

During the Classical ballet era, the new form of dance, *ballet d'action* dispensed with the masks previously used in social dance halls, ballrooms, and courts, and drew on the dancer's emotions along with the movement and music to convey the story. The first dance pointe shoe was used in 1681. This iteration had a heel, which remained part of the design until the mid-18th century when heels were removed to allow more flexibility for leaps. Shoes were revolutionized following the French Revolution and the predecessor of the classical pointe shoe made its debut in "*La Sylphide*" at the Paris Opéra Ballet at the start of the Romantic era. The flat pointe shoe enabled the dancer to dance on the tips of their toes, giving an ethereal appearance of grace and weightlessness but were extremely uncomfortable. Russian ballerina Anna Pavlova is credited for altering her shoes to create a box for the toes, thus the age of modern pointe shoes commenced in the early 20th century with more support for the dancer's foot. Fun fact: this style shoe needs to be 'broken in' by the dancer and you will often see dancers beating their shoes to break them in and avoid discomfort.

While formal costumes relaxed somewhat as the Classical era began, they remained restrictive due to corsets, layering, and heavy materials. This did not shift for another century when Jean Georges Noverre demanded lightweight costumes for fluidity. This was the Romantic era and with it came the Romantic **tutu**, a multi-layered, bell-shaped skirt that created a soft, flowing look, and the skirt length shortened to above the ankle to show off **pointe work**. The tutu continued to shorten throughout this century and in 1870 we began to see the development of

Figure 1.2 Romantic and Classical tutus with pointe shoes (credits in appendices).
Source: Photograph by Sue Fenty.

the **classical tutu**: a short white skirt of layered tulle that flares out to reveal the leg and allow for jumps. The next major shift in costumes wouldn't be until the 20th century when we began to see leotards and tights onstage.

Figure 1.2 illustrates a romantic style tutu on the left, created for the Borovansky Ballet's *Coppélia* (1953), and prima ballerina Lucette Aldous' classical tutu for the role of Aurora in *The Sleeping Beauty* (Sydney Opera House, 1973) on the right. In front of the classical tutu is a pair of pointe shoes worn by Dame Margot Fonteyn (1974).

Figure 1.3 shows three original Ballet Russes Costumes worn in their Australian tour of *The Firebird Suite*.

Figure 1.3 Ballet Russes *The Firebird Suite* (1929) Costumes (credits in appendices).
Source: Photograph by Sue Fenty.

BALLET RUSSES

Serge Diaghilev's Ballet Russes (1909) was a renaissance in the dance world creating a new aesthetic as he incorporated an ensemble of refugee dancers in the corps de ballet, burgeoning stars in his principal company, up-and-coming composers, and avant-garde artist-designers. The company was defined in the early years by its grandeur and opulence. They toured extensively, influencing the arts internationally and producing shows that are still in repertoires today. Diaghilev was a visionary who firmly controlled all aspects of the production and had a gift of recognizing raw talent in artists.

Ballet Russes produced the first abstract, non-narrative ballet, heralding a new period in dance, the Neoclassical era. Nicolai Rimsky-Korsakov's *Scheherazade* and Igor Stravinsky's *The Firebird Suite* were also game-changers in the genre. Three *Firebird* costumes from the tour to Australia are pictured in Figure 1.3, courtesy of the Museum of Performing Arts, Perth, Australia. Diaghilev forged important collaborations with artists including Alexandre Benoit, Pablo Picasso, and Henri Matisse. Post-World War I the company embraced the new artistic innovations of cubism and futurism which Diaghilev brought to the stage in the historic ballet *Parade* and, finally, in the 1920s, after a period of near financial ruin, the elaborate costumes gave way to more simple designs.

The company moved to Monte Carlo in 1922, recruiting dancers from around the world. The shape of dancers transformed during this time as Diaghilev became selective about body type, employing slim, long-limbed female dancers. This set a precedent that continued until only recently when the norms began to give way to more diverse shapes. He continued to engage talented artists during this period, and in the final years of the company, gave the young choreographer George Balanchine an opportunity to create work. Balanchine would go on to become one of the most influential choreographers of the 20th century, creating the School of American Ballet in 1934 and co-founding the New York City Ballet in 1948.

Fun Fact: George Balanchine brought ballet to Hollywood with his choreography for MGM movies in the 1930s and 1940s. His work can be seen in *The Goldwyn Follies, On Your Toes, and Star Spangled Rhythm*, among others.

MODERN DANCE

Professional companies relinquished space for the pioneers of Modern Dance in America at the turn of the 20th century. Modern Dance pioneers rejected the rigidness of ballet and wanted to promote serious dance, not the frivolity of Vaudeville. Stepping out in the late 1890s was innovator Loie Fuller who experimented with stagecraft, fluidity in costumes, materials, and even lighting. She was an inventor and used gas lighting to create effects on her silk costumes. Fuller held the patent for the first mix of chemically created lighting gels, slides and luminescence salts used for lighting effects. "Two of her most famous works are *Fire Dance* and *Lily*, both stunning," according to Sandra Kaufmann, former Martha Graham Dance Company member and Director of Dance, Loyola University Chicago. Fuller's dance concentrated on arm movements incorporating sticks to extend their length and fabric effects.[28] Isadora Duncan, considered the mother of Modern Dance, was inspired by classical Greek art and philosophy. She was a teacher and a solo performer who rejected the ballet costumes and corsets in favor of simple tunics that revealed the shape of the movement. Her emphasis was on a more natural flow of movement. Ruth St Denis explored Eastern styles of movement, philosophy, and design and was known for her cultural dances internationally. With her partner Ted Shawn, she created the Denishawn school (Los Angeles) and company that nurtured the next wave of Modern Dance leaders, including Martha Graham, Mary Wigman, Lester Horton, Doris Humphrey, Charles Weidman, and Agnes DeMilles.

> *A group of early modernists including Anna Sokolow, Jane Dudley, Sophie Maslow, and Mary Anthony worked with the New Dance Group (New York City). Originally formed by students of Mary Wigman, it expanded to include dance artists from many different techniques seeking to make social change through art. Their motto 'Dance is a weapon in the class struggle' applied to their vast activities presenting new choreography, offering classes and creating programs about the needs for social reform.*[29]

By the end of World War II, dance artists did not have the same pressure of convincing an audience to take them seriously, so their dances could be abstract and experimental. The second wave of Modern Dance choreographers were trained by earlier visionaries. Merce Cunningham and Erick Hawkins emerged from the Graham company. Paul Taylor, Pearl Primus, Katherine Dunham, Hanya Holm, José Limón, and Twyla Tharp were all in this second generation. All of these artists became influential choreographers. Of this group, we recognize Katherine Dunham as having created the first African American modern dance company, and Alvin Ailey's company as one of the first to welcome dancers of diverse cultural backgrounds, while also celebrating the talents and heritage of African-American artists.

From a more production-based perspective, Hawkins is noteworthy for incorporating masks in his work. Merce Cunningham notably developed collaborations with composer John Cage and avant-garde artists, experimenting with chance, which informed his unique approach to performance. His philosophy of the autonomy of design, music, and dance elements in a piece was controversial. This theory, in concert with the use of chance, resulted in pieces that were performed in different combinations with no prior notice to the company. They would simply arrive at the venue and be given the combination to perform. As stage managers, we'd like you to let that sink in and see if you can imagine how these shows might have been managed.

> *One of Merce Cunningham's most influential strategies was his use of chance and randomness as a creative tool. Cunningham would often flip coins, roll dice, or even consult the I-Ching to guide the way he structured his choreography. This strategy, also favored by John Cage, challenged traditional notions of storytelling in dance. Cunningham described randomness as a way to free his imagination from its own clichés, counterbalancing his own rigorous creative process with unexpected moments of wonder.*[30]

CONTEMPORARY DANCE LIGHTING

The 20th century was an exciting time for dance companies in the US, as many newly formed, cutting-edge companies made their debut. Contemporary Dance emerged in the mid-century as a direct result of the pioneers of Modern Dance, and blends elements of other styles of dance. Its focus is on floor work rather than pointe, and can incorporate ballet, jazz, lyrical and modern. Alongside this was the innovation of technology. Here we will base the discussion more on how lighting changed the way dance was performed, lit, and also stage managed.

From the beginning of recorded dance history, lighting has been an element. However, lighting design for dance has had a much shorter history. We acknowledge the innovations of dancers like Loie Fuller who advanced work in this area. Adolphe Appia, a European scenographer, best known for scenic designs for Wagner's operas, developed theories on mise-en-scene, three-dimensional use of space, and lighting theories of color, the interplay of light and shadow, intensity, and distribution (focus) of light. An innovator, his chief contribution to theatre was "the creation of physical space through lighting."[31] Stanley McCandless was considered the father of American lighting design in the 20th century. He began as a student of architecture and developed house lights for Radio City Music Hall in the 1930s that used ellipsoidal reflectors. These new lighting units were the predecessors for the ellipsoidal spotlights used in most theatres in the US for the rest of the 20th century. His theories included angled overhead lights at equal distances with cool gel in one and warm in the other to create a more naturalistic effect. Finally, we must also mention Jean Rosenthal who, born in 1912, was a pioneer in theatrical lighting. A lighting designer for Martha Graham in 1929, Rosenthal argued that lighting design played an integral role in production in its own rite. Prior to this, it was handled by the scenic designer in association with a stage electrician. Rosenthal recounts in her book *The Magic of Light* (1972) "Dancers live in light as fish live in water."[32] This one sentence might help paint a picture of how lights and bodies might interplay. We recognize this particularly as the stage manager has historically been responsible for lighting the dance when a designer was not touring.

> *Early in my career, touring as a stage manager with dance companies in the 1980s and '90s meant lighting the show (or re-lighting if you were fortunate to work directly with the designer on the original performance). Dance lighting directly informed our work.*
>
> – Sue Fenty

If you are stage managing dance, you must understand the interplay of the lights. There are still companies that require the stage manager or production manager to recreate the light, whether this is due to size of the company or budget, or a myriad of other factors, which we discuss further in Chapter 7: Repertoire, Repertory Companies, Co-productions, and Touring.

Side lighting, or booms, changed not only what the dancers' bodies looked like onstage, but how we organized and managed the backstage areas. The stage manager's cues, presets, and running lists would now include changing gels during a performance and monitoring safety around the physicality of lighting boom positions and cables. With the development of sidelights in design, we saw fewer front spots, depending on the repertoire. A dance lighting plot generally includes an overhead rig of high sidelights, backlight, and top light. Front of house lighting and torm positions are also used, but it is arguably the sidelights that are the hinge pin to the design. This is because sidelight sculpts the dancers' bodies, giving them more dimension and, in ballet, ensures the legs are lit beneath the dancers' tutus. Figure 1.4 illustrates a typical dance lighting boom focus. Figure 1.5 shows lighting designer Christine A. Binder's interpretation of how sidelight illuminates a dancer's body in her pencil drawing: *Dancer in sidelight*. Scenery is often minimal in contemporary dance, using cycloramas or an RP screen, a black curtain or backcloths, plus legs and borders. Each wing that the dancers enter from will generally contain a boom position. While followspots are still in use, particularly in story ballet, they are used less in contemporary dance.

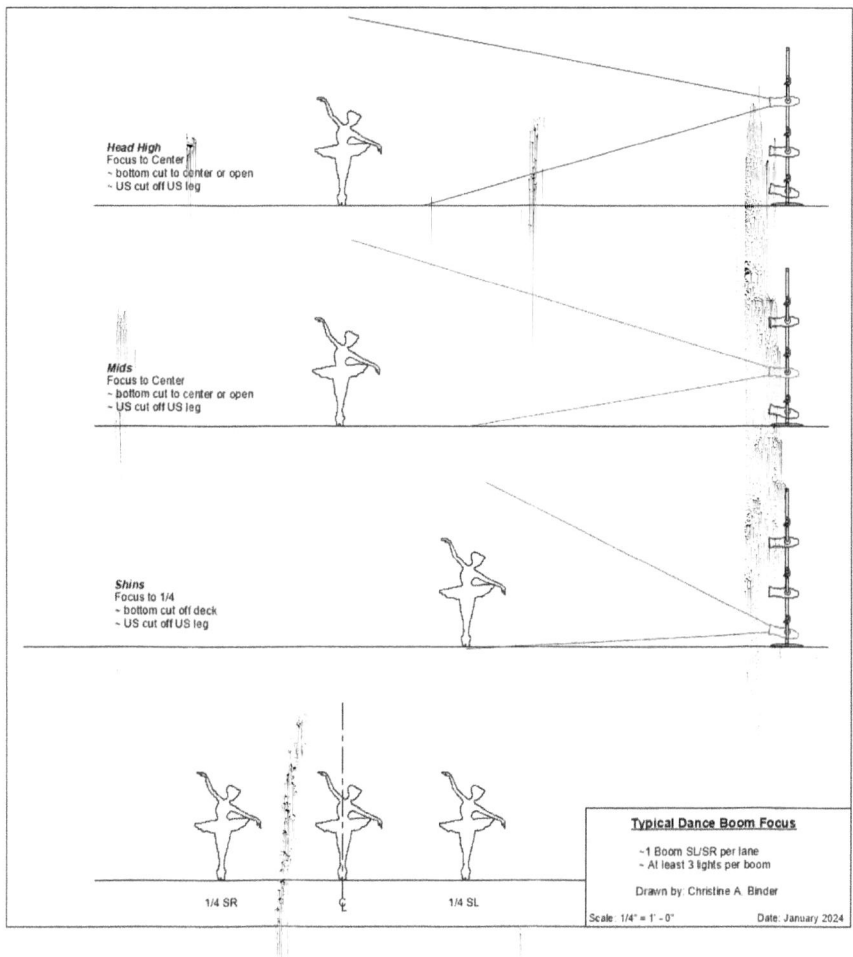

Figure 1.4 Typical Dance Boom Focus.
Source: Image created by Christine A. Binder.

Other dance lighting designers you might want to access for historical background include Thomas R. Skelton, Nicola Cernovitch, Jennifer Tipton, James F. Ingalls, Natasha Katz, and Howell Binkley.

NOTATION

The notion of recording a written record of a piece: notating, scripting, or writing dance movement as it occurs in time and space of the work, could be considered an aspect of choreography, but is generally called dance notation or choreology. When referring to the two specific codified methods commonly used to record movement, we use choreology as developed by Laban or Benesh. Labanotation or Kinctography Laban was developed by Rudolf Laban in 1920 and first published in 1928. Based on descriptions of movement through spatial models and concepts, the Laban method considers direction, weight, speed, and flow. Joan and Rudolf

Figure 1.5 *Dancer in sidelight.*
Source: Image created by Christine A. Binder.

Benesh created the Benesh system of choreology in the 1940s. This notation system documents the body within space, using symbols on a music staff. Benesh invented choreology as a non-verbal description of movements that can be used to accurately reproduce a dance or ballet. These systems will be explored further in Chapter 4: Studio Rehearsals.

The recording of movement as a tool for stage management is referred to as blocking notation or dance blocking, which is interpreted from a production perspective. This can incorporate movement, timings, gestures, technical specifics, and design elements.

The earliest samples of Western notation attempt to document courtly social dance, according to Mark Franko. Known as Renaissance tablature, letters, representing steps, were placed on a musical staff to show timing with the music. The designated alphabet symbol for the step referenced the name of the step, for example R was used for *révérence*.[33] This style of shorthand bears a commonality with current stage management notation methods.

The earliest published document was Michel de Toulouse's dance manual, *L'art et instruction* 20 *de bien dancer*, in the 15th century. In 1700, Raoul Auger Feuillet first published *Chorégraphie, ou l'art de d'écrire la danse*. In the pages of these booklets are samples of birds-eye view blocking, similar to modern methods of recording patterns of dance blocking using blocking squares. The purpose of these early documents was for students to learn the specific dance steps. It is unlikely that the notations were employed in ways that were in line with what we currently call stage management.

STAGE MANAGING DANCE

Here we take a moment to consider the stage manager within the contemporary dance world from the mid-20th century. With the proliferation of dance pieces designed to tour, and companies making their living moving from place to place, many dance companies employed a hybrid technical position to accompany them. Either the stage manager or a lighting designer would recreate the lighting with either a touring lighting package, or, in smaller companies, using whatever lights the venue had. The designer/stage manager would tour with the gels, and sometimes gel frames, and gobos. They would call all cues and assist the company as pre-determined in their contract or verbal agreement. This individual would attend minimal rehearsals after the piece had been choreographed, or in the last week before the company went on the road. Cues were written out or created on a typewriter until the late 20th century, when access to computers and printers became more common. While it was possible to tour with an electric typewriter in the later part of the century, many did not as it was cumbersome. Therefore, touring involved folders with either handwritten pages, graph paper, or a pre-typed list of cues and could be adapted 'on the road' with a pencil. Alongside the cues, the stage manager would notate pertinent blocking in relation to cues, either in longhand or shorthand diagrams. Few were versed in the choreologist methods listed previously, as this system was based on specific dance/body movements and gestures, it was often left to the ballet team of choreographers and directors. Show reports were either typed at the venue or handwritten in a pre-printed template, if required. Rehearsal reports were not commonly part of the documentation system at all. The stage manager's toolkit was stocked with pencils, erasers, sharpeners, tape, a splicing **block and blade** to repair reel-to-reel tape, and stopwatches. For dance, a stopwatch (or two) was a necessity.

Responsibility for sound recordings was commonly in the stage manager's purview as well. While the stage manager may not have been responsible for content, they were oftentimes responsible for booking the recording studio, transporting the recordings for shows, and potentially running the audio deck. Historically in this period, music was recorded on reel-to-reel tape, with **leaders** placed internally to separate and designate cues.

Fun fact: Management of reel-to-reel audio media was an important stage management job, particularly in dance touring contracts.

1. At the end of a season, the reel-to-reel tapes required reversing the direction they were wound on the reel to preserve the magnetic imprint of the tape. The danger was that if this didn't happen the recording could 'print through' from layer to layer damaging the soundtrack.
2. If traveling through airports was part of your tour path, the stage manager needed to ensure that security metal detectors (or any source of electromagnetic fields) did not come into contact with the tapes. This was something to take seriously as few touring stage managers would risk arriving internationally with audio show reels that had been erased in transit!

As the stage manager developed into an integral role in dance in many companies, they truly had to be a jack of all trades ready to jump in and help with the set-up, care for the dancers, assist the choreographers with any technical aspects of the show and, in some cases, pull the curtain, lay the floor, cue the lights, and run the sound. In our personal experiences, wardrobe did not fall into these contracts as they could often be handled by dancers.

While responsibilities may have shifted in the intervening years, the size and funding of each company may play a role in what your job duties are. So set your assumptions aside and keep an open mind to how the role of a stage manager might be reframed in different phases of production. You may find a great deal of value in adapting to dance genre-specific requirements!

EXPECTATIONS OF THE STAGE MANAGER

We wanted to begin this journey with a look at the past to establish a foundation for the work ahead. Both dance and opera are steeped in history and tradition, and yet, they are both evolving reflections of the times. The stage manager is a part of that history and tradition, evolving with the times as well. Whether we began as performers who stepped off the stage because someone was needed to open a curtain or were bystanders who jumped in to use our organizational abilities to help mount a complex production, we've offered our skills throughout the history of both genres as they made their impression upon the stage. For the stage manager, where dance and opera differ from traditional theatre, the stage manager is seen primarily as a member of the production team rather than the creative team. In a rehearsal for a play, the stage manager may be asked for their artistic opinion; however, that is not likely to happen in an opera rehearsal, and as you'll learn in dance, the stage manager is not typically involved in the early rehearsal period. In both genres, you'll be expected to conduct yourself in the rehearsal hall as you would in a theatrical rehearsal in terms of communicating and documenting production needs, but that's where your assumptions come to an end. You will work with a new team of artists, creatives, and supporting roles throughout the pre-production, rehearsal, and performance periods. Enjoy this new set of colleagues who are all there to ensure that you're putting up a successful production. The chapters that follow will introduce you to these colleagues, followed by practical instruction on how to navigate these new waters.

ACKNOWLEDGMENTS

The authors wish to acknowledge and thank the following experts, historians, and specialists for their advice on this chapter: Christine A. Binder, Susan Giles, Sandra Kaufmann, Ivan King, Jonathan W. Marshall, Megan Parker, Deborah Robertson, and Angela Swift.

NOTES

1 Fazio, L. (2017). *Stage Manager: The Professional Experience Refreshed*. New York: Routledge.
2 Swift, Angela. Associate Professor-Educator of Musicology, University of Cincinnati, College-Conservatory of Music. Personal email communication, November 9, 2023.
3 Ibid.
4 Grout, D. & Williams, H. (2003). *A Short History of Opera*. New York and Chichester, West Sussex: Columbia University Press. https://doi-org.uc.idm.oclc.org/10.7312/grou11958.
5 Ibid.
6 Ibid.
7 Ibid.
8 Ibid.
9 Ibid.
10 Fisher, B. D. (2003). *A History of Opera: Milestones and Metamorphoses*. United States: Opera Journeys Publishing.
11 Ibid.
12 Ibid.
13 Ibid.
14 Ibid.
15 Ibid.
16 Ibid.
17 Ibid.
18 Ibid.
19 Park, Elena. The Ring Transformed. https://www.metopera.org/user-information/nightly-met-opera-streams/articles/the-ring-transformed/.
20 There are several articles on the Machine on The Met's website https://www.metopera.org/discover/articles/rise-of-the-machine/
21 Fisher, B. D. (2003). *A History of Opera: Milestones and Metamorphoses*. United States: Opera Journeys Publishing.
22 Ibid.

23 Ibid.

24 Wikipedia contributors. Treemonisha. Wikipedia, The Free Encyclopedia. Revised November 25, 2023. https://en.wikipedia.org/w/index.php?title=Treemonisha&oldid=1186808184.

25 André, N. (2018). *Black Opera: History, Power, Engagement*. Illinois: University of Illinois Press.

26 Ibid.

27 Edgar, H. "Discriminating Ears: Critical Receptions of Blackness in the Music of George Gershwin and William Grant Still." *Nota Bene: Canadian Undergraduate Journal of Musicology*, 11(1) (2018). https://doi-org.uc.idm.oclc.org/10.5206/notabene.v11i1.6618.

28 Kaufmann, Sandra. Former Martha Graham Dance Company member and Director of Dance, Loyola University Chicago. Personal email communication, July 27, 2023.

29 Ibid.

30 Merce Cunningham Trust. https://www.mercecunningham.org/about/merce-cunningham/#:~:text=Shelley%20Eshkar%201997-,The%20Collaborator,mood%2C%20and%20structure%20of%20music.

31 Anderson, R. (2017). "The Appian Way." *AA files*, 75 (2017), 163–182.

32 Rosenthal, J. & Wertenbaker, L. (1972). *The Magic of Light*. New York: Theatre Arts Books.

33 Franko, M. "Writing for the Body: Notation, Reconstruction, and Reinvention in Dance." *Common Knowledge* (April 2011) https://doi-org.uc.idm.oclc.org/10.1215/0961754X-1188004.

CHAPTER 2

Organizational Structures, Personnel, and Communication

Most performing arts companies have a similar operational structure. There is a board of directors that provides high-level oversight of the organization, then there are a variety of administrative, production, and creative personnel who run various aspects of the daily operations. These include artistic directors, executive directors, development, marketing, facility operations, etc. in administration; scenic, props, costumes, wigs/makeup, lighting, sound, stage management and media, etc. in production; and directors, choreographers, conductors, designers, musicians, and performers in creative. We placed stage management organizationally in the production category, but in terms of functionality, stage management plays a much more critical role as a hub of communication among many if not most areas of the organization.

In the following chapter we'll discuss some organizational differences you might find in dance and opera companies. Most of these differences will be found in the production and creative subsets of the organization. However, we'd like to note that not all companies are structured the same. Size, artistic mission, and historical practices will have a significant impact on organizational structure. We advise all stage managers to never assume one company will function the way the last company you worked with functioned. Throughout this book we will stress the importance of asking how your current employer does things so that you can align expectations to set yourself up for the best way to serve the production and the organization. Even in the same company, if there has been a major turnover in administrative leadership, the way the organization functions may also shift. It is best to remain flexible and adaptable to new ways and ideas. Additionally, we'll introduce several theatrical unions that function outside of the organization but have a significant bearing on the practical operation of production. Finally, tied to both your colleagues within the organizational structure and external influences, we'll discuss communication which is key to the stage manager's success in any field.

DOI: 10.4324/9781003098812-2

ORGANIZATIONAL STRUCTURES

The core of the organizational structure in both opera and dance is similar to what one may find in a theatre. The size and funding of the company will determine the number of roles on staff; however, here we will provide a general list of positions you may encounter in a ballet and/or opera company. Note that the terminology may change regionally or from company to company. As noted at the beginning of this chapter, there are administrative, production, and creative teams. Administration oversees the governance of the organization, conducts all business, and provides the artistic mission of the company. At the helm of many opera companies, you may find a staging director or conductor, whereas in a dance company, you are likely to find a choreographer. This is not an absolute, but a general observation. In production, you will find many familiar personnel, with exceptions in both genres in the music department and in ballet wardrobe, where you will find larger teams to create specialist items such as tutus or headpieces, and the addition of a shoe/footwear coordinator. There also may be a specialist managing the dance floor, and an array of medical specialists in attendance to support physical and mental health. Sometimes we'll see a change in terminology from what we're used to in theatre. We'll note those exceptions as well. The biggest difference, of course, will be seen on the creative front and in the performers. Let's begin in the rehearsal hall.

THE CREATIVE TEAM

An opera is a story told through music. The orchestra and the singers make the musical composition through which the story is told. As such, the conductor plays a critical role in bringing these two often large groups together into a beautiful blend for the ears. Out of respect, the conductor is almost always referred to as the **maestro/maestra**. However, in a dance company you are more likely to use the term **principal conductor** or **music director**. You do not typically refer to the conductor in a dance company as the maestro; however, if in doubt, ask them how they'd like to be referred to, or it may appear in their contract.

> On many opening nights, I would introduce my husband to the maestro as 'Maestro,' to which my husband said, 'You never tell me their name,' I replied, 'I don't need to know it, they're the Maestro.'
>
> – Michele Kay

The **staging director**, much like a director in a theatrical production, is "an individual engaged to create and direct the staging for productions according to the design concept as agreed by the EMPLOYER."[1] Although the staging director is the artistic visionary for the production and hence a key decision maker, in opera, their decisions may be superseded by the conductor. When there is a controversy between the staging and the aural composition, the aural composition may take precedence. This is very different from the relationship you'd find in musical theatre and one that can surprise even a seasoned stage manager. An example of this may be seen in staging if the director wants a performer to face upstage while they are singing. If the performer loses visual contact with the conductor, they may ask the staging to be changed so that the singer can maintain that visual contact, or so that their voice plays out to the audience and not upstage.

> As a stage manager, you should make note of when singers are facing upstage or offstage so your team can track video monitors that broadcast the conductor to maintain that visual contact.

The same does not hold true in dance where the **choreographer** sits at the top of the artistic decision-making hierarchy. The work is the choreographer's vision, and most decisions will be led by the choreographer. Dance takes many forms, from new works to story ballets, so the level of collaboration with the music director and other members of the creative team can vary greatly. This would hold true for opera as well, especially when devising a conceptual work. In both opera and dance, the staging director and choreographer may also be the head of the organization, such as the artistic director, or they may be a guest to the company. When working with a guest your role as stage manager will be key to helping them perform at their best for the company. Remember, as a guest, they will want to put their best foot forward in order to be hired again. The stage manager can play a crucial role in ensuring the success of the head of the creative team. Again, we'd like to stress that not all organizations function the same, and not all organizations' missions are the same. The more adventurous the mission, the more likely the roles are to be blurred or less defined on the creative team.

Stage directors and choreographers will work with the design team in a predictable fashion throughout the design process, though technical rehearsals will run a bit differently from what is typically encountered in a theatrical production. That will be discussed in Chapter 5: Technical Rehearsals.

Inside the rehearsal hall you will find many personnel who will support the process. In a dance company the **rehearsal director**/ballet master or mistress will run the studio and work closely with the choreographic team, coaching dancers, and maintaining the integrity of the dance work. They are also responsible for creating cast lists and schedules and rehearsing alternate casts and replacements. Since many companies are transitioning from the title ballet master or mistress, we will refer to this position as rehearsal director throughout this book. You may also have a **choreologist** whose primary job is to record dance moves or teach a ballet from recorded choreology notes. Additional ballet staff may include dance coaches and guest teachers for company classes.

Next, you'll find the **repetiteur** who will run through sections of dance or music with the performers. A repetiteur may be found in either genre. As we'll discuss later, opera singers must come to the first rehearsal with their music memorized; however, many opera companies employ **vocal coaches** to work with the singers as needed. You may also find music or vocal coaches in the room for young artist program singers, covers, or chorus. For these performers there will also be a **chorus director**, formerly titled chorus master, though that title has fallen out of favor in many companies. The chorus director is responsible for teaching the chorus their music. Unlike the principal singers, the chorus is taught their music during music rehearsals. In an opera rehearsal, there may also be an **assistant staging director** who will assist the director. Some duties may include tasks such as running scenes with the chorus, directing a scene, or taking notes. The assistant stage director is usually responsible for keeping the official record of the staging. In larger opera companies, the assistant director may stand in for the director to remount a production from the repertory, as discussed in Chapter 7: Repertoire, Repertory Companies, Co-productions, and Touring. As you'll see later when we discuss unions, the staging director, the assistant staging director, and the stage management team are all members of the American Guild of Musical Artists (AGMA), the union governing opera and dance in the United States. In larger opera houses, the assistant staging director may run the rehearsal, e.g. scheduling and updating paperwork, in lieu of a stage manager who will be more involved once the show moves to technical rehearsals and performances. In addition to the assistant staging director and stage management team, there may be a **super captain** employed by the company. This person typically falls outside of the union agreements and oversees the supernumeraries (described later). They may track hours and assist with reviewing staging with the supers.

As mentioned earlier, the music staff are critical members of the creative team. At the helm is the conductor who will work very closely with the choreographer to set **tempi**. There is also often an **assistant conductor** who will usually conduct staging rehearsals when the conductor is not present. They may also conduct offstage chorus or banda, and some performances as well as cover rehearsals. There will also be a **rehearsal pianist** for all opera rehearsals, and sometimes there will be multiple pianists to cover all the rehearsals. The stage manager may be asked to track the rehearsal pianists' hours and submit those to Human Resources or company management for tracking purposes. In a dance rehearsal, you may have a rehearsal pianist or you may be rehearsing using pre-recorded tracks. Dance company classes often use pianists as well, however, this may not be the same person as the rehearsal pianist. There will be more discussion on this in Chapter 4: Studio Rehearsals. Rounding out the music staff and depending on the size of the company, you may have a **music librarian**. They are responsible for coordinating the music parts for the orchestra. They will also store the music if it is owned by the organization. If the company has a music librarian, this may be where the stage manager obtains their score or cuts. There may also be an on-staff **piano technician** who will care for and tune the pianos and harpsichords that are used in rehearsal and performance. If the company does not have a staff piano technician, they will surely have a relationship with a local technician.

THE PERFORMERS (MUSICIANS, DANCERS, AND SINGERS)

In the United States, most sizable dance and opera companies will employ musicians for the orchestra who belong to the United Federation of Musicians union. Among the union members, you'll find the **union steward** who is responsible for monitoring compliance with the rules from the collectively bargained agreement between the organization and the union, as well as members' attendance, hours, and temperature/humidity in the orchestra pit. The stage manager must introduce themselves to the steward who is usually a member of the seated orchestra to coordinate technical rehearsal and performance protocol. In larger companies there may also be an **orchestra manager** who is responsible for ensuring the comfort of the orchestra, including coordinating the orchestra set up with the local props crew. Within the orchestral structure, they may be responsible for taking attendance, setting scores on stands, adjusting instrument configurations in studio rehearsals, organizing transport for instruments to the venue, and so on. Finally, once you are in performance, the stage manager must introduce themselves to the **concert master** or first chair violin as they will be responsible for tuning the orchestra prior to each performance and each act within the performance.

> Check with the Director of Production to see who is responsible for setting up the orchestra. In our experience, the properties department often does this, placing chairs and music stands for each instrument as dictated by the conductor's pit plot.

Next, let's look at the performers. We'll discuss dance and opera separately in this section.

OPERA CASTING

An opera singer will prepare several roles that are within their vocal range with their personal vocal coach for their **repertoire**. They can then market themselves as knowing that role for casting. The performer will continue to develop the character and their personal style of singing the role the more often they are cast. These roles become the performer's repertoire. Repertoire fit within the vocal ranges of the performer. Vocal ranges are bass and baritone, tenor, mezzo-soprano, and soprano. Each of these ranges tends to come with a type of character and are broken down into descriptives for each vocal range. Bass/baritone singers carry the bottom, the buttery low notes. There are **bass** (Leporello in *Don Giovanni*, or Sarastro in *The Magic Flute*), **bass-baritone** (Wotan in *The Ring Cycle* or The Dutchman in *The Flying Dutchman*), **dramatic baritone** (Scarpia in *Tosca* and Rigoletto in *Rigoletto*), and **lyric baritones** (The Count in *The Marriage of Figaro* or Figaro in *The Barber of Seville*). Moving up the scale we get the tenors or the high end of the lower register. Here we have the heroic Wagnerian **heldentenors** (Siegfried in *The Ring Cycle* or Tristan in *Tristan and Isolde*), the powerfully voiced **dramatic tenors** (Cavaradossi in *Tosca* or Pagliacci in *Pagliacci*), the romantic, leads, the **lyric tenors** (Rodolfo in *La Bohème* and Alfredo in *La Traviata*), and finally the fast-moving **coloratura tenors** or Rossini tenors (Count Almaviva in *The Barber of Seville* or Tonio in *The Daughter of the Regiment*). Then there are **countertenors** who are males who sing in

Figure 2.1 Vocal types.

falsetto at the very highest of their range similar sounding to the mezzo-soprano (Xerses in *Xerses*). Next, we move into the higher vocal parts or typically female range by first looking at the **mezzo-soprano** or **mezzo**. We begin with the **contralto** which is the very lowest range of the female voice (Ulrica in *A Masked Ball*), then the powerful **dramatic mezzo** (Ammeris in *Aida*, or Azucena in *Il Trovatore*), next are the **lyric mezzo** who are often cast in the secondary roles (Sesto in *La Clemenza di Tito* but then there is the grand exception of Carmen in *Carmen*), at the top end of our mezzos are the **coloratura mezzo** (Rosina in *The Barber of Seville* or Ariodante in *Ariodante*). **Pants roles** or **trouser roles** are often cast out of the mezzo; these are male characters who are sung by women (Cherubino in *The Marriage of Figaro*). Finally, at the top of the vocal range are the **soprano** – they sing the highest notes. We again have a division among the soprano beginning with the powerfully voiced **dramatic soprano** (Isolde in *Tristan and Isolde* or Brünnhilde in *The Ring Cycle*), the oft romantic lead or **lyric soprano** (Musetta or Mimi in *La Bohème* or Bess from *Porgy and Bess*), and finally, the queen of them all, the **coloratura soprano** who sing the highest of high notes, really fast (The Queen of the Night in *The Magic Flute* or Zerbinetta in *Ariadne auf Naxos*). Performers can change their repertoire if they are at the border of their vocal range. Age also changes the voice. Performers such as Maria Callas were made famous for their repertoire. Knowing that a singer is performing a role from their repertoire helps us appreciate why we cue singers onto stage for each entrance, more on this in Chapter 5: Technical Rehearsals. A performer may be singing their fourth Count Almaviva in the calendar year. Perhaps even on the same set that was rented by a previous opera company. Knowing this, we can appreciate that we are doing the performers a tremendous service by helping them remember *this* version of *Barber of Seville*.

Broadly speaking, the cast is broken down into size of role:

Principals are the lead singing roles in an opera.

Chorus function as a group both vocally and in staging and scheduling. They are typically divided by voice type and will be cast based on the needs of the opera. For example, the chorus in Rossini's *Il Barbiere di Siviglia*, or *The Barber of Seville*, only has low range voice types, e.g. bass, baritone, tenor; whereas *Tosca* has all vocal parts and children.

A **comprimario role** is a singing role that is smaller in scope than a principal. They are typically cast out of the chorus and can be scheduled with principals, separate from the chorus calls.

Actors are cast members with speaking parts who do not sing. Not all opera companies call them actors, sometimes they are grouped with the supernumeraries.

Supernumeraries or "supers" are cast members who don't sing or speak. They serve an important role in moving the story along as messengers, servers, footmen, officers, etc.

Children can be members of any of the above groups. There are many operas that have a children's chorus, such as Handel's *Hansel and Gretel*. The children's chorus is usually treated similarly to the adult chorus in terms of scheduling and casting. There are other operas that have children who have principal parts, such as Britten's *The Turn of the Screw*. Sometimes to eliminate the complexities of having children in a production, an opera company will cast a soprano to sing the roles of the soloist children.

Dancers (in opera!) are used when there is a complex dance beyond basic movement. For example, the waltz in Johann Strauss' *Die Fledermaus* can usually be accomplished by the chorus, whereas Act 3 of Amilcare Ponchelli's *La Gionconda* ends in a short ballet, *The Dance of the Hours*. Depending on the company, the dancers may be unionized, and their hours governed by an AGMA agreement, so the stage manager will need to know this information before they begin rehearsals.

DANCER LEVELS

Depending on the dance company structure, dancers may work as an ensemble and be listed as company artists, dancers, or artists. Whereas, in more traditional hierarchies, you might encounter a division such as the list below. These designated levels can reflect both seniority and talent and have specific contracts with associated conditions and pay scales. Not all levels are employed in all dance companies. For example, Soloists may replace Senior Artists.

Principal Dancers are the highest level of dancer in the company and perform the principal roles.

Senior Artists also known as **first soloists**, perform lead character roles and select principal roles, and understudy principal artists.

Soloists are considered the rising stars of a dance company and perform smaller soloist roles, understudying senior artists.

Coryphee also known as **second soloists,** are young artists showing talent that are highlighted in the corps de ballet.

Corps de ballet is the first level within a dance company, also known as **artists**.

Character Artists sit separately within this hierarchy. They are generally senior artists, or of a similar level, who have a certain amount of acting ability. In many cases, character artists do not dance in the main company. These dancers are cast in specific roles such as Drosselmeyer in *The Nutcracker Suite* or Dr. Coppelius in *Coppélia*.

In both our experiences, we have worked with organizations that promote **young artists** programs which are training programs. Often the members of the young artists programs will **cover** principal singers' roles or may have productions of their own that are generally either smaller in scale or may be touring productions for young audiences. Chorus members may also serve as covers or understudies for principal roles. Some larger dance companies may have schools associated with them. These dancers may serve aside the corps de ballet but be titled separately, one such example is the "second company." Again, like other young artist programs, members of the school company may perform in mainstage productions as well as have smaller-scale productions that showcase their talent separately from the main season.

ADMINISTRATIVE AND PRODUCTION PERSONNEL

While many of the administrative and production personnel will be similar to what you would encounter in a traditional theatrical production, in both opera and dance you will find some new collaborators in the organizational chart. A key member of the administrative team is the **company manager**. While the company manager may perform many similar tasks that they might in a theatre company, such as housing and travel, they will likely also be doing considerable work acquiring **work visas** for international performers and creative staff. Both opera and dance companies hire a large complement of artists from around the world, so company management has an added layer of complexity when bringing performers from other countries to your organization. Likewise, if the company is touring internationally, the company manager will assist company members with securing work visas abroad. This job is not for the faint-hearted, be kind to your company manager.

Physical and vocal **health and wellness** is paramount to the livelihood of the performers in dance and opera. The support team for the performers can include any number of associates depending on the size of the company. If these health professionals are not on staff, many companies will have a relationship with a local practitioner or advisor. A sampling of these critical health associates includes physical therapists, Pilates instructors, performance psychologists, rehabilitation specialists, massage therapists, sports science specialists, nutritionists, health and wellness coordinators and consultants, orthopedic consultants, and ear/nose/throat specialists. In addition to these, you may now have a Covid-19 Safety Manager or team to address wellbeing surrounding the coronavirus pandemic.

While **development/philanthropy** and **community engagement**, or **education departments** are again found in theatre companies, you may find that your involvement with these groups is more than you have previously experienced. Most opera and ballet companies are in the not-for-profit sector of the industry, and galas and events are vital to their existence. Both our authors have worked with the development office on gala productions of varying scale from full performances offering a variety of the rep alongside a lush dinner to run-out solo performances at a donor's home. Supporting development and community engagement works to everyone's benefit as the funds and friends raised through these events provide substantial contributions to the operational budget associated with running an arts organization. Instruction on stage managing galas and events could fill an entire book in the toolkit series! The short version of the story is: it is rehearsal, tech, and performance all rolled into a few hours. Work hard, work fast, it won't be perfect – move on. Speaking of hours, if the event involves performers from the company that are in rehearsal or performance, you will need to account for their work hours in both your daily and weekly schedule. For example, the company may need to both travel to and perform in an event on the same day. Depending on the distance traveled, that may take up a full rehearsal segment or even all the rehearsal segments allotted in the day. When you are reviewing the schedule during prep week, be sure to ask about any special events and more importantly, how they will impact the rehearsal schedule. And then…make sure the staging director knows!

The core of the production team will again resemble positions you are familiar with from theatre companies, however, please be aware that terminology can vary, and in many opera and dance companies, the production manager is called the **director of production**. In the organizational flow chart, you report to them. They may have several team members on their staff, serving in a variety of roles, but essentially, they are the hub of production-related activity, inquiry, and communication. Additionally, many companies will have resident production or creative team personnel, e.g. a resident lighting designer. Functionally, they will be the lighting designer, or overseeing the lighting team and assisting guest lighting designers acclimate to the company. An oddity you may find in opera is the **rehearsal/scheduling department** that is often responsible for scheduling. If there are several shows rehearsing simultaneously, the stage management team will be asked to send a daily schedule to the rehearsal department noting plans for the following day, and the rehearsal department will coordinate all the schedules along with fitting requests from the wigs/make-up and costume teams.

Rounding out the production department in opera, you will have a **supertitles/surtitles operator** or **team**. This person or group may be responsible for acquiring, editing, and/or running or calling the supertitles. The supertitles are projected translations to help the audience understand the story being performed. Supertitles can be projected on a screen or may be an LED screen, either way, someone is at the other end of the system clicking a button to make the titles change and someone else, or maybe the same person depending on the size of the company, will be creating the supertitles book. Generally, stage management is not responsible for making the book or running the supertitles, but, as you will find our mantra throughout this book, ASK! Incidentally, calling supertitles is a great job for a stage manager who reads music. If you are calling the supertitles, you are likely calling them to a union stagehand who is doing the actual operation of the supertitles.

You may be working with staff who are associated with the venue, not the company, including venue managers, crew, ticketing, and house managers, to name a few. Ask the director of production what the chain of communication is with the venue. They may want you to work through them on some matters but go directly to the venue on others. There is no one-way to work with the venue staff.

UNIONS, UNIONS, UNIONS

While you yourself may not currently be a member of a trade union, chances are you will be working with several unions in these performance fields. You may be asked to join a specific union when you are hired. AGMA has taken the lead in representing performers at many dance and opera companies in the US. Here, the stage manager will generally belong to the same union as the performing artists; however, there are some dance companies where the performers will be AGMA, but the stage manager will be unrepresented.

In addition to being conversant with your own union rules, you must be knowledgeable about the unions representing the musicians and crew. Information about the stipulated union rules regarding breaks, length of days, and overtime is paramount for a stage manager to know to do your job competently and efficiently. Unlike the Actors Equity Association, the union representing stage managers and actors in plays and musicals, which negotiates several agreements with groups that represent many theatre companies, AGMA negotiates its agreements with each individual company. As such, it is important to get a copy of the collectively bargained agreement (CBA) for that company prior to signing your contract, or at the beginning of your pre-production, so you know what rules you will be operating under. If you are a member of the union, you can access the agreements online. You cannot assume that the rules are the same from company to company as they have been negotiated to suit the members who live in that city and work at that company.

> Pro Tip: *Our AGMA union rules prohibit dancing on concrete floors, even covered in marley.*
> – Sandra Kaufmann, former soloist with the Martha Graham Dance Company

Let's look at who is covered by which union.

AGMA covers singers, dancers, and staging staff in opera, choral performance, and concert dance. Each of the agreements are collectively bargained agreements that have been negotiated by AGMA with each of the producing houses.

Covering more than 80,000 musicians in the US and Canada, American Federation of Musicians (AFM) is the largest union of musicians in the world.

The American Guild of Variety Artists (AGVA) was founded in 1939 to represent performing artists and stage managers, including The Rockettes and stage managers at Radio City Music Hall.

Founded in 1893, the International Alliance of Theatrical Stage Employees (IATSE) represents theatrical stage employees, moving picture technicians, and arts and allied crafts of the US, its territories, and Canada.

> Pro Tip: *Learn the names of your crew from the top of the morning (or at least the ones who will be working directly with you). It is probably about a dozen people at most, and for someone who earns their living learning complicated calling sequences, this is not hard. The upside is that it will instantly humanize the activities of the day. We are all just humans trying to make a show happen.*
> – Isabel Martinez Rivera, Associate Director (former Production Manager), Les Ballets Trockadero de Monte Carlo

COMMUNICATION

INTERNAL COMMUNICATION CHANNELS

Communication is the backbone of an effective stage manager in any genre of performance. Here, we won't go into detail as you have no doubt well and truly covered this aspect of your job in foundational stage management classes, books, and practice. However, interpersonal communication within dance or opera companies can have variations that veer from theatre companies or other genres of performance. Live performance brings with it various histories based on ritual and tradition. Communication approaches are dictated by time-honored decorum that is contextual. In this section we explore a few of those variations.

> Guiding principles for any communication:
> 1: Be Professional.
> 2: Be Respectful.
> 3: Language matters.
> 4: Be Inclusive.
> 5: Be Intentional.

DANCE-SPECIFIC COMMUNICATION CHANNELS

During the rehearsal process with a dance company, you will have three main lines of communication:

1. The Production Manager / Director of Production
2. The Choreographer / Choreographic team and/or Director
3. The Rehearsal Director

Each of these individuals provides different information that you will need to do your job effectively. They will each have their own expectations of you, as well. Nurture these relationships ensuring a collaborative and healthy atmosphere. While it is true you will also interact with numerous other roles, these are your central points of communication as a dance stage manager. Take note that dancers are not on this list! The stage manager usually does not directly brief dancers on many issues. In most cases, communications will go through the artistic team or be noted on the call board when necessary.

The production manager is your link to the technical aspects of the show. You may or may not attend production meetings, depending on the company and where the team is in their process. Instead, you may be asked to attend staff meetings which include production within the overarching company discussions. You may sometimes be invited to design meetings with the choreographer and designers, but this is less common, and unlikely if you are brought in later in the process. Make time to get to know the designers and keep them updated on relevant matters such as an upcoming studio run in rehearsals. In some companies, the choreographer or rehearsal director will invite the designers directly, so make sure you are also kept in this loop. Again, a healthy working relationship with the choreographer, rehearsal director, and production manager will ensure you are in the information loop of such activities.

Additionally, across any genre, make an effort to embrace each company's specific protocols, particularly if you are new to the team. These procedures have been developed over time and are ingrained historically and culturally within the operating systems of the company. If you are a resident stage manager, you may recognize a need to revise and/or streamline processes for better efficiency. Walk gently here and discuss any changes with the departments that may be impacted by new processes to ensure everyone is on board. While you may occasionally add a component to the company's processes, it is unlikely you will change them altogether. It is your perspective that will likely shift within the learning curve of getting to know the community and working culture of your new team.

EXTERNAL COMMUNICATION CHANNELS

External communication channels will include your collaborators, as listed in the organizational structure earlier. The orchestra, media, venue, and union representatives will be your main contacts. Much of the procedural external communications may go through other channels, for example through the director of production and artistic team. In many cases, you will be updated when needed rather than initiating the conversations. The exceptions are your direct communication in the theatre with union stewards, orchestra managers, media calls in the theatre, and venue management.

FINAL THOUGHTS

In this chapter we've introduced you to the members of your team, external collaborators, and a variety of unions associated with these genres. We've also given you background information on the artists, artistic team, and their contributions to a production. Now let's prepare to enter the rehearsal space with the next chapter, Pre-production.

NOTE

1 "The Basic Agreement between The American Guild of Musical Artists and The Dallas Opera." *American Guild of Musical Artists/AGMA.* https://www.musicalartists.org/contracts-and-agreements/contracts/opera/agreement-158/.

CHAPTER 3

Pre-Production

Pre-production is one of the most important times in the cycle of the stage manager's work. Like any other genre of live performance, success in managing the production is all in the preparation. Dance and opera are no different. The more work that is done in advance of your first rehearsal, the more prepared you will be for the rehearsal period. Pre-production is the period when you dissect your show on a granular level so that you know it in the minutest detail, from multiple perspectives. Being prepared and knowing your show allows you to stay alert and observant in rehearsal to respond to notes that come from the artistic team, the music department, the production staff, and the cast. Knowing your show allows you to predict potential trouble spots and be flexible and adaptive to the changes that rehearsal always brings.

For the stage management team, the lead up to rehearsals is an intense phase of preparatory work. This includes meeting with key production personnel to set expectations, document design, preparing the prompt book or calling score for rehearsals, scheduling, and preparing the rehearsal space/s. In dance you may find that you join the team later, once rehearsals are in progress, so you will have to incorporate the tasks we associate with pre-production later in the process. We'll discuss that further towards the end of this chapter and in the next chapter. For the moment, in order to be inclusive of both disciplines and the variations within them, we will lay out common expectations and how to organize your time (and spreadsheets) to achieve results.

MEETING THE TEAM

Whether you are a part of the resident production team or working with a contract-based (freelance) company, your start date will be determined when you negotiate your contract. In an opera company, that may be a week to a few days in advance of the first staging rehearsal for the principal performers. However, in dance, if you are not the resident stage manager for a company, you may be brought onto the production team one to two weeks before *technical rehearsals* begin, so your 'pre-production' timeline should be adjusted to work alongside the scheduled rehearsals and meetings. In this case, other personnel such as the production manager, wardrobe, company management, and/or artistic team have been managing schedules, casting, press calls, and fittings to date.

When you arrive, your first meeting should be with the company manager who will advise you of the company's key personnel policies. In some dance companies, the rehearsal director may fulfill the role of company manager. They will also either have a cast list for you or direct you to the artistic department for that information. In either case, be sure to ask if anyone in your cast has any specific contractual agreements you should be aware of, or releases for the term of their contract. For example, an artist who does not appear in an opera until Act 3, may not begin rehearsals until well after the rest of your company. Likewise, you'll want to know if any of the artists have negotiated a **release**, or scheduled time off, that occurs during the rehearsal, tech, or performance period as this will affect scheduling.

Your next meeting should be with the director of production, sometimes called the production manager or the technical manager, for a full briefing on production protocol and procedures, an overall company calendar, a tour of the premises, including the rehearsal studios and theatre, and introductions to the resident production and administrative staff. If you are joining a dance company after the company has been in rehearsal, then you will also be introduced to the creative team and dancers. Once you've met the key production and administrative team members, it's time to discuss expectations. Remember, expectations need to be a two-way conversation. The company will have expectations of you and the stage management team, but you should be clear with your expectations as well, outlining what you need to successfully do your job.

Reflecting on our advice as we began this book, "you don't know what you don't know" so we encourage you to think critically about what your job is. Start at the macro-level and work towards the micro-levels of responsibility. There is a certain amount of investigative work in stage management, so approach new jobs as fact-finding opportunities to learn as much as possible in a short amount of time. If you are joining a team later in the process, this approach will reveal a stage manager with a professional attitude and keen observation skills as your first impression with the company.

As both genres present repertoire pieces, it is suggested that you check with the production manager at the start of the process to locate any existing documentation such as a stage manager's marked score, cue lists, show running sheets, props lists, videos, photos, designs, and any other show-specific documents. Once you have acquired any pre-existing information, you then begin the process of creating the stage manager's book and show paperwork. Additionally, the stage manager must understand the physical requirements of each art form to adequately prepare a space for creative activity to take place safely.

Note: As terminology varies regionally and by genre, for our purposes in this book we will refer to the calling document as the **SM Score** or **SM digital cue sheets** (a.k.a. prompt copy), acknowledging there is usually a production book with associated SM paperwork. As we move into a greener version of stage management, we suggest that these associated documents are created and stored in share files online, rather than printing where possible.

> Before you begin pre-production, check to see if there is a prompt book, SM score, or any pre-existing documentation for this production.

GETTING STARTED

First things first, now that you know the key production personnel and have working knowledge of company protocol, it's time to get to know your show. Acquaint yourself with the opera or dance piece: Listen to the music. If possible, see a production or watch a video of a production. Take a moment to enjoy the piece before you start dissecting it for information. Giving yourself time to experience the music and story will make you a better stage manager and collaborator. The audience is not coming to see your paperwork, they are coming to see the opera or dance; likewise, the stage director, choreographer, conductor, design team, and cast are not presenting your amazing paperwork, they are telling a story. Taking a moment to enjoy the piece viscerally, will help you help your collaborators share their vision.

> If you don't have access to your company's archives, you can try a resource such as the Metropolitan Opera on Demand.[1]

Note: Some historic recordings that you will find online or in the archives of opera and dance companies may depict offensive and culturally insensitive stereotypes and/or outdated production practices. Although most companies no longer participate in these practices, their archival videos may contain offensive material.

MUSIC

In both dance and opera, it is vital that you are working with the correct **score**, sheet music, and/or audio recording as, in many ways, it is the framework of the piece. In Chapter 2: Organizational structures, personnel, and communication, we were introduced to the music librarian or coordinator. This is your first port of call if you are working with a company that employs someone in this position. The music librarian can provide specific details on the arrangement and any changes made to the score. You should also be able to request a copy of the score from them, being specific on which score you will work from. The piano score is used in rehearsals and represents the full work in terms of length and melody. The conductor's score contains all instrument parts. It is much larger and might be a challenge to follow, particularly if you are new to following a score. However, if you are seeking a specific part, for example, the trumpets in a certain section, it might be useful to have access to a copy.

Generally, the stage manager will use a piano score. It is more manageable, and you can annotate specific instruments where needed. Although there may be several publishers to choose from, it is helpful to work from a common version of the piano score. In an opera, ask the stage director which score they'll be using so you can reference common page numbers during rehearsal, or check in with the rehearsal director or rehearsal pianist in dance rehearsals. Then, let everyone on the team know which edition you will be referencing in your paperwork. Common **opera publishers** are Bärenreiter, Boosey & Hawkes, Ricordi, and G. Shirmer, Inc.

Along with the score, a stage manager will use the audio recording to learn the music of the show. Although operas have lyrics, the score you are working out of may not have the language your production is performing, so you should always endeavor to call from the music, and not rely on the words. The majority of dance scores will not have a lyric line to follow, so be sure you have acquired the same audio recording that the creative team is using in rehearsals. Your timings and understanding of the piece will be based on this. Again, in dance we suggest consulting the rehearsal director, who will be running the rehearsal room. Also confirm that the full recording will be used since there may be sections or movements in the recording that will change or be omitted in the orchestration that is to be used for performance. This is vital information in preparing your SM Score.

If you are working on a dance piece that has been created using recorded music and no score is being referenced by the artistic team, then be sure you've secured a copy of the music being used in rehearsals. It is unlikely in this case that you will make an SM Score for calling. This may come as a surprise to some, but it is actually *not unusual!* Instead, you will call from a cue spreadsheet, 'longhand' descriptive notes, or from blocking cue sheets; we will detail these later.

> Pro Tip: *Few skills in stage management can be practiced outside of the job itself. Reading scores, however, is a skill that CAN be practiced outside the job and you should take advantage of this! When I was first starting out as the resident stage manager for a professional ballet company, I would go to the library and check out scores and accompanying CDs (pre-Spotify days!) for famous ballets. I spent a couple hours each weekend sitting in my apartment, listening to the music, and following the score. Reading music was a muscle I needed to exercise, just like any other muscle in my body. The practice of reading unfamiliar scores helped to hone my ability to sight-read music, and I was much more confident when the company did their first big story ballet with a full orchestra under my tenure as the production stage manager.*
>
> – Evangeline Rose Whitlock, Stage Manager

BUILDING A WORKING SCORE

Once you have the correct version of the score and/or audio recording, you can begin the process of preparing your book. Whether you choose to create a bound paper score, a digital version of the piano score, a digital spreadsheet, or dance blocking sheets to call the show, layout is key. Ultimately, you need to find a layout that works for you, but we have a few suggestions based on what has worked for us in our careers. In dance, although you may use a score for a story ballet (a.k.a.

narrative ballet), it is common to not use a score to call modern or contemporary pieces; however, in opera, you will always call from a score. You will find examples of an opera score, a ballet score, a dance digital call spreadsheet, and dance blocking cue sheets later in this chapter. It is suggested in these last instances that the stage manager has a score available to reference if working with an orchestra, for stage calls.

If the show is a 'remount' and you have been given a pre-existing stage manager's score with cues, it is your decision whether to use the existing book or create your own show tool based on this documentation. This might be a great opportunity to rewrite the book in a digital format!

- Decide whether you will create the calling book digitally or in hard-copy.
- If you are using a hard copy, decide whether you will use a one-sided or two-sided score. A two-sided score is more environmentally friendly and will be easier to maneuver in and transport. Some opera stage managers will use the publisher's score instead of making a copy, but that is not our preference.
- Set up your book to suit your own needs.
- **Cuts**, **adds**, and **repeats**.
  - Check with the music department to confirm cuts or changes to the score. In an opera score, it is common to mark a cut by striking through the music with a diagonal line, typically these are red. Then note "Vi-" at the beginning of the cut and "-de" at the end of the cut (Figure 3.1a). "**Vide**" is Latin for "see or refer to" and is therefore used to direct you from the beginning of the cut to the end of the cut. If a large section of the music is cut, leave it in the hard-copy score and paperclip the pages together. Sometimes cuts get "opened up," meaning, they are added back in, so it's best not to remove these pages. If you have imported the score into a digital format, you can keep these pages in a separate folder or at the end of your pdf document.
  - Sometimes an aria will be cut or added to an opera based on the ability or knowledge of the singer. If an aria or piece of music is added to the score, be sure to get that addition from the music department and add it appropriately to your calling score.
  - Likewise, some **operetta** style operas such as the canon of Gilbert and Sullivan will note all refrains within a song under the same piece of music. The authors suggest copying the piece of music as many times as there are repeats of the section of music. This will make cue notations much clearer later on.
  - In both opera and dance it is useful to copy any repeats and insert these as extra pages into the score. This gives you the ability to make cleaner blocking pages without overcrowding a page with two versions of the movement.

This is your original score, which should be kept pristine. Make a working copy of this original for yourself and any additional copies for assistant stage managers or designers from this score. Keep the original in a separate folder and update with additional cuts, adds, or changes as necessary. Keep this unbound, so you are able to make single or double-sided versions depending on the person requesting

38 PRE-PRODUCTION

Figure 3.1a Score page from *The Magic Flute* showing a cut notation.

PRE-PRODUCTION 39

Figure 3.1b Score page from *Dialogue of the Carmelites* showing markings for timings, rehearsal numbers, and time signatures.

Source: *Dialogue of the Carmelites* page created by Rosie Burns Pavlik.

the copy. If you are calling from a tablet or iPad, then save the clean score as a pdf which can be uploaded to a variety of programs for annotation.

CREATING THE STAGE MANAGER'S SCORE

- Tab the acts, scenes, arias, specific dances such as a pas de deux, or any section that is rehearsed often for easy reference.
- Input any available information into the book that will help you manage technical rehearsals later or assist when calling the show. This includes scenic elements or props used in scenes, preliminary lighting and sound cues, scenic transitions, wardrobe quick changes, and so on.
- If you are new to opera, it can be very helpful to work through the score highlighting each character's name or initials as they sing. You can pick a color for each principal character and highlight their names throughout the score. This will allow you to see quickly when that person is singing. This may seem busy to an experienced opera stage manager, but to a beginner, it can be a lifesaver to help you quickly find a placement in the score when a character's name is highlighted.
- Next, find the entrances and exits for each character. Whenever a character makes an entrance or an exit, place a mark in the margin of the SM Score. Be warned, some composers do not give you this information. At first, you may need to make some guesses. For example, you may notice a character has begun singing, but they hadn't been singing before. This should indicate a recent entrance to the scene. Likewise, if someone hasn't sung in a long time, then they may have exited. Make a note and mark it as a question to confirm later, or this information may be found on an archival video. Once you add the timings (described later in this chapter) to the SM Score, you can also add a tab or sticker approximately three to five minutes prior to each performer or chorus entrance to indicate their "**page to stage**" which will be discussed in Chapter 5.
- It can also be handy to highlight rehearsal numbers and time signature changes in both dance and opera scores (Figure 3.1b).
- Insert timings (Figure 3.1b) into the score for future reference. 30 second timings are suggested for opera. The physicality of dance prompts the suggestion of 15 second timings in the score.
- Finally, add any important identifying information. This should include contact details for the SM and/or Company in case this important document becomes misplaced!

> Opera artists are generally called to the stage two to five minutes before their entrance cue.

HOW TO WATCH THE ARCHIVAL VIDEO

If the composer did not provide written prompts for entrances and exits, this is when you turn to another production of the opera or dance. If the company has produced the opera or dance previously, then watch that archival video. If the opera company is renting the set from another opera company, then see if that company has an archival video of the production you may use. Or, if the stage director has done the opera before, see if you can locate an archival video of that production. You may not find an archival video that exactly matches the circumstances of your production, but any information is better than no information.

Just like a stage manager must read a play from beginning to end before starting to dissect it for information, an opera or dance stage manager should watch the archival video from beginning to end. This will give you a complete view of the story. Next, go back through the video with your score and confirm the placement of all entrances and exits. Here we refer to the placement of the entrance or exit within the score, not the location on the physical set. Note all entrances and exits that you see in the video. This may take some time as archival videos can be of varying quality and it can be challenging to determine who is coming and going, especially when you don't know the show very well. You can also note props that you see that you're certain will be used in your production. For example, in *La Bohème*, the character Mimi always enters the garret in Act 1 carrying a candle. We know this because she and Rodolfo sing about the candle and in furthering the story, their love ignites. But a servant carrying a tray may simply be a conceit of the stage director of a production. It's usually easier to note the prop and ask if it, or something similar, will be used in your production and cut it later than it is to ignore it and leave it off the props list.

TIMINGS

Once you're confident with the placement of the entrances and exits, the next step is to review the video to note timings in your SM Score paying close attention to cuts in either the score or the archival video. Getting timings is as basic as it seems: at the downbeat of the music, start a stopwatch. There are two ways to note timings. Style #1: every :30 seconds make a mark in the score. Then, once you've reached the end of the act, go back to write the actual timings. Style #2: instead of making a mark and going back to add the numerical notations, add the numerical notations from the beginning. This may be easier once you've done timings a few times. In addition to the :30 second timings, note the time of each entrance and exit as this will be critical information for costume quick changes later on.

Note: Timings are written like this, :30, 1:00, 1:30, 2:00, 2:30, 3:00, 3:30, etc. until you reach the end of the act. Start again at zero at the beginning of each act.

If there are cuts in the video that will not be in your production, then find another video or audio recording to pull the timings. If your production has cuts that are not in the video, then you can simply pause your stopwatch and then restart it once you reach the end of the cut. Earlier in this chapter the authors noted not to remove the cut music, but rather, to paperclip it. You can follow that cut music now to know precisely where to restart the stopwatch when you reach the end of the cut.

> Remember, your SM score is a living, working document! Treat it with care, store it with intention, and make changes as necessary as the show evolves.

DOCUMENT DESIGN

Why spend time on document design? How your work is presented goes a long way in how the company perceives the stage management team is managing the production. If your paperwork is presented neatly, timely and in a way that is easy to understand, it generates trust. The company (cast, crew, creatives, administration, producers) feel well supported. They know that the stage management team has done the work, understands all aspects of the show, and 'has their back.' Is this a proven theory? Possibly not, but with 70 combined years of experience between the authors of this book, we feel that this is the case. Taking time to create documents that are thorough, accessible, reliable, and easy for everyone to follow will pay dividends. Every well-thought-out document further supports the theory that the stage managers are dependable and know the show well enough to lead the team safely through unplanned and unexpected moments in a production.

Take time creating documents that represent the team. Choose visuals, logos, format, and colors that will become your 'brand' moving forward in the production. Theming documents presents a coherent and intentional design choice. Add the *show headers* to note show title, document title, company, and *show footers* to note document version and date, directing staff in opera and choreographer in dance, and author (stage manager).

OPERA-SPECIFIC PAPERWORK

WHO WHAT WHERE

At its core, the Who What Where notes the time and location of each entrance and exit of every performer, plus notes what they are wearing and if they are carrying any props. A complex Who What Where will also include offstage actions completed by the running crews: deck electrics, props, scenic, wardrobe, and wigs.

Where to Begin?

The stage manager can build the preliminary Who What Where during pre-production as much of the information can be found in the score, on archival videos, and through information from the production departments. What differentiates operas from plays is that the composers often don't give you as much information about the characters as a playwright does. Plus, there is a strong likelihood that the lyrics in the score will not be in your native language, or not in the language your company will be performing. So, reading the lyrics is not always as easy as reading a play. What do you do? How do you get started?

Creating the Document

- Using a spreadsheet program such as Microsoft Excel or Google Sheets, create a document with eight columns.
- Use the column headers in Figure 3.2, and be sure to set your document up to repeat the column headers on every page.
- **P/S/M = Page / System / Measure.** Although it is not always possible, it is helpful for the production team, stage management team, and directing staff to work

P/S/M	Time	Who	What	Where	Props	Costumes	Notes

Figure 3.2 Sample of column headers for a Who What Where.

out of the same version of the publisher's score. Doing so allows the stage management team and assistant staging directors to 'be on the same page' when creating paperwork. When noting the Page/System/Measure, you note the page of the entrance, which system or staff the entrance occurs on, and which measure within that system indicates the moment of the character's entrance.

- **Time = Chronological time of the entrance or exit.** Remember those :30 second timings? Use the timing that is closest to the entrance or exit.
- **Who = Character.** Note the character's name who is making the entrance or exit. In a complex Who What Where the department or crew person doing an offstage task, e.g. Wardrobe, or Props would be a 'who.' You would follow this pattern through 'what' and 'where' as well.
- **What = Action.** What is the action the person is taking? This is typically an entrance or exit. For exits, many stage managers like to italicize the entire row. This gives visual emphasis to the character's exit which can sometimes trigger a wardrobe change. If adding crew actions to the Who What Where, the crew member's actions would be the 'what,' e.g. Open SL1 door for Tosca's exit.
- **Where = Location.** What is the location of the entrance or exit? This is usually noted as a stage direction such as SL1 (stage left, wing 1). Sometimes at this early stage, you do not know where the character is entering, simply leave this cell blank until the information reveals itself in rehearsal.
- **Props = Props being carried by the character.** Don't forget to include swords or letters or coins that may be in a pocket.
- **Costumes = Costume currently being worn at the entrance.** Typically, the stage manager only notes what the character is wearing upon their entrance to the stage. When the character exits, note "no change" if they will be wearing the same costume upon their next entrance or "change to" if they will be wearing something different for their next entrance. If the character is re-entering wearing the same costume as their previous entrance, then note "same" in the costume column to indicate that there has been no change of costume. More on this later.

Combining the Information from the SM Score and Videos into the Who What Where

You now have the basic beginning of the Who What Where. At this point, you have the timings and the entrances and exits noted in the score, so it's time to add that information to the Who What Where. Using the score, start at the beginning. Note the page/system/measure and timing for every character's entrance and exit on a new row. Also, just like a stage manager would do for a play, note any stage props that a character is carrying. Do this for the entire opera. You will have blank cells in your spreadsheet this early in the process, for example, you may not know the location of the character's entrance until you get into staging rehearsals. Costume information may not be apparent from the score or the video unless you are remounting the production and using the same costumes. For that information you'll need to talk to the costume department.

Work with the assistant staging director to update the Who What Where daily. Store the document in a shared folder so the stage management team can update it frequently, keeping accurate information on entrances which will be needed by the assistant stage managers to cue the performers onstage during rehearsal, tech, and performance and by the wardrobe and wig/makeup departments to track costume and wig or hair changes.

> Stage managers cue the singers onstage for every entrance.

FIRST ENTRANCE TIMINGS

Use the information from the Who What Where to create the First Entrance Timings. This document notes the timing of the first entrance of each character and therefore each performer. You'll share this document with the wig and makeup and the wardrobe departments so they can set call times for the cast during performances. The First Entrance Timings document can be made as a spreadsheet or a word document and should have three column headers: Entrance Time, Performer Name, Character Name. If the performer plays multiple characters, then the name of their first character.

> Most opera companies have a wig and makeup department who does each principal performer's makeup and hair for each performance. Show calls will be discussed in more detail in Chapters 5 and 6.

COSTUME PAPERWORK

The next stop for the stage management team is to meet with the costume department. Costumes may be designed new for your production, they may be pulled from the company's stock, or they may be rented from a costume rental company or another opera company. If the opera company is using their own costume stock or renting from another opera company, then either the costume department or stage management may have costume paperwork. If the costumes are being rented from a costume rental company, then the stage management team will need to work with the costume department to develop costume paperwork for the production.

Where to Begin?

As noted earlier, the stage manager should first meet with the artistic staff, company management, or casting to get a **full cast list**. Casting could include principals, chorus, actors, supernumeraries, children, and/or dancers. Ask for the vocal parts information on the chorus, that is, how many bass, baritone, tenor, mezzo-soprano, and soprano singers are in the chorus. Also, if there are comprimario roles in the opera, ask who has been cast in these roles. Refer to Chapter 2: Organizational structures, personnel, and communication for casting definitions. The artistic department will also provide you with a schedule of services (more on this under 'Opera Scheduling') and any schedule conflicts for each group or individuals within the cast. Set that information aside for now.

Take the cast list back to the costume department. If the costumes have been rented or are being pulled from the company's stock, check to see if chorus parts have already been assigned based on the size of the rented or pulled piece. Sometimes the casting assignment is dictated by the costume rental package. For example, in Act 2 of Puccini's *La Bohème* there are townspeople and shopkeepers. You want to check with the costume department to see which rented costume has been assigned to which chorister. That information will be critical for the stage director when it comes to staging the scene in Cafe Momus. Obtaining this information ahead of time will eliminate questions later and help expedite staging. An opera staging director once jokingly called this information the Who Wears What. Now that you know who wears what, you can add that information to the Who What Where.

There are two methods for including costume information in the Who What Where.

- Style #1 (Figure 3.3): Title the costume and note it as such in the Costume cell. For example, "Townsperson #1" or "Shopkeeper #1," or "Tosca Dress #1."
- Style #2 (Figure 3.4): Provide detailed information for what pieces make up "Footman #1." When providing detailed information, always be consistent by describing the costume from top to bottom, inside to out. For example, what is the person wearing on their head, torso, legs, and then feet. Also, when listing layers of clothing, start at the skin and work outward, for example, T-shirt, white, Collared Shirt, blue, Vest, brown, Bow tie, brown, Overcoat, tweed.

P/S/M	Time	Who	What	Where	Props	Costumes	Notes
32/2/2	27:00	Character A	EN	SR 1	Box groceries	Footman 1	

Figure 3.3 Who What Where with costume as title.

P/S/M	Time	Who	What	Where	Props	Costumes	Notes
32/2/2	27:00	Character A	EN	SR 1	Box groceries	Footman 1: Fedora, T-shirt, white, Collared Shirt, blue, Vest, brown, Bow tie, brown, Overcoat, tweed, underwear, Trousers, tan, Socks, black, Boots, black	

Figure 3.4 Who What Where with detailed costume information.

The benefit of Style #1 is its simplicity. Extensive detail may not be needed early in the rehearsal process and may actually be cumbersome as edited information comes in from the costume department following fittings. Early on, the titled shorthand may be sufficient information to work through staging. However, once you move to stage and are working with the wardrobe and wig departments, you may need to provide the detailed information so that you can note costume or wig changes.

PROPS AND SCENIC PAPERWORK

First, ask the technical director or production manager for the most up to date and accurate ground plan. Set this aside for now, you'll come back to it later when you tape-out the rehearsal space.

Next, following a similar process for the costume paperwork noted previously, you first need to assess whether your show is being built new, rented, or pulled from the company's stock. If the props and scenery are being rented or pulled from the company's stock, then there may be existent paperwork. Check the stage management archives or the props and scenic departments. If there is no existent running paperwork, see if there is at least an inventory of items. A good inventory will note scenes when the props and scenic pieces are used, detailed descriptions of the items, quantity, photos, and maybe even the character/s who use them.

> *I once stage managed a Don Giovanni which used a rental set. The props paperwork that came with the rental package was a list of nouns indicating the items in the rental package, e.g. goblet, tray, flowers with no indication as to when the items were used or who used them, descriptions, or quantity. This encounter helped me understand the value of thorough paperwork.*
> – Michele Kay

Since so many opera companies rent the set and props, you will begin to recognize different stage manager's paperwork and even what you consider to be "good" and "bad" paperwork. Don't worry, we've all created "bad" paperwork at some time in our career.

Where to Begin?

If there is archival paperwork, compare it to an archival video, if available, to confirm that the paperwork is accurate. Be mindful that if your production has a different stage director from the one who directed the production in the archival video, then specific staging, e.g., entrances and exits, may vary from the archival video. If there is no archival production, then consult the internet for someone else's version of the opera. The important thing is to get an idea of the story and how the characters in the story use and interact with the props and scenic elements. It's not perfect, but because operas written prior to the 19th century often do not indicate props or scenic pieces, having someplace to begin can be tremendously helpful to get the ball rolling and help you not feel overwhelmed. Remember, at this point you are working in draft!

When viewing an archival video for props and scenic items, be prepared to stop and start the video <u>often</u>. In addition to props and scenic elements that are onstage at the beginning of each act or scene, you are also looking for any prop that enters or exits the stage with a performer, and any time a prop exchanges hands from one performer to another or is left onstage by a performer. For example, keep an eye out for exchanges of letters and coins, characters taking drinks from a tray or hiding a letter in a desk.

> Do not try to do everything at once! Be prepared to watch an archival video multiple times to pull the specific information you are looking for. That is, watch the video one time for timings, another for entrances and exits, a third for costumes, and a fourth for scenic and props. Multiple viewings will also help familiarize you with the music, flow, and pace of the production.

Returning to the Who What Where

Use the Who What Where to help you track props that performers bring onstage or offstage with them in the column you have previously labeled "Props." You do not need to provide detailed descriptions of props in the Who What Where; however, if you do not have a good **Props List** from the archival documents, we recommend creating one now and providing detailed descriptions of each prop including quantity needed and character who uses the item in that document. The stage management team will continue to update the props information in the Who What Where throughout the rehearsal process.

> It is common to divide inputting duties for the Who What Where among the stage management team members and assistant staging director. For example, one assistant stage manager may be responsible for updating costume information while another is responsible for updating props and scenic, and the assistant staging director is updating entrances and exits.

One final note on pre-production paperwork in opera: if the opera is a new piece, and it is in a language that is known to you, then you are likely to be able to retrieve entrance/exit information as well as props and some scenic information from the score itself. This is more common in operas written during or after the 20th century. If the opera is brand new to the canon, then you should enquire if there have been audio recordings made by the composer from which you can pull timings. If there aren't any recordings, then you should assign a member of the stage management team to note timings during early music rehearsals. But the composer is likely to have noted entrances and exits more clearly than their predecessors.

CAST-RELATED ITEMS

There are some small-cast operas, however the bulk of the canon written during and prior to the 19th century often have large choruses and even full ballets or dance sequences mid-opera. To help you get acquainted with the performers prior to their arrival in the rehearsal studio, it can be helpful to create a **Face Sheet**, a visual who's who. Most company managers, artistic departments, or casting directors will have headshots for all performers in the company. Ask for copies of the headshots then save them in thumbnail size into one document noting the performer's name and character above or below each thumbnail. Create separate sheets for principals, chorus, children, supernumeraries, and dancers. This can be very helpful to the stage management team, the assistant staging director, and the staging director as they get to know the cast. It can also be helpful information for the wardrobe and wig departments when the production moves to stage for technical rehearsals. Finally, you could create a separate face sheet for the creative and production teams which can help you and the cast know who's who when guests join you in the rehearsal hall.

Additionally, it is common practice to make **nametags** for all performers to wear during rehearsals. Although they may cost a bit more, we recommend using pinned nametags rather than stickers as they can be reused multiple times and across multiple productions. Ask the staging director if they'd prefer character names or performer names, and if they'd prefer voice types or roles for the chorus noted on the name tags. Although nametags are not typically used during principal staging rehearsals, they are regularly used for all performers during chorus and combined principal/chorus staging rehearsals. The stage management team will lay out the nametags at the top of each rehearsal and collect them at the end of the rehearsal.

Finally, create a **Sign-in Sheet** for each performance group: principals, chorus, children, supernumeraries, and dancers. Some stage managers will print an individual sheet for each day, allowing a section for notes on the sign-in sheet. However, this wastes an awful lot of paper. With the ease of creating a free QR code online, many stage management teams have moved toward using this digital method. Use your preferred search engine to search "create free QR code." You will find instructions on how to link the QR code to the URL for a form, such as a Google Form. Create the linked form, generate the QR code, copy and paste it into a document, and post it on the callboard. When the performers arrive, they simply scan the QR code with their smartphone and input their name. The form will automatically timestamp the entry which is critical to track hours for some employees such as the chorus. Recording arrival times is critical to helping human resources track chorus pay. Per some contracts, the chorus member's pay may be docked if the member arrives late to rehearsal or performance. Always check with the human resources department to see how they'd like you to communicate chorus hours to them.

> Ask the artistic administrator or company manager how they would like you to report chorus or performer hours. Typically, the chorus works on a pre-arranged schedule and is paid hourly, so if they are late, their pay may be docked. The timestamp from the QR code makes this very easy to track and report.

> Green Tip: Create a QR code sign-in, it saves paper and is a more sanitary option.

DANCE-SPECIFIC DOCUMENTS, BLOCKING, AND TASKS

The stage manager is responsible for generating, posting, and distributing a number of documents over the course of a production. Within the company structure, it is important that you have an idea of which documents are expected from the stage manager, as this varies by genre and company. For instance, in a typical ballet company, the rehearsal director creates the daily schedules. The stage manager will have little input in this system. Yet, in another company, you might encounter a different style of rehearsal management where it makes sense for the stage manager to assist and distribute schedules.

> If you have not worked in these worlds before, find out what your responsibilities are and who else on the team might have stage management-style work in their purview to prevent duplication of work or misunderstandings.

TASKS IN APPROACHING PRE-PRODUCTION DOCUMENTS

- Meet with the director of production/production manager and rehearsal director or ballet staff to identify your responsibilities within the team.
- Determine your work schedule and rehearsal attendance.
- Access prior stage management files to gain an understanding of the style of documentation the company is accustomed to receiving from the stage manager.
- If you are working on a piece that is part of the company repertoire, access a performance video and any show-specific files.
- View the archival video to understand the narrative of the ballet and/or flow of the dance piece, and then dissect it into production elements by creating a production analysis spreadsheet.
- Separate the production analysis columns into preliminary show paperwork for each department.
- Design your preferred blocking and score-backing sheets.
- Create your SM Score integrating your score-backing sheet.
- Begin your general SM paperwork, covering any lists or documents that have not been created in advance of your arrival by the ballet and production teams.

> You will have a better comprehension of the dance piece if you create the production analysis yourself. An opera-style Who What Where spreadsheet may also be used to analyze the production.

Scheduling Your Workday and Gathering Information

As you will likely start your contract after the company has begun rehearsals, your pre-production tasks will be organized around rehearsals. Check the rehearsal schedule and manage your days so you are taking full advantage of the remaining rehearsal time before the company moves to the stage. For example, schedule meetings and any document/score work during the company class time and prioritize run-throughs of the ballet and specific rehearsals.

Observe as much as possible, documenting everything. If the dancers or ballet team have been setting the props and furniture pieces in rehearsals, find out if there is an existing props list. If not, begin preparing one as soon as possible. Learn the dancers' names quickly. There is usually a company list online with photos for you to use as a reference, or you could ask for a recent performance program to create a facesheet. Learn the language in the room (studio) and use it. Go through your pre-production check list to see if there are any documents that another team member has already completed or has underway. Use your carefully honed observation skills to find out as much as you can about the production and the company. Stage management incorporates a vast amount of 'detective work' to be successful. Do the work, you will be glad you did. As with any production, the amount of detail you know about the overall show will be revealed by the ease in which you are able to manage when things don't go to plan.

Now look at the micro level, for instance, music: Is there an orchestra? Are you working with a conductor? Has the music been pre-recorded? Is there a rehearsal pianist? What arrangement is being used in rehearsals? Is there a score available? By breaking down the minutiae of each component, you will create a list of questions to take you further into what documents you will need to create. If you are working from recorded music, you'll need a list of tracks or starting points in the digitalization of the arrangement. From this list you can create a **score reference 'cheat sheet'** that will be invaluable in the process. Figure 3.5 shows how you might populate this cross-reference sheet, putting score details and recorded music timings at your fingertips.

P/S/M	Score Ref #	Track or Audio File #	Recorded Music Time	Act/ Scene	Movement/ Action	Cast	Set Notes	Notes
5/3/5	148	1	2:27	I, 1	Duet	Rudolfo & Marcello	Attic: Topof Show	Scarves Required
6/6/4	200	1	3:03	I, 1	Marcello's Solo	R & Marcello	No Change	Stove lit
13/4/4	425	1	7:30	I, 1	Colline Enters	R, M, Colline	No Change	Wind effect
17/6/6	558	1	10:25	I, 1	Quartet	R, M, C, Schaunard	No Change	Over sofa

Figure 3.5 Score reference "cheat sheet" for dance.

Accessing Production Documents

To determine what production documents are necessary on your work 'to do' list and their order of priority, we suggest heading straight to the company callboard to see what information is posted. You will find a great deal of detail there about the company, ballets in rehearsal, schedules, and casting. Start with what is most readily available. What information did the production manager (or whoever your supervisor is) give you? Are there schedules on the notice board to view? What information do the schedules contain? This is where you start. Don't make work for yourself simply because you are a stage manager and a certain type of paperwork is what you would normally do. Find the relevance in each document you create.

Figure 3.6 is an example of a daily schedule or call sheet for a dance company created by the rehearsal director. The layout is clear and effective. It reveals specific production information: the names of the dances and/or sections being rehearsed,

West Australian Ballet
Rehearsal Schedule

Wednesday
25 / October / 2023

	Studio1		Studio2		Studio3	Studio4
10:00	Class	10:00		10:00		10:00
10:15		10:15		10:15		10:15
10:30		10:30		10:30		10:30
10:45		10:45		10:45		10:45
11:00		11:00		11:00		11:00
11:20		11:20		11:20		11:20
11:35	Sugarplum, Sugar Prince	11:35	Flowers	11:35 Soldiers, Rats		11:35
11:45		11:45		11:45		11:45
12:00		12:00		12:00		12:00
12:15		12:15		12:15		12:15
12:30		12:30		12:30		12:30
12:45		12:45		12:45		12:45
1:00	Sugarplum, Sugar Prince Clara, Dross	1:00	Doll Boy	1:00		1:00
1:15		1:15		1:15		1:15
1:30		1:30		1:30		1:30
1:45		1:45		1:45		1:45
2:00		2:00		2:00		2:00
2:15		2:15		2:15		2:15
2:30	Snowflakes	2:30	Dross, Clara	2:30		2:30
2:45		2:45		2:45		2:45
3:00		3:00		3:00		3:00
3:15		3:15		3:15		3:15
3:30		3:30	Children's Rehearsal	3:30		3:30
3:45		3:45		3:45		3:45
4:00		4:00		4:00		4:00
4:15	Spanish	4:15	Fritz and Clara join at 4:15	4:15		4:15
4:30		4:30		4:30		4:30
4:45		4:45		4:45		4:45
5:00	Arabian	5:00		5:00		5:00
5:15		5:15		5:15		5:15
5:30		5:30		5:30		5:30
5:45		5:45		5:45		5:45
6:00		6:00		6:00		6:00

Figure 3.6 Dance daily call sheet.
Source: Craig Lord-Sole, Rehearsal Director, West Australian Ballet.

when the children's company will join (and potentially, chaperones), character names, how many rehearsal studios will be active, breaks, and the time, length, and location of the daily company class. To supplement this document, the rehearsal director has supplied rehearsal casting information, indicating which dancers are to learn which roles.

There are many variations to what information might be presented in the daily call. Ballet companies often work ahead, so if you are employed on a specific show, you may find that there are certain hours in the daily schedule allocated to another production that is in rehearsal. For instance, time may be allocated for a 'remount' or creation of a future show or tour. Details of these additional pieces and casting will be available on the company callboard. You may also note which personnel are running the rehearsal/s (choreographer, rehearsal director, associate choreographer), ballet-specific terminology used by the choreographer, and how they choose to label sections of the ballet for rehearsal purposes. For example, Act 3 pas de deux, finale, fight scene, café, dream sequence, and so on.

ARCHIVAL VIDEOS AND ANALYSIS

Dance companies work with a repertoire, meaning many of their ballets have been produced before. Show paperwork already exists for the repertoire ballets and should have been retained by the company in their archives. If this is not the case, there will likely be an archival video recording that you can gain information from. Be sure to familiarize yourself with the stage management files and all show or ballet-specific documents on hand. Even if you are working on a new piece, look at the style and type of documents previously archived by the stage manager. A browse through archived stage management files will show the type of information that the company finds useful to keep, and how they are accustomed to viewing the information. Don't be too quick to change format as you may be asked to revise in order to match the pre-existing style as the company standard. Historical show reports will also give you information about the business of the company.

Next, watch the archival video if one exists, as described earlier in the chapter. Similar to reading a new script, you should view this video for the first time for your enjoyment and to understand the narrative and flow of the piece. On the next viewing you can begin breaking the show down into elements following along with any existing paperwork. A word of advice, if you are following a previous stage manager's blocking notes for cue placement, it may take a few viewings of the dance video to identify the actual cue points as notating dance can have many variations. Allow yourself time and patience to do this. If no prior paperwork exists, create a production analysis spreadsheet (Figure 3.7), dissecting the piece for timings, props, entrances, scenery shifts, and fly cues. You will add detailed lighting cues later.

Production Analysis

Time	Dancer/Character	Ent	Ex	Scenery	Flies	Props	Lights	Costumes	Notes
0:50	Drosselmeyer	DSR		Inside house Christmas Tree	Curtain out	Presents Cane	Follow spot, blue gel	Cape, suit, black shoes, hat	XC to tree
2:20	Clara	DSR					Follow spot, pink gel	White dress with pink bow, flat ballet shoes, coat	X to Dross.

Figure 3.7 Dance Production Analysis.

Set up your spreadsheet with timings in the left column, then characters, entrances, and exits and then add the design elements in the following columns. Always leave a section for notes. You can add a column later for score references using the P/S/M notation system to make the document more comprehensive if you are working with a score. Adapt the document to suit your needs, for example, if you don't have moving scenery the scenery column could be deleted. As with creating a Who What Where, watch the video a number of times to discover what has been included in the choreography and design. Note, if the show is not in repertoire, is a reworked production, or a new piece, you are less likely to use this style paperwork in pre-production as a familiarization tool. Instead, you will develop your spreadsheet throughout the rehearsal process. The production analysis or Who What Where can be used to begin the creation of individual department show plots/tracks for the technical team. It is still early in the process to complete show paperwork, you will need to attend rehearsals to populate all areas of the form. Nevertheless, begin them. You should create preliminary versions of all tracks, as shown in the sample paperwork. Technical rehearsal will be upon you before you know it! If you have all of the show running templates started, you will only have to fill in the blanks when you've gathered enough information to determine how the show will run.

DANCE BLOCKING SHEETS

Alongside the score, the Who What Where is arguably the most important document in your stage management toolkit for opera. This parallels the production analysis and entrance/exit plot that you might find in drama. However, there is not a formal genre-specific equivalent in dance. The Who What Where is a fantastic tool that could certainly be carried over into the dance world, and probably is by some stage managers who prefer it to a production analysis. As a dance stage manager, you need the information that these tools prompt easily accessible, but how else might the information be presented? Dance blocking sheets can offer a more visual depiction of the same information. It's important to understand that the stage manager does not take blocking notation for the dancers or company, the rehearsal director will do that. This is for your reference as a stage manager. What information do *you* need to be successful in your work? That is how you should approach creating and populating dance blocking templates.

What follows are three methods of notating blocking, with more of a dance focus.

Creating Football Blocking Sheets

The first style is called *football blocking*. It is quite simply a page with 12–15 small rectangles that serve as stages, and space for relevant show information. Add horizontal lines for wings, and any crucial scenic elements if desired. Creating 'football blocking' templates can be as simple as setting up a series of 'stages' using the underline key on your computer or drawing and copying mini stages, to working with more elaborate drafting programs. Figure 3.8 shows a version of stages with SR and SL leg masking,

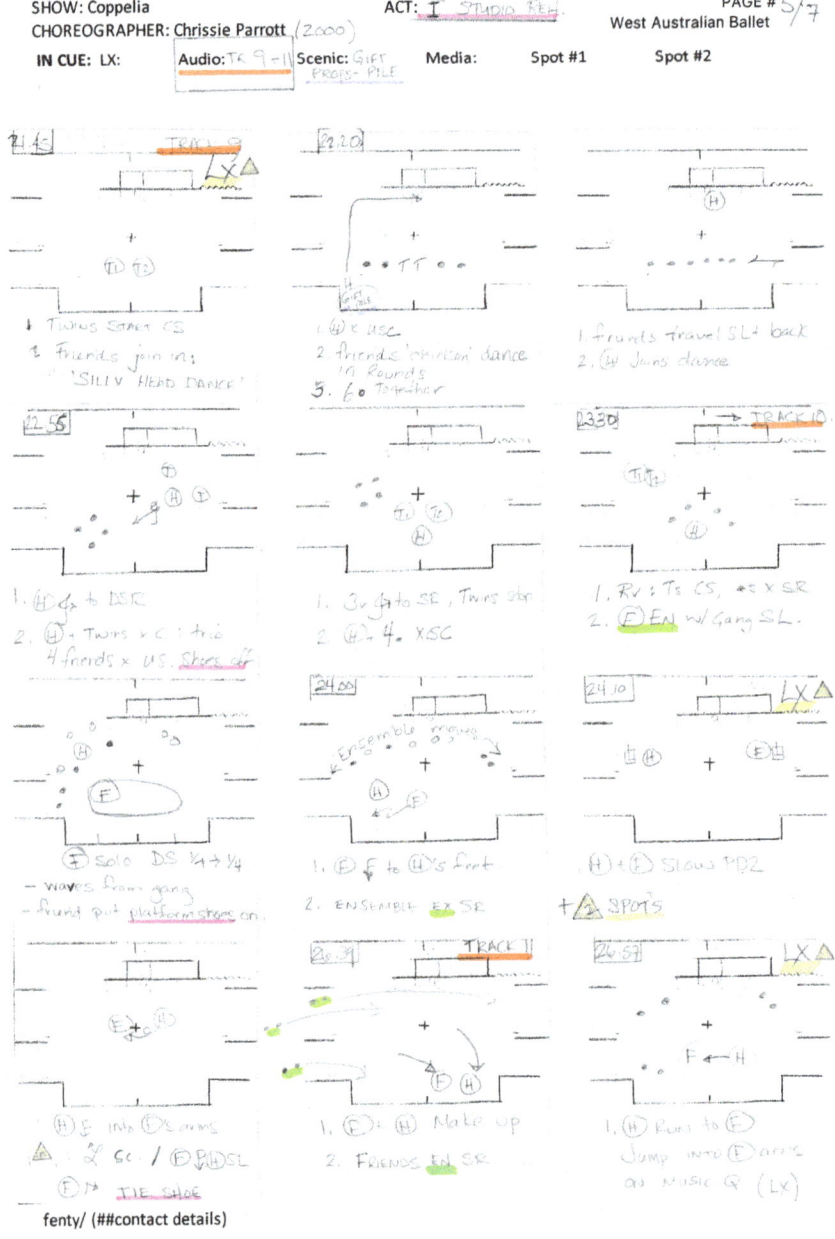

Figure 3.8 *Coppélia* Studio Rehearsal blocking squares.

Source: Created by Sue Fenty.

and enough blank space between the 'stages' for you to add valuable information. It allows a visual 'birdseye view' diagramming the structure and flow of the piece.

While the basic premise of the system seems simple, what you populate it with can save you huge amounts of time in cross-referencing information. You might also consider color-coded highlights for easy reference. For instance, in Figure 3.8, the green highlights are used for all stage entrances, props notes are blue, yellow signifies lights, orange is sound, and pink shows costume notes. We will revisit these blocking sheets in the next two chapters, exploring how, when, and why you might add any show-specific information. For the moment, in the pre-production phase of your work, simply create the document templates and either upload to an iPad for digital notation or make copies for future rehearsals. Once you have a system that works for you, it's easy to recreate or simply make copies for future productions, saving time in your upcoming shows.

> If you have access to an archival video, you can practice your blocking skills with this tool to create a working set of blocking diagrams. A word of caution: there may be revisions in the rehearsal room or alterations to the choreography on the day of the video, so be sure to check this work against the choreography in the studio. It's suggested that content is gathered in the rehearsal studio for several reasons that we will discuss in Chapter 5.

Score Backing Pages with Blocking Notation

The second style is a score backing page (Figure 3.9). This might be as simple as a single line dividing your blocking from called cues, to more sophisticated

Figure 3.9 *La Bohème* dance score with backing page.
Source: Created by Sue Fenty.

show-related documents with set layouts, scenic/props notes, and cue descriptions. What is the ideal layout for a blocking sheet? Whatever works for you and is easy to follow for others. Since you are creating the document, we encourage you to be intentional about any inclusions. If you've ever created a blocking sheet for a script, consider what you liked about it. Which sections did you use? What might you change or leave out? Would it be beneficial to have a small ground plan in the template design or do you like the flexibility of open space? The reality is you should create the pages to suit how you work!

With this style of blocking, not all movement will be included in the notation. Larger movement points such as entrances and exits, **divertissements**, solos, **codas**, lifts, and any blocking that might signify a cue point should be included. If you are trying out a score backing page for the first time, you might choose a more basic design, and then revise the layout for your next show. Consider the information you will want at your fingertips either in technical rehearsals or in performance and try to design a template that is clear, not over-crowded, flows well, and gives you enough space for all your information including paging calls, cues, and stand bys. Some stage managers prefer cues noted in the music. If that's you, then you can still use the cue column for cue descriptions or notes regarding the cue placement or call.

Figure 3.9 shows a column-style division of the backing page, with allocated space for current cues across the top (the cues you should already be in onstage when you turn to this page), timings, blocking, cues to be called, and any notes. This backing page is designed for *you* to call the show, so be intentional about the specifics of layout. You can determine which side of the page you will put cue notes, which side the music will be on, and so forth. In Chapter 5 we will explore this style backing page, and how the information it prompts can benefit the stage manager during technical rehearsals.

Dance Blocking Cue Sheets

The third style of blocking that we'll share is a combination blocking and cue sheet.

This flexible format lends itself to quick cue notation on shows that have little tech time. All documentation is listed on a single page format, with columns for cues and either longhand blocking, diagrams, or a combination of the two, as pictured here. In this case we've included a score reference column as well as a clocked time column.

This template sits nicely on a clipboard leaving room at the SM calling desk for a notebook, running list, phone for SM show apps, and a stopwatch (or two!). This is a 'go to' format for one-day dance events because it is so easy to edit and no 'print out' is required.

> Green Tip: Upload the single page template to your iPad or tablet so you always have a copy on hand. Pairing this with a compatible digital pencil means you are always prepared to call a show with your preferred cue sheets, and with the environment top of mind to boot!

PRE-PRODUCTION 57

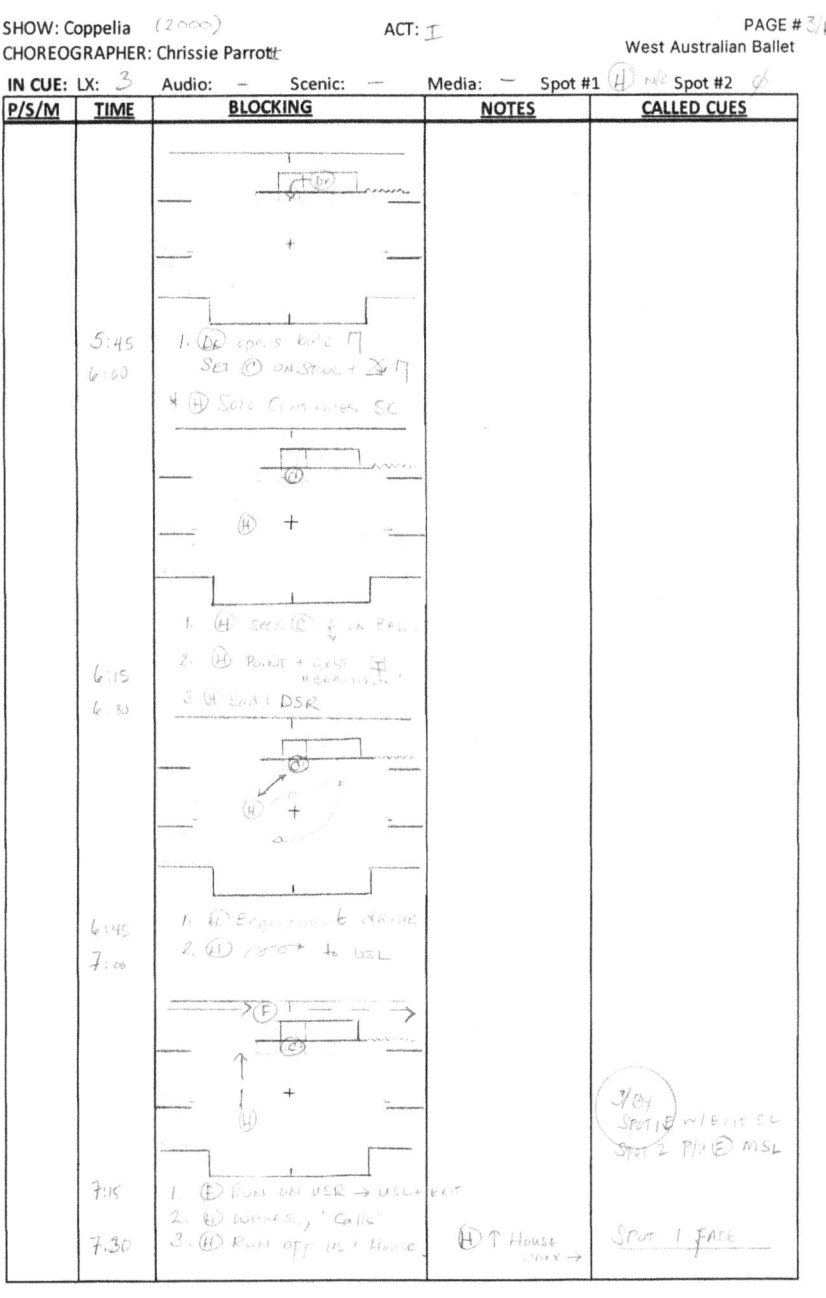

fenty/ (##contact details)

Figure 3.10 *Coppélia* Act 1 blocking cue sheet.
Source: Created by Sue Fenty.

Longhand/Spreadsheet Blocking

If you plan to write out the blocking notes in longhand, a spreadsheet style might work best for you. The challenge will be to be able to quickly find your place within your notes, so be sure to plan out markers for yourself. You can begin by inputting

THE HELIX PROJECT

TIME	Timecode	Segment	Action	Projection Image	Notes	Cues
12:34	3:00		Audio " Interesting"		6s purple strip mid	LX Q 12 GO
	3:10		D move from C/ stand	fade to skeleton parts	Music	
	3:30		D at USP: diag cross to DSR			S/BY LX 13
13:27	3:50		music segues		3/6s LX X to shins	LX Q 13 GO
	3:50		D at SC	Daz looking upstage	AUDIO: speaking	
	4:20					S/BY LX 14 - 18 & VID 4 & BARRE
14:20	4:46		Audio "Moving"		6s purple strip	LX Q 14 GO
	4:48				Music	
14:38	5:03		Exit to SL	Daryl looking at audience	LX: 3s - sides	LX Q 15 GO
	5:09		End of music	fade out	LX: 3s FTB	LX Q 16 GO
		4. EQUILIBRIUM	IMMED FOLLOW fade out		Richter: Piano	VIDEO 4 &
			Together	Video IN, fade up	10s Build CS	LX Q 17 GO
	0:00		D: offstage			(Pass Barre)
	0:10		D En with barre			
			D arrive at CS			LX Q 17.3 GO
			Barre work CS			
	1:20		end of footwork, tight 5th			LX Q 17.5 GO
			raise bar over head, turn			
16:00			Exit SL/ when offstage		6 sec FTB	LX Q 18 GO
				footwork	Deck: Collect barre	
				knee		
				legs		S/BY LX 19 - 21 & VIDEO 5
				feet		
	2:16			fade out		
			Daryl in DSL wing			VIDEO 5 &
			Together		2s DSP small box	LX Q 19 GO
17:02	0:00	5. OXYGEN	start DSL		Philip Glass	
	0:04		D Turn Head for move:		6s path along arrow	LX Q 20 GO
	0:06		(Anticipate move up arrow)		LX 20.9 F/On 2s	
	0:07		walk USL			
			to floor			

Figure 3.11 SM Digital Call Spreadsheet.
Source: Created by Sue Fenty.

blocking and timings into an Excel spreadsheet. Put headers in where the sections change so you have the ability to jump around the document with ease. Figure 3.11 shows a completed SM digital call spreadsheet. In this version, the blocking is referencing what is necessary for cueing. However, as you begin your documentation process, you should put more detail in so you can place cues and stand bys and find your way through the piece as it develops.

> Pro Tip: *When putting together your digital prompt copy, include anything that will make it easier for you to follow the piece and manage technical rehearsals and shows. You just have to make it as straightforward as possible to follow the ballet, call cues and still be able to respond to unexpected moments in the show that take you away from the calling desk.*
> – Fiona Boundy, The Australian Ballet, 1998–2015

OPERA BLOCKING

While notating blocking for dance can be quite complex, preparation for recording blocking for opera is not that different from a play or musical. One notable difference is that in many opera companies, the assistant staging director is responsible for the official record of blocking. This does not mean that the stage manager does not need to record blocking too, but what the stage management team records is less detailed and used more for tracking entrances, exits, larger moves that may indicate a light cue placement during tech, and props tracking. Whereas in recording blocking for a play or musical, you need to be very detailed with every physical move of each performer, in opera, the stage manager is looking for broader movements of groups.

WHERE TO BEGIN?

You have already begun to build your SM Score. You have created either a hardcopy or digital copy of the score, inclusive of cuts, adds, repeats, or alterations as dictated by the music department. Now you need to decide whether to create a two-sided score with inserted blocking pages, or a single sided score with a blocking page per page of music. In the time of digital scores, this choice is less relevant than if you are using a hardcopy score. Be forewarned, opera scores are already quite large so when you create a single-sided score with opposing blocking pages like you might for a play, you may find yourself with a very cumbersome SM Score. With the availability of digital options, you could insert a blocking page for each page of the score, but even digitally, it can make page-turning absurdly quick when you're looking at a score that has one system of music per page for several pages.

> *For a production of Tosca I went with a more traditionally theatrical method and put a blocking page in for each page of music. I learned this the hard way that this created an unwieldy score, and ultimately had to put each act into a separate binder to make page-turning manageable – that was three separate binders!*
>
> – Michele Kay

When stage managing a play or musical, it is common to insert a blocking page for each page of script or score. However, performers tend to have much more active movement in plays and musicals than they do in operas. It is important to consider the incredible internal machine of the opera singer: controlled breath and considerable concentration. An opera singer uses every muscle in their body to produce not only the quality of sound but the quantity of sound to fill the performance venue. Opera houses in the United States range from 1200 to 2800 seating capacity, and an opera singer fills that space usually without amplification and often over a sizeable orchestra. Although we cannot see a great deal of physical movement, they are working at the strength and stamina of a professional athlete to fill the theater with their voice. For the stage manager, this translates to minimal blocking, therefore minimal blocking pages.

> Opera singers do not regularly use microphones for amplification.

A typical blocking page in an opera will look very similar to one used in a play or musical, with a miniaturized version of the ground plan for the act or scene and room to write descriptions of the performer's moves; however, the blocking page will be copied onto both sides of the sheet. As noted previously, you'll probably choose to insert these *only* when there is a need to note blocking or significant cast movement.

PREPARING THE REHEARSAL VENUE FOR THE COMPANY

Preparing the rehearsal spaces and green room for dance and opera require the same basic components as any other style show: a safe, clean space to warm up and rehearse with amenities, hospitality, hygiene supplies, and first aid. In both dance and opera, the company requirements and specifics of the genre may mean that the rehearsal room is already set up, or partially set up, before you join the team. Whether in their own premises or a short-term rental studio, these companies will look for a large rehearsal room (preferably large enough to encompass the stage playing area and wings) with a specific floor type and infrastructure such as dressing rooms, restrooms, showers, storage, office/s, a sound system, a tuned piano, plenty of chairs, tables, good lighting, a callboard, music stands, a way to regulate the studio and change room temperature, a kitchen area, filtered water, and so forth. Whatever is not provided by the venue will have to be brought in by the production team or company management. To best support the art form, you must understand the physical needs of the artists and genre-specific rehearsal equipment and safety requirements. Also note that there may be company staff or venue personnel who look after, stock, and maintain all or some of these items – or it might fall under the SM duties. Be sure to find out where your responsibilities lie.

> Pro Tip: *When renting a rehearsal studio, if you plan to have the performers tap dancing, you must arrange that in advance. Most studios require protective flooring to be laid to cover their existing floors.*
> – Nancy Pittelman, Stage Manager, Radio City Music Hall

SETTING UP THE OPERA REHEARSAL SPACES

Setting up for an opera rehearsal is not that different from setting up for a musical. In addition to taping out the floor and setting up rehearsal prop tables and costume racks, you will need to pay close attention to the needs of the music staff. Both the conductor and the rehearsal pianist will need light to see their music and be positioned in such a way as to be easily see and be seen by the performers. Typically, the conductor or maestro will be at the front of the room, center stage. The piano will be to one side of them with the piano arranged so that the pianist can see the conductor and the singers, a table for the staging director and assistant staging director will be set-up to the other side of the conductor. As the conductor's score and the rehearsal pianists score can be quite large, it is necessary to make sure that both the conductor's music stand and the pianist's music stand are large enough to fit the score. There are specially sized conductor's stands designed for this, but you can solve the problem of a standard music stand by adding a 24" x 18" piece of Luan. This same size piece of wood can usually be placed on the piano's music stand to make it hardy enough to hold a score. Again, you may need to clip a music stand light to these boards to ensure that your conductor and pianist can see their music. If you are using music stand lights, you also need to have power located near the conductor's stand and the piano. Be sure to tape down any cables to prevent trip hazards.

Some operas use a harpsichord for recitatives, or mildly underscored dialogue. If you have a harpsichord or piano forte in your rehearsal hall you will need power and a dehumidifier for the instrument; the ideal humidity for a harpsichord is between 50% and 60% humidity. Harpsichords are notoriously bad at holding a tune, so if this instrument is in your rehearsal studio, it will need to be tuned often. You'll get to know your piano technicians well and rely on their expertise to help you maintain healthy instruments in rehearsal.

One last note about rehearsal hall set-up. The assistant stage managers will spend most of their time located either stage right or stage left, so that they can easily track props and costumes, but more importantly so that they can cue performers onto the stage. Ensure that your teammates have what they need to successfully do their job. This may include additional music stands.

SETTING UP THE DANCE REHEARSAL SPACES

Dance studio specifics include a specialized dance floor and surface covering, wall mirrors, ballet barres, and a tuned piano and/or sound system. A 'sprung floor' is preferred in dance as it is designed to absorb shock, preventing potential injury to the dancers. Generally, studio floors are designed with this element incorporated. If not, the floor may be too hard and unforgiving for the physical movement required. In this case, a temporary sprung floor might be installed. Larger ballet companies will often own and travel with their own floors. Whether using the studio floor or adding a sprung component, it is topped with a vinyl performance floor cover, commonly known by brand names such as Marley (US), Tarkett (France, Europe, Australia), or Harlequin (UK, Asia). This special flooring will have specific care etiquettes depending on the company. These include protocols such as:

- Do not wear stiletto heels or street shoes on the dance floor.
- Do / Do Not use **rosin** on the floor (this is company and venue-specific).
- Do not use soap or floor mopping detergents on the floor surface.
- Dancers should not use body oils or hair wax when doing 'floor work' (where skin or hair comes into contact with the floor). This could create a slip hazard for the dancers that requires immediate attention.
- There are various beliefs in how best to clean the dance floor and counter risk hazards such as floor areas with 'slippery patches.' These include mopping with a clean mop head that is not used on other surfaces and using very hot water in the bucket. Alternatively, you might add specific products to the mop water, such as a designated amount of methylated spirits or products such as 'Slip No More.'

> Always check with the team responsible for the floor before adding any product to the floor surface.

Many studios have full length wall mirrors and installed ballet barres attached to the walls. There will also be a number of moveable barres for class. Studios may have full length curtains that can be pulled closed over the wall mirrors when not required. Some have rolling mirrors that can be turned around or stored when not in use.

If you are setting up the room for dance, you will need chairs at the front and a few music stands. Production tables are not generally used in dance rehearsals. There will usually be a video camera set up for recording rehearsals, and a playback system. These are all fairly standard items associated with dance. Additionally, your company may allow the use of rosin in the studio. Not all companies/theatres allow rosin on their dance floor, so be sure to check with management before supplying a rosin box, rosin and a file.

While not directly your responsibility, the stage manager should be aware of the optimal temperature for the rehearsal studio, as it affects the company. During the rehearsal process you may be asked to check on the temperature with the venue if the system does not appear to be functioning properly. Keep in mind that the controls may not be easily accessible, so make sure you know how to contact the appropriate person if there are issues. It is also handy to know this information when moving to the stage or touring. Variations in temperature might result in a cold rehearsal or performance space, which could lead to injury if the dancers' muscles do not remain warm. Your company may have a few area heaters or fans available for use in these circumstances; however, these items should be checked by the venue staff or technical manager for electrical compliance before use.

In addition to the predetermined dressing rooms and showers, dance companies require an area for massage therapists, physiotherapists, and first aid/medical. Even if your company does not provide these services on staff, you will likely need a space in the event they are called in for sessional work. In this instance, a dressing room or a shared space might be workable if there are space limitations. For instance, a prop running room may be used if it is big enough and allows for privacy at certain times within the rehearsal day. Not every company will have this option but being aware of the requirement is important so other alternate options might be addressed. While you as a stage manager may not be responsible for setting up or acquiring this space, you might be posting the daily massage sign-up sheet or moving props from a shared space.

> Don't forget to assign dressing rooms for the artistic team and any guest choreographers or coaches!

TAPING THE FLOOR

After you have checked the basic room set up and noted the rehearsal layout, you will want to tape the floor as this is standard practice in both opera and dance for company members to learn their blocking/choreography within the actual usable performance space. For an opera rehearsal, follow standard operating procedures you'd use for any play or musical. Dance, however, follows different rules.

> If you are working on a three-act opera, use a different color tape for each Act. It is common practice in a US opera company to tape Act 1 in red, Act 2 in white, and Act 3 in blue. The red/white/blue color scheme is quick and easy to remember.

If dance studio floor/s have not been taped out, check in with the artistic team to see what elements they might want taped on the floor, and ask about any layout preferences or requests. If taping is required, it is beneficial to mark masking (side legs) and only the corners of any furniture or set pieces that impede on the dance space. Consideration of the wings is an important component of the dance tape-out as it affects all entrances. These need to be accurate. Additionally, you will consider how much floor space is required for the artistic team in the front of the room. Confirm placement with the rehearsal director or ballet staff before taping the edge of stage.

In addition to taping any scenic pieces, curtains, and flying scenery positions, for dance rehearsals you will mark the center-center point of the space with a + mark, and upstage and downstage center T's at the edge of the dance floor, then quarter marks (small LED hooded lights may be used for this) and eighth marks if they are a preference of the company. Make sure you are placing your marks in relation to the working space of the stage, not necessarily the stage itself or proscenium opening. Check with the artistic team to see what their reference mark requirements are. If rehearsals started before you joined the team, it is likely that center and quarter marks are already in place.

Note: The floor surface gets a lot of use throughout the day, as well as daily mopping, so be sure your marks won't come up on the bottom of a performer's shoe, or on a mop. A preset check list with all floor marks should be referenced before each rehearsal/tech rehearsal/show to ensure spike marks are still in place. For dance,

Figure 3.12 Dance center and quarter marks.
Source: Photo by Sue Fenty.

use spike tape for the initial marks, and then cover these with a piece of clear vinyl dance floor tape, such as Marley tape, to secure them to the floor. Replace any tape marks showing signs of rolling or peeling back. This is a warning sign that the tape might be pulled up if a dancer pulls their foot across it in the movement of the ballet.

> Pro Tip: *When visiting a rehearsal or performance space during a sight survey, give special attention to the floor surface. Dancing on concrete is very different than dancing on a sprung floor. Flag any areas of concern where the floor may feel uneven or the surface is compromised in any way. If possible, have a choreographer test out the surface wearing the performance shoe so you can determine if the floor will need Marley, rosin or something else. Make a note of where the seams of the floor hit in relation to the edge of the stage and note any other architectural features that can serve as guideposts or landmarks for the dancers.*
>
> – Nancy Pittelman

WATER AND HOSPITALITY

Consider the number of cast and their requirements. For example, dance requires a substantial amount of drinking water available in the studio due to the physical nature of the work, and room temperature water is preferred to chilled water for both opera and dance. It is also good to have a source of hot water for tea. Designated water bottles are always a good choice for dancers because they can fill them at the start of any given rehearsal and travel with them around the studio without potential safety spills.

> Green Tip: Reusable water bottles present an environmentally friendly choice for the company.

All coffee/tea and hospitality supplies should be located in the green room and not the studio or rehearsal space. This may be the responsibility of the stage manager, the company manager, or venue staff depending on the company.

FIRST AID

In dance or physical theatre, the potential for possible injury in the workplace is greater due to the intense physical movement involved, so first aid is quite a different matter when compared to many other genres of performance. Even the team contracted to perform first aid can vary. Your first aid kit will include items that cover more than emergency situations. For example, strapping tape, instant ice packs, and a store of reusable ice packs – frozen peas are often on standby as a preference for a cold pack – heat bags, lozenges, muscle ointments, and so on. Note: any shared items should have specific Covid-safe company protocols or single-use dispensers. Supplies should be checked on a regular basis, as you might be surprised how quickly some of the items will need to be replenished.

In an opera rehearsal, it is a good idea to keep lozenges in large quantities on hand. And although it is not a first-aid supply per se, ask your singers what kind of tea they prefer – vocal comfort and care is critical. Ask the company of performers what they need to feel supported.

Most larger companies employ first aid/medical staff. Smaller companies may expect the stage manager to monitor first aid supplies. This, however, is company-dependent, in some instances a company manager or another designated team member will take on this responsibility. Either way, there should be an approved list of first aid supplies that the company will pay for and a clear understanding of who will dispense. This can be a 'gray area' and will change depending on the rules of the company, and laws of the state or country, so be sure to ask for clarity on what you are permitted to supply. We suggest acquiring an approved written list from the company if you are asked to provide medications. This list may change in touring circumstances which we will discuss later in the book.

> As a professional stage manager, it is recommended to obtain first aid certification.

OPERA SCHEDULING

The last thing you need to do before rehearsals can begin is build the rehearsal calendar and create a weekly or daily rehearsal call template. Although many opera companies have specialized rehearsal scheduling departments, some companies rely on stage management to do the rehearsal scheduling, so it is important to know how to put together a calendar and do the daily scheduling.

In many opera companies the chorus is comprised of local singers who may have day-jobs. They may be members of a union such as AGMA or they may not be unionized. Either way, an opera company typically casts the chorus for each opera from the pool of chorus members for the entire season. The company will draft a **Schedule of Services** for the chorus for each opera in the season. You will need to get this Schedule of Services from the artistic administrator, casting director, or company management. The schedule will note each day and time that the chorus is called for music rehearsals, staging rehearsals, technical rehearsals, and performances. These are the *only* days that the chorus may be called, you may not make changes to this schedule without prior approval by the director of production as changes to the Schedule of Services can come at a considerable cost to the company. Typically, chorus calls are in three-hour blocks and have a regular pattern, such as Monday and Wednesday evening and Saturday afternoon. You will also need to ask if there are any limitations to costume fitting calls. Supernumeraries often follow the chorus schedule but confirm this with your director of production or artistic administrator.

> You will also receive a Schedule of Services for the Orchestra.

CREATING THE SHOW CALENDAR

The **Show Calendar** is an overview of the entire process from the first chorus music rehearsal through closing night (Figure 3.13). You will need to talk to the director of production for key information such as technical rehearsals and the performance schedule, and the artistic administrator or company manager for performer's schedules, such as arrivals for out-of-town performers. Use a basic calendar format or create

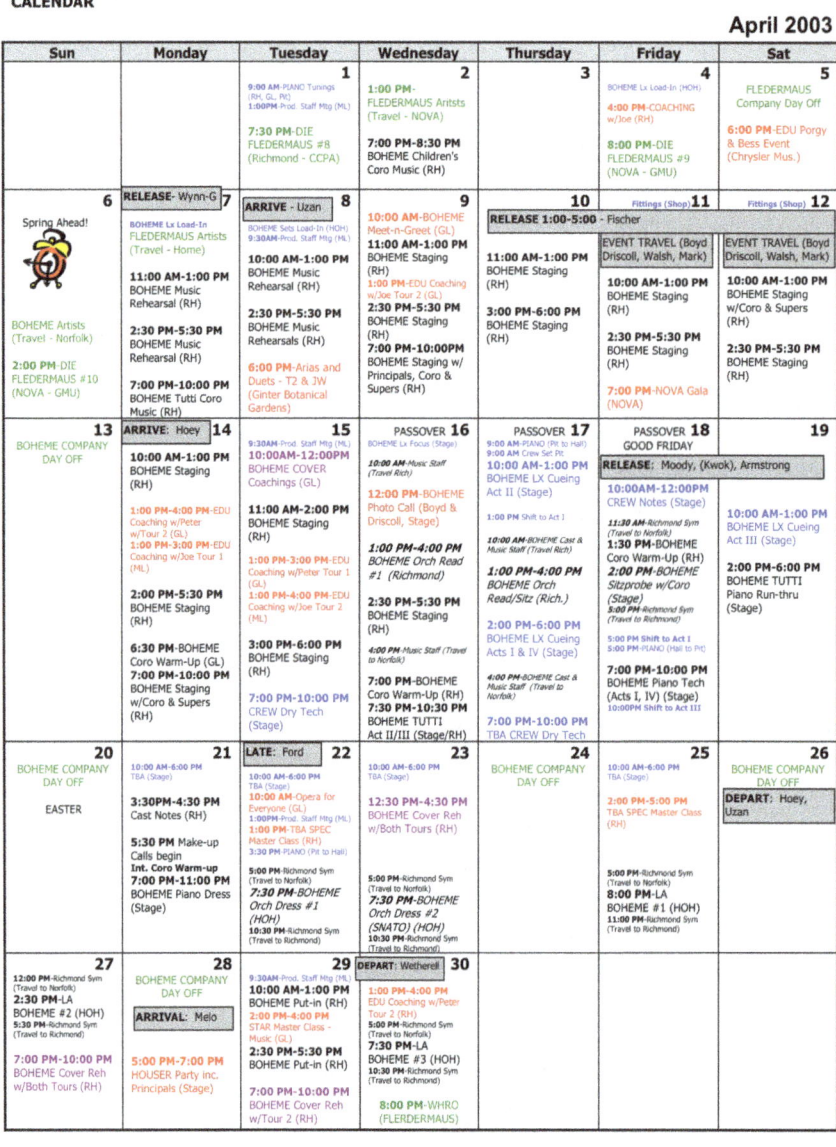

Figure 3.13 Calendar for the opera *La Bohème*.

Source: Created by Michele Kay.

a block-style calendar using either tables in a word processing program or a spreadsheet. If the opera singers are working on an AGMA contract, you will need to consult that company's collectively bargained agreement for specifics regarding rehearsal hours. Still, considering the strain on the performer's voice, even a non-union company will often follow union standards. Typically, principal singers are only called for 36 hours of rehearsal per week, or six hours per day, working in two, three-hour chunks with a meal break between those chunks. Take note, on days with chorus staging rehearsals, stage managers may work three sessions on that day, for example, the morning and afternoon with the principals, and the evening with the chorus. For the calendar, you should note six hours of principal music or principal staging rehearsals per day prior to tech. Although standards of working practices are changing, most opera companies still work six days with one day off per week. The day off is often Sunday. Confirm the day off with the director of production or the AGMA agreement.

If you are working with union stagehands (IATSE) or musicians (American Federation of Musicians), you will need to ensure that your schedules adhere to the rules set forth in their collectively bargained agreements as well. Work with the director of production to ensure your calendar follows these unions' rules, especially regarding working hours and breaks during tech or any time these colleagues may be integrated into rehearsal.

> Always confirm performance dates and times with the Box Office!

- ADD performance dates/times.
- ADD technical rehearsals, including Piano Tech, Piano Dress, and Orchestra Dress.
- ADD principal music rehearsals.
- ADD principal staging rehearsals.
- ADD chorus (and supernumeraries) Schedule of Services.
- ADD orchestra Schedule of Services.
- ADD children and dancer's rehearsals, if used in your production.
- ADD any artist release information to the calendar – ask for this information from the company manager, artistic administrator, or director of production.
- ADD any promotional or special events.
- ADD days off, including any holidays that are recognized by the company.

The first few days of any opera rehearsal period are usually dedicated to music. With the exception of a new opera, opera singers must come to the first rehearsal with all their music prepared. Most opera singers prepare for a role for many months, and then once that role is in their repertoire, they will continue to perfect their singing of the role as they perform it for many years. Therefore, principal music rehearsal is not for learning the music, it is for the conductor and the performers to work together to create this production's version of the role. Ideally, two to three days should be dedicated to music with the principal company and the conductor. Discuss the specifics of each day's call with the conductor, working in chunks to minimize any individual performer's vocal exertion. Likewise, the chorus will have been working music with the chorus director for two to three sessions prior to the principal conductor's arrival. There is often a session scheduled for the chorus to sing with the principal conductor prior to the beginning of staging rehearsals. Following the two to three days of music rehearsal, you'll begin principal and chorus staging rehearsals. Be forewarned, operas will often rehearse out of show running order to adhere to the chorus Schedule of Services.

Once you have it all blocked out, confirm the calendar with the director of production and then with your staging director and conductor. Next, work with the conductor and the staging director to map out the daily rehearsal schedule for the first few days of rehearsal. We suggest planning the daily rehearsal calls a week at a time to give the performers the ability to predict how their time is going to be used each week. This courtesy allows them to prepare appropriately for the week and plan their lives outside of rehearsal accordingly. It is important to create an environment of mutual respect within your company; honoring the performers' time is a great way to demonstrate that you care about them as human beings. That being said, we also recognize that planning rehearsal a week at a time can be challenging, if not unrealistic. Even if you do not share the weekly with the cast, you may want to create one for you and the director to use for planning.

OPERA DAILY CALL

As noted elsewhere in this toolkit, there may be a rehearsal or scheduling department who makes the daily call. If that is the case, then you will need to work with your director to set the next day's schedule and get that preliminary schedule to the rehearsal/scheduling department. Ask them when they need this information by in order to effectively do their job. If the stage manager is responsible for the daily call, be sure to check the AGMA rules that set the perimeters for the daily and weekly calls. With those in mind, we make these suggestions:

- ADD Rehearsal numbers in addition to Page/System/Measure to indicate what is being rehearsed. Remember, opera singers come to rehearsal already knowing their music, so they may not all be working out of the same score. Rehearsal numbers tend to be consistent across publishers and editions. In Figure 3.14 you can see these noted in boxes.
- ADD conductor, assistant conductor, and rehearsal pianists to the schedule. In Figure 3.14 you can see the conductor call times noted in parentheses under the cast called for each segment as well as on the right side under "First Calls."
- There may be items outside of rehearsal such as vocal coachings that need to be accounted for in the daily schedule. Discuss those with the conductor and consider creating a separate section for them in the daily call. It was our practice at this company to add the Coachings to the Schedule and as a separate section called "Coachings." You can see this in Figure 3.14.

LA BOHEME VIRGINIA OPERA

DAY: Thursday
DATE: April 10, 2003

RELEASES:

SCHEDULE:

Time	Activity	Location	Personnel
10:00	Staging, Act I, pg. 1-14 Reh 01 – Reh 06 & Act IV, pg. 238-246 Reh 01 – Reh 05	RH	Boyd, Youngblood *Covers: Greene, (Wood)* *(Saunders, Walsh)*
11:00	Staging Act IV, pg. 246-262 Reh 06 – Reh 12		ADD Greene, Murphy *Covers: (Honeycutt, M. Williams)*
11:30	Review Act I, men only		ADD Fischer
1:00	**BREAK**		
2:00-2:30	Coaching w/Peter & Joe	GL	Boyd, Driscoll
2:30	Staging, Act III, all	RH	Boyd, Driscoll, Simpson-Hoff., Youngblood *Covers: Brewer, Greene, Hermon, (Mitchell), Wood* *(Saunders, Walsh)*
3:15-4:00	Coaching w/Peter & POD	GL	Greene
4:00	Staging, Act IV, pg. 262-end Reh 12 – End	RH	Boyd, Driscoll, Greene, Murphy, Simpson-Hoff., Youngblood *Covers: Brewer, Hermon, Honeycutt, Mitchell, M. Williams, Wood*
TBA	Act II		
5:30	RELEASE Dan Saunders		
6:30	**END OF DAY**		

FIRST CALLS:

Jonathan Boyd	10:00
Karen Driscoll	1:30 wigs
Alan Fischer	11:30
Eric Greene	10:00 cover
Tim Honeycutt	11:00 cover
Raul Melo	n/c
Terence Murphy	11:00
N'Kenge Simpson-Hofmann	2:00 wigs
Eric Strong	n/c
Melvin Williams	4:00 cover
Brandon Wood	2:30 cover
Grant Youngblood	10:00
CHORUS	n/c
CHILDREN	n/c
SUPERS	n/c
Dan Saunders	10:00
Joe Walsh	10:00

COACHINGS:

	w/PETER M. & JOE W. or PATRICK O.
2:00-2:30 GL	Boyd & Driscoll (JW)
3:15-4:00 GL	Greene (POD)

COSTUME FITTINGS:
1:00-1:45... D. Kidd
4:00-4:30... E. Hall

WIG FITTINGS:
1:30-2:00... K. Driscoll
2:00-2:30... N. Simpson-Hoffman
2:55-3:15... E. Greene

MEETINGS/OTHER:
9:00-10:30 LCD Meeting (Bene. Rm.)

5 Distribution: POST: SM, Canteen, Production, Copy Room & Front Desk
10 HARDCOPY: Dir., AD, PSM, ASM, PA, Peter M., Dan S., Joe W., Wigs, Costumes
EMAIL: HOH Staff, Cast, Chorus, Supers

Figure 3.14 Daily Call Sheet for *La Bohème*.
Source: Created by Michele Kay.

- ADD artist releases to the daily schedule so everyone knows if someone will be missing from the rehearsal that day. There is a box at the top of the daily to add Releases. On this day, it looks like no one had a release from rehearsal.
- If available, you may want to include Covers. Again, at this company, it was our practice to invite covers to all rehearsals. Covers on Figure 3.14 are noted in blue.

FINAL THOUGHTS

By the end of your pre-production work period, you and the stage management team have met the key production, artistic, and administrative personnel, and maybe the performers. You have reviewed any archival videos and documentation from the company or begun original documentation of your own. You have begun key production paperwork that will be critical to accurately track all entrances, exits, props, costumes, and scenic pieces in rehearsal. You have created your SM Score, including any changes to the music and inserted blocking sheets. You've taped the floor, obtained rehearsal props and costume pieces, and made the rehearsal studio/s safe and comfortable for the performers and a space where the artistic team can create. And, depending on the genre, you've created the overall calendar. Now review everything you have done with the choreographer and rehearsal director, or staging director and conductor to ensure that you are ready for rehearsals to begin.

In the next chapter we'll move into music, staging, and dance rehearsals, beginning with the first rehearsal and ending with the final room run of the show.

ONLINE TEMPLATES

We have included resources on Routledge.com, you can check in for templates and samples at: www.routledge.com/9780367566579.

NOTE

1 Metropolitan Opera on Demand. https://www.metopera.org/season/on-demand/.

CHAPTER 4

Studio Rehearsals

During the rehearsal period the stage manager often takes on the role of organizer. Responding to the artistic staff, they collaborate with the creative team, Maestro, staging director, choreographer and/or rehearsal director, ensuring a safe and productive workspace for staging, music, or dance rehearsals. However, the personnel responsible for specific functions may vary. For example, the rehearsal schedule may be dictated by the artistic team or a specific administrative team rather than generated by the stage manager, so there is a divergence from a 'normal' theatrical rehearsal process. For the dance stage manager, this phase of production is very different when compared to 'traditional' theatre, putting into question the stage manager's expectations and assumptions of the role. Yet, in opera, the rehearsal process is very similar to that of traditional theatre with a few specific differences that are unique to the needs of an opera rehearsal. Since the dance stage manager's responsibilities are less formalized, we will begin with detailing what their experience might look like, and then move on to the more formal opera stage manager's processes to share a glimpse of what to expect in each discipline.

DANCE REHEARSALS

Dance rehearsals do not take the same format as a drama, and the stage manager may not even be on contract for the all-important 'first rehearsal.' Still, beginning any creative process is an exciting time for the creative team and dancers. Formalities that apply to other genres such as design presentations may not be incorporated in the first rehearsal, but, rather, might be shared later in the first week, or later in the process through visuals rather than formal presentations. In the dance world, the first rehearsal is an introduction for the choreographer, dancers, and rehearsal director/s, and is likely to be centered on the choreographic vision and casting goals.

UNDERSTANDING YOUR ROLE

When working with dance companies, the stage manager may be asked to assist with preparing the studio for rehearsals, if on contract early in the production. However, the stage manager does not facilitate rehearsals, or 'run the room' in the same way that they might in theatrical productions. This may be a challenge to some stage managers when entering the dance genre for the first time, as it does not align with more traditional assumptions of the role. According to US Actors' Equity Association, the definition and duties of a stage manager under the professional guidelines of Equity state "Stage Managers are leaders and collaborative specialists who prioritize and advocate for the production and its entire process commencing with pre-production."[1] Further, the definition notes that stage managers and assistant stage managers, "Coordinate and facilitate all rehearsals, calls, and performances before and after opening."[2] While AGMA contracts vary and are company-specific, the role still carries the weight of rehearsals by definition. For example, one opera agreement states

> STAGE MANAGERS and their assistants are those persons hired by the EMPLOYER to be responsible for the coordination and operation of rehearsals and performances as directed by the EMPLOYER. Further, the STAGE MANAGER will be responsible for 'calling' those rehearsals and performances on the stage in the theater.[3]

However, in a dance production, the stage manager's core responsibility is managing and running *technical* rehearsals and performances and the safety of the dancers within those phases of production. The importance of the dance stage manager understanding their role and responsibilities within any company is paramount to their success and requires a shift in both perspective and approach if you are coming from a standard theatre background, or most other genres of performance. Each studio rehearsal phase will be unique to the choreographic team of the show, but once the company moves to the stage, processes follow a general schedule or order of events.

In previous chapters, we've covered the role of the rehearsal director. It is in the rehearsal phase of the production that the stage manager must be very clear on their own responsibilities, as well any overlap with other collaborators, such as the rehearsal director, to work cohesively within the team. The stage manager's role will adapt with the company and duties will vary, so consider reframing not only how you experience studio rehearsals, but how you fit in with the existing dynamics of the team. Where your expertise is needed in the room will be determined in collaboration with the rehearsal director. Additionally, communication with the dancers is generally channeled through the rehearsal director or choreographic team.

ATTENDING STUDIO REHEARSALS

It is useful to consider that the stage manager's main task in attending studio rehearsals is *preparing for technical rehearsals*. This includes creating the documents suggested in pre-production, learning the show by familiarizing yourself with the music, choreography, dancers, venue, archival information and videos, and intricacies of all design elements. While the stage manager may not have a 'hands-on' role in the studio, it is crucial to attend rehearsals to discover entrance points and all production-related information. Additionally, you will assist, where needed, with any technical or scenic information and potential furniture or props moves. Whether a new production or a repertoire piece, choreography may change at any time throughout the process. This is determined by the choreographer and ballet team in response to the company performing. An additional cautionary note is that, with several casts per show, the choreography and tempi may change from cast to cast.

Attendance in the rehearsal room not only clarifies the production for you as a stage manager, it can also provide background information as to why certain choices or directions are made in the studio. This background knowledge is useful not only in technical rehearsals but can impact your response to unexpected moments during performance. As a rule, in all live performance, the more you know about the production, the better equipped you will be to handle potential show-stop situations.

Your first rehearsal on any contract may fall anywhere in the flow of the dancers' rehearsals for a production. Therefore, you should be introduced to the company at your own first rehearsal (not the show's first rehearsal). In the first instance, unless you have a very limited number of rehearsals to attend, we suggest taking time observing the processes within the rehearsal room. Note who is in the room, who is operating sound or accompanying on piano, what documentation is being used, and the language of the studio. Is there a callboard in the room or elsewhere? What information do the dancers have access to? Observe how 'scenes' are run. You may be watching a small portion of a scene, movement, or dance, say three minutes of a pas de deux, or ensemble work that will be added to a principal dance segment. How much music is the rehearsal director giving the dancers before their intended rehearsal segment starts? There is usually a run up or 'count in' to ensure all artists are prepared for the work they are about to contribute to. This may be a few measures of music, or a specific point that naturally falls in the music, or the start of a rehearsal track. This information will be important when you are determining potential starting or 'pick up' points in technical rehearsals, and something you should be cognizant of in all rehearsals. Begin to note these moments in your score, on your score reference sheet, and/or in your blocking notation sheets.

> Pro Tip: *Stage managers should tune in to what the choreographers have named each section ... Pay attention to the way the choreographers are counting the sections; this will keep communication clearer when discussing other elements. For instance, the choreographer may say 'lights shift after 2 (8s) of the big cross.'*
> – Nancy Pittelman

The dance rehearsal day will begin with a **company class**. This is the physical warm up for the dancers. A coach, guest teacher, or rehearsal director will lead the class from the front of the room calling out the expected movement. They also determine, and sometimes demonstrate, the dance combinations that the dancers will replicate in the floor segment of class, sharing the rhythm of the movement by clapping their hands or snapping their fingers, along with any musical accompaniment. Generally, stage managers do not attend class.

There will be a break after class before formal rehearsals commence. The schedule will be dependent upon the number of productions currently rehearsed and acts or pieces within those shows, as well as number of rehearsal studios being utilized. Ballet staff will determine this, and you are encouraged to speak with the rehearsal director about the needs in each room and which rehearsals you will benefit from most. Rehearsals will generally include all casts for the specific sections, so they learn at one time. In this case, the first cast is on the floor with the second and third casts standing upstage of the taped floor, also learning the movement. This section will be rehearsed several times, so there is time to learn/notate the movement if you miss something the first time. Of course, processes vary, so this is only one sample of what the rehearsal day might look like.

Full-length ballets may require the stage manager's presence in the studio from the beginning of the rehearsal process. If this is the case, the stage manager may be asked to assist with specific responsibilities such as operating an audio playback system for runs or sequences, thus presenting an opportunity to familiarize yourself with the show's music-dance interplay. Audio playback programs enable cue sequencing in the audio file and have a visual time display that is invaluable as a reference for the stage manager. Whether you are operating the system yourself or observing, engagement with this tool provides a level of specificity, informing potential cue sequences in the rehearsal phase of the production. It's important to know your way around some of the more widely used software programs such as Q-Lab.

> Pro Tip: *If you are running the rehearsal music from a pre-recorded track, put the track in a multi-functional playback app such as Tempo Slow. This allows you to create pick up points within the track as well as modify the tempo without changing the pitch. This is also a great tool to share with the dancers who may want to change the tempo when working on the details of a certain section while doing their homework.*
> – Nancy Pittelman

The stage manager will actively participate in running the room during full run-throughs. This will come in the form of setting and running props tracks, setting/checking top of show presets, and calling out specific cues such as lights, flying scenery, and pyrotechnics. Discoveries are made during these rehearsals, including possible limitations or parameters dictated by specific scenery pieces, flying sequences, costume changes, and so on. As a stage manager, you may begin to flex your creative problem-solving muscles through observation and collaborative discussions. You will ultimately be responsible for the safety of the cast during the stage rehearsals and performances, so it is important to identify possible challenges and/or hazards in these early runs of the production.

As there are likely to be more than one studio running rehearsals simultaneously, your time will be split. Open conversations with the rehearsal director will assist you in determining where your time is best spent on any given rehearsal day. Check in with the ballet staff and ask questions, particularly if you are new to this genre. There is often a shorthand between creatives, both verbal and visual. You may observe this in many ways; through abbreviated dance movements, gestures, sounds, sung music, or informal names or words that reference specific sections or choreographic moments, for example. Try not to make assumptions and ask for confirmation where needed.

> Pro Tip: *Humor is so important, don't be afraid to laugh … Ask questions if you are unsure of something. There is no stupid question.*
> – Craig Lord-Sole, Rehearsal Director, West Australian Ballet

NOTATING DANCE MOVEMENT

Once you have observed a portion of rehearsal and made relevant notes on cast, music, and any props, costumes, scenic, and/or other production elements, it's time to take out your blocking sheets or SM score and begin to notate movement. If you've had some dance performance training or choreographic experience, you may be familiar with choreology, including the Benesh style of movement notation or **Labanotation** (a.k.a. Kinetography Laban) that were introduced in Chapter 1. Utilized by ballet directors and choreographers to analyze and record dance movement for documentation purposes and coaching or remounting ballets, these are two very different systems; one uses a music staff to record body movements and the other enlists a series of signs and symbols concentrating on movement in relation to space, rather than 'codified dance steps.'[4] While some stage managers might be trained in these styles of notation, it is not common as the systems rely heavily on in-depth understanding of the physicalities of the movement. There are also a number of hybrid styles of notation that have their origins in these systems. Figure 4.1 illustrates how vastly different these systems can be. The first is written by Craig Lord-Sole, rehearsal director at West Australian Ballet, while the second is created by Sandra Kaufmann, former Martha Graham Dance Company member and Director of Dance, Loyola University Chicago. Both systems are unique and highly effective forms of notation. Along with this, contemporary practice has been trending towards digital cameras to record the choreography of rehearsals for some time.

While blocking notation methods vary, we begin by sharing one version of recording blocking in the rehearsal room that incorporates more universal stage management symbols in its notation. If you are working with a score, begin by following the music. You already have 15 or 30 second timings that you noted when you were learning the music, so this is a good reference for your overall timings, or to record in a football/diagram style blocking sheet showing the choreographed dance patterns. In the early stages of learning the show, the timings will help you sync with the rehearsal pianist or audio recorded music when you join rehearsals

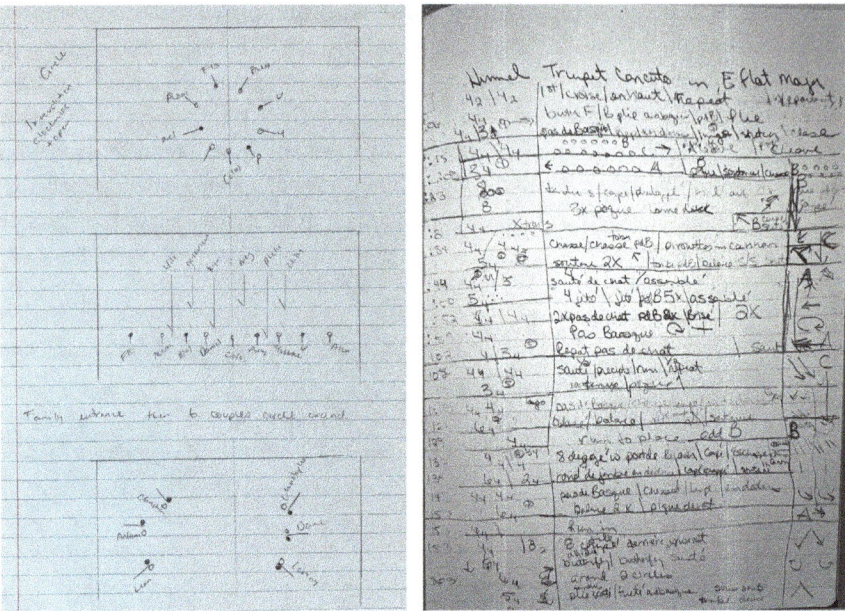

Figure 4.1 Choreology samples.

Source: Created by Craig Lord-Sole (left) and Sandra Kaufmann (right).

and, also, keep you from getting lost when following the score. Later, when you are moving from working with recorded audio or a rehearsal pianist to working with an orchestra, the timings will be beneficial when you are looking for specific music sections during technical rehearsals. You may also notice the tempo changes throughout the rehearsal process if there is an accompanist in the studio, catering to the dancers learning the work and potentially accelerating as they become more familiar with the movement. This, of course, will impact on your timings.

The information recorded on your blocking sheets should include major shifts in movement, entrances and exits, changes in music, lighting cues as they are plotted, specific props, scene transitions, costume quick changes with times, moments of isolation on stage, **corridors**, solos, **pas de deux**, full stage coverage, and so on. This information is incredibly useful during lighting sessions – particularly when dancers are not called, which will become apparent in the next chapter as we translate this information in technical rehearsals.

> Pro Tip: *When setting up your call sheets for dance, especially contemporary dance, it can be all too easy to say, 'ah, I know this, I don't need to write the choreography down.' Resist that urge!!! You don't want to leave something to chance in the pressure of tech and in performance. If you have everything codified as much as you can, it frees up brain space to deal with unexpected problems that may arise in performance.*
>
> – Evangeline Rose Whitlock

STUDIO REHEARSALS

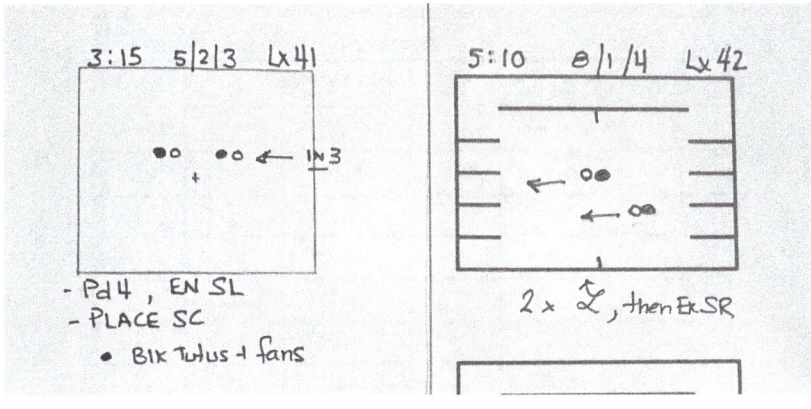

Figure 4.2 Two styles of dance blocking squares.

The stage represented in Figure 4.2 shows two diagrams of blocking. In the first diagram, four dancers: two male, two female, enter from stage left, wing 3, for the pas de quatre (dance for four, notated as Pd4, using the language in the studio). The female dancers are wearing black tutus and carrying hand fans. Their music is timed to start at three minutes, 15 seconds in the piece. The entrance triggers lighting cue 41. The word 'place' infers that we will wait for the dancers to set in position prior to the music cue. There is also a score reference listed in Page/ System/ Measure (P/S/M) format.

The second diagram notates the exit of the couples, and all affiliated details. When deciding what information you might include here, consider what might assist you in managing technical rehearsals and placing cues.

> Don't forget to include a blocking and cue shorthand symbol sheet at the start of your documentation to ensure a smooth transition in unexpected circumstances that might require a substitute or swing stage manager. (Figure 4.3)

A NOTE ON COLLABORATING IN DANCE REHEARSALS

While the stage manager's involvement in studio rehearsals varies from company to company, if you are employed at this stage of a dance production, it is vital that you attend a number of rehearsals throughout the process. The stage manager's presence is important not only to learn the piece, but for you to be an active collaborator, engaging in the production and continually learning and updating information for yourself and others via your documents and, importantly, building trust with the company. This is not intended to mean that you should attend every moment of every rehearsal. If you are not required to fulfill a particular duty, then choose which moments make the most sense for you to attend. What do you still need to learn? Would the repetition of what might be a difficult section to call be

Dance Blocking Symbol Sheet

Dance Specific		General Movement		Stage or Cue Related	
Ⓐ	Character name reference letter	EN	Enter	IN 1	In Wing 1
•	tutu/female role	EX	Exit	IN 2	In Wing 2
○	tights/male role	X	Cross	TOS	Top of Show
(symbol)	Lift	(symbol)	Lean	CTN	Curtain
(symbol)	Jeté	K	Kneel	OS	Offstage
(symbol)	relevé	S	Sit	DS	Downstage
f	frappé	S	Stand	US	Upstage
pir	pirouette	h	Hand	SL	Stage Left
◊	plié	2h	Holding hands	SR	Stage Right
ep	en pointe	gest	Gesture	SC	Stage Center
chori	choreography	(symbol)	Off	DB	Downbeat
ara	arabesque	(symbol)	On	VIS	Visual Cue
(symbol)	Fish dive	fr	From	SPEC	LX Special
Pqt	Piqué Turn	→	Go To	ANTIC	Anticipate
(symbol)	Turn	↔	Go to & Return	IMMED	Immediately
(symbol)	Lie down *Head in the direction of arrow	--→	Secondary Movement	HS LX	House Lights
(symbol)	Crouch	sh	Shoulder	S/BY	Stand by
(symbol)	Fall	wr	Wrist	LX	Electrics
(symbol)	Circle (spin)	⊕	Circle (Formation)	FTB	Fade to Black
(symbol)	Raise	P/U	Pick Up	B/O	Blackout
Rx	Repeat	(symbol)	Put Down	N/C	No color
R	Reverse	(#)	Count/ Time	Ax or Snd	Audio or Sound
(symbol)	Face (SL) *nose in the direction of T	/	Then, Next	QC	Costume Quick Chg
Pd2	Pas de deux	//	At the same time	Ø	Snap/ bump 0 Counts
Pd3	Pas de trois	(symbol)	Open	—	Backdrop
Pd4	Pas de quatre	(symbol)	Close	Balc	Balcony
div	divertissements	(symbol)	Up/Downstairs	Fl	Floor
Var	Variation	w/	With	(symbol)	Corner
Cpl	Couple	w/o	Without	⊓	Door
1/4 '	Quarter mark	(symbol)	In/Out	(symbol)	Chair
(symbol)	Line	"action"	Mime action	(symbol)	Ramp
* Revision of 1991 Blocking Symbol Sheet: Fenty, S					

Figure 4.3 Dance Blocking Symbol Sheet.

Source: Created by Sue Fenty.

useful? Is there a section of music you are having trouble following? These may be your priorities, along with any run of act or show. Learn the piece well enough to determine how different elements will translate to the stage. Re-frame what you experience when you walk into a rehearsal studio, especially if you are walking in after the process has started.

A daily check-in with the rehearsal director top of day will not only inform your decision on which rehearsals to attend, but also provides the opportunity for you to offer your assistance at any of the upcoming rehearsals, this builds rapport within the team. The rehearsal director can then request you are there for scene change moments or to clarify technical specifics, as well as keep you informed of developments in the studio. It is in these discussions that you will also determine the appropriate time to tape the floor, and what scenic or prop pieces are required. Generally, a fully taped layout is not a requirement in ballet rehearsals. Important inclusions are wings, and anything that might restrict the flow of the dance in any way.

Additionally, your relationship with both the choreographer and the rehearsal director will help keep you in the loop when any special guests are expected to arrive in the studio. If you are working with live musicians, at some point the conductor will join rehearsals. Timing is dependent on contract and/or location of orchestral rehearsals. If possible, try to be in the room when the conductor is in attendance as there is much to learn on these days regarding specifics of tempi, any planned casting rotation, and language used within the artistic team. The lighting designer will also attend rehearsals to learn the movement for their light plots and cues. Lighting is an incredibly important element of dance, so it is vital to keep the designer informed on any potential run throughs. Note that this information may be channeled through the rehearsal director, similar to the daily schedule. The lighting designer will potentially start booking cues with you in the studio, so always be prepared to take these notes. Where possible, the stage manager should plan to attend any rehearsals the designer is at, thinking strategically about where you might sit in those rehearsals to hear any cueing information.

During the rehearsal period, you may also have the opportunity to attend production meetings. Take full advantage of this opportunity to learn about the technical aspects of the show. Additionally, make it a priority to have regular contact with the production manager as the build and load-in progress. This link will be vital to inform you on a variety of details as you prepare the show documentation for technical rehearsals. For example, the production manager, being in constant communication with the heads of departments, will know when any physical changes to the set, stage or backstage layout are being discussed. Having this information as soon as it is considered, rather than waiting for an email or production meeting, will save time and energy when you are creating your show tracks and preset sheets.

CREATING SHOW DOCUMENTATION

Once you have an idea of how the production will flow, you can create and update show paperwork. If you are a stage manager who likes to work within the structure of a production analysis document or Who What Where, you will be filling in valuable information throughout the studio rehearsal process. By the time the company is running the piece, you should have learned enough information to

TIME	OP	TYPE	CUE	LOCATION	ELEMENT	ACTION	NOTES
0:43:06 Man improv DS- "Conducting" - VARIATION 20 (1:10)							
	WAB HD MX	Q	SPOT		White Cloths	Spot cloths coming in	Watch out for cast
	WAB HD MX	Fly	FLY Q30	L21	WHITE TABS #1	IN	To deck / Speed Medium
	HD FLY	Fly	FLY Q31	L24	SMOTHER #2	IN	To deck / Speed Medium
	MX 1	Fly	FLY Q31.5	L52	WHITE TABS #2	OUT	Follow on / To Mid dead #2
	ASM 1	DECK	SET	USCS	Day bed	Set on spikes	Once SMOTHER #2 IN (FlyQ 31) Give "SET" to SM once bed and cast set
	HD MX (FLY 4)	MX	SET	USCS	Day bed	Set on spikes	Once SMOTHER #2 IN (FlyQ 31)
	FLOOR LX	LX	SET	USCS	Unique Hazer		(immediately after fly 31)
	FLOOR LX	Q	OPERATE		Smoke machine USCS		from behind smother #6
	FLOOR LX	LX	STRIKE	USCS	Unique Hazer	Clear USC Unique hazer	Signalled by DT /OR/ before fly 32
0:44:16 Angels - VARIATION 21 (Canone alla settima) (2:42)							
	HD FLY	Fly	FLY Q32	L24	SMOTHER #2	OUT	Medium speed
	DRESSER 1	WARDROBE	COLLECT AND	PS 2	Red trousers	Hand red trousers and collect black trousers from Man

Figure 4.4 Excerpt from Comprehensive Run Sheet: Goldberg Variations.

Source: Created by Hugo Aguilar Lopez, Production Stage Manager at West Australian Ballet.

know the mechanics of the show and your spreadsheets should be populated with scenic moves, costume changes, entrances and exits, and anticipated follow spot cues. This information can now be extracted for individual running plots and a **comprehensive run sheet**. In Figure 4.4, Production Stage Manager Hugo Aguilar Lopez shares a comprehensive run sheet that includes tabs for different elements of the show, as well as streamlining his process by creating timesaving shortcuts that automatically generate individual crew tracks.

Prepare as much of this information as you can during rehearsals because once you move into the theatre, the process will run quickly, with little time to update. Additionally, speak with the rehearsal director to create dressing room allocations and check with the company manager to see if any of the artists have stipulated special requests/requirements for their dressing room: i.e. location, size, amenities, etc. The dressing room assignments will need to be circulated in advance and shared with the wardrobe team. Any quick costume changes should be discussed well in advance of the first stage rehearsal as they may require purpose-built quick change rooms side stage. As with many shows with larger casts, side stage 'real estate' is of premium value and should be discussed interdepartmentally at a production meeting so that all departments are clear on the dancers' requirements as well as the technical requirements. In some instances, these are drawn into the stage plans. As a stage manager, it is not your responsibility to manage this, but be aware of, to participate in the process collaboratively as decisions are being made. For instance, if you hear a quick change mentioned in the rehearsal room, and no room has been allocated you could bring this to the attention of the production manager to ensure it does not become a problem later in your technical rehearsals.

> Since the stage manager does not typically create rehearsal reports in dance, clear communication in production meetings, emails and direct conversation is essential!

CONSENT-BASED WORK

> *'Check yourself first' is a comment I use when working on intimate scenes between two people. I have conversations around consent on a daily basis.*
> – Danielle Micich, Intimacy Director

Consent based touch, intimacy, and violence has taken on new protocols since 2017 in response to the #metoo movement. Rehearsal rooms in many genres have updated procedures around consent. Opera approaches are in-line with those used currently in traditional theatre. However, it should be noted that dance may handle consent in a different manner as all of their work is physical and usually based on specific choreography. There is a current movement to create practices that give agency to dancers around consent, but the conversation and reality seems to be that it will take a number of years for this to be achieved. Currently in dance you are less likely to see a specific person designated as an intimacy facilitator in the room, but it is important that everyone is safe, so there is more discussion on consent-based touch ahead of us. We spoke with specialists in consent-based intimacy practices across a number of genres. Danielle Micich, Sarah Lozoff, Molly Tipping, Kristina Fluty, and Samantha Murray are based in the United States, Australia, the UK, and Europe, and shared with us some of these complexities, insight, and advice in order to create an awareness of practice and, importantly, the reasons behind the variations.

Danielle Micich is the Artistic Director/CEO of the contemporary dance company Force Majeure in Australia and also an intimacy coordinator (IC). Note that terminology varies, an intimacy coordinator is film-based in the US, and other titles including intimacy director, facilitator, designer, and/or choreographer are used in live performance. 'Intimacy Professional' is a catchall term that is being used to cover all delineations.

> *Currently the dance industry has not developed protocols for Dance Intimacy. It has safe dance practices, but this does not include contact, improvisation and intimacy. My skills as an IC have been engaged for film, tv and theatre companies and fortunate for Force Majeure and any artist engaging with us, they are held within a safe space and supported in all content being developed appropriately, especially enhanced or intimate scenes.*
> – Danielle Micich

Dance is a disciplined art form, with dancers starting their training at a very young age. They are often taught through touch-based lessons, following all verbal and physical instructions rather than voicing opinion or practicing agency. Molly Tipping, a somatic practitioner and consent educator specializing in anxiety, embodiment, and the performing arts, spoke about power dynamics and voice.

> *Dance is slowly waking up to the calls for consent. Dance schools have removed hands-on corrections, universities offer touch corrections if requested, conferences are speaking to consent, and companies are hiring intimacy co-ordinators.*
>
> *But a simple truth prevails – dancers are trained not to speak – literally and metaphorically. The dance class is mostly a voiceless space for students. And traditional hierarchical power dynamics further condition the silence. Dancers, often praised for their etiquette, compliance, and discipline undergo intense training designed to make pliable their body. With this, however, they also learn to override their pain, fatigue, physiological urges, and threat responses, with some teachers asking students to 'leave their emotions at the door.' These methods de-robe the body of the person and further prime dancers for silence.*
>
> *A more complex fashioning also occurs in the creation of the 'neutral body.' In a quest to liberate, de-sexualise and in some cases de-gender the human form dance can aspire toward the borderless and boundaryless body. Arms, buttocks and genitalia lose distinction and sexually sensitive areas become neutralised.*
>
> – Molly Tipping, Somatic Practitioner and Consent Educator

Sarah Lozoff is one of three collaborators who developed the US-based company IDID: Intimacy Direction in Dance. Sarah stresses two points when considering intimacy in dance:

> 1. *Dancers, in most instances, have an incredible amount of control over their bodies, however, can often experience less agency than other performing artists.*
> 2. *Every count in dance is choreographed. However, moments such as kissing often are not. If we break down those moments and choreograph them as well, we not only create a better working environment, but also better, braver, more specific storytelling.*
>
> – Sarah Lozoff, Intimacy Director

Additionally, post-pandemic, the need for intimacy direction seems essential for some to create braver spaces. Sarah, who has been engaged by American Ballet Theatre and RudduR Dance in New York City, commented that post-Covid 19 there was a dichotomy with more fear around closeness, intimacy, and touch, while artists were also yearning to be connected. This was particularly true as performers began to shed their protective face masks in the studios, so it was important to facilitate a "brave way to make art" at an intense time.[5]

Kristina Fluty, Associate Professor at The Theatre School at DePaul University, is a professional dancer and choreographer who has been involved in consent-based processes over a period of 25 years. This exposure has impacted her own work. Based in Chicago, Kristina is a dancer/collaborator with Molly Shanahan/Mad Shak, where they practice 'consent forward' in rehearsals.

> *We always check in with each other before we begin to work about how we are doing physically, mentally, emotionally. Before doing any touch-based processes (frequently), we also pause to make sure we are all on board with what is about to happen. If that process includes improvisation, we tell each other where we are okay with being touched on our bodies, as well as with what quality (firm, light, direct, etc.). The improvisation always has parameters, as well, such as 'we are going to explore shoulder and knee contact that melts into an embrace.' This mode of working prepared me well for choreographing intimacy in theatre, even though we were not considering it 'intimacy choreography' in our dance processes.*
> – Kristina Fluty, Dancer, Choreographer, and Intimacy Facilitator

As a stage manager you might not be directly involved in the intimacy work or even witness the consent discussions, as this again depends on the company. Danielle relies heavily on a stage manager in her process, and also requires documentation in the form of blocking and rehearsal reports, which are less common in dance. One note from several of the facilitators is that the work takes time, in the same way a fight call would, so this must be factored into the schedule.

> *It's an investment that pays back tenfold in the long run. If you short cut, it will compound, and you'll find that problems will arise quickly that are difficult to resolve.*
> – Danielle Micich

Both Danielle and Sarah note that intimacy rehearsals and consent discussions are a time investment that will pay back in the long run. The specific protocols may even have shifted by the time the stage manager joins a company for technical rehearsals, so you are witnessing the end product, not the full procedure.

> *Take time to establish boundaries at the beginning of the rehearsal process and make sure those boundaries are both respected and allowed to change. This allows for trust to be developed, which can encourage greater risk taking during the creative process. Once in tech, the dancers will have practiced the 'longhand' enough that they'll have developed a shorthand, requiring far less time, in their consent checks.*
> – Sarah Lozoff

Power dynamics in the rehearsal studio is different in dance, as we have previously noted. So be clear on what your responsibilities as a stage manager are in this process. At the very least, you will be a contact point for dancers if choreography does not go to plan. But be aware that you may not be the first point of call, as the stage manager is often considered production and not a company member. We advise that you practice approachability in any situation.

Samantha Murray, an Intimacy Coordinator based in the UK and Europe also brought copyright into the discussion. On many ballets, there is specific copyright on content. Therefore, requests for alterations to any movement may be complicated, or not permitted. Samantha questions, if 'no' is not an option, are you really seeking consent? This is one of the complexities in navigating agreement frameworks in dance.

> *A relevant question that emerged was how does consent-based practice interact with choreographed and copyrighted movement and touch? In contemporary performance, where work might initially be co-created with one set of dancer's parameters, how does this successfully transfer to a new set of performers? Similar to the copyrighted movement in ballet, how might a production navigate personal touch preferences as applied to what is essentially body as script? For stage managers, the responsibility of navigating performer safety and agency within a protected, codified canon leads to the question of what strategies, if any, can respect both the creator content and self-led boundaries, both in rehearsal and real-time performance?*
> – Samantha Murray, Intimacy Coordinator

A consideration for stage managers to bear in mind when working with a company incorporating moments of intimacy and/or violence in a production is agency and the voice of the performer. If these have not been actively invited into a traditional dance space in the past, then a dialogue around consent may be challenging for some. Molly suggests what may be needed is a deep and nuanced industry discussion that addresses "how we accidentally train consent out of our dancers." She, along with the team we spoke with, is optimistic on what the future holds and says emphatically: Watch this space! As a stage manager, we suggest always keeping in the forefront of this issue that protocols are fluid and even as procedures are noted down as a guiding framework, there will be adaptations to be made as we continue to navigate this important topic.

OPERA REHEARSALS

The role of the stage manager in an opera rehearsal is very similar to that of the stage manager in a traditional theatrical production. Our job is to run the rehearsal room, track and communicate daily notes to and from the production teams and directing/creative staff, and prepare for the technical rehearsals. Let's look at those major functions and how they differ from traditional theatrical productions.

FROM PRE-PRODUCTION TO FIRST REHEARSAL

Now that we have created the production book and relevant paperwork and prepared the rehearsal space and production calendar, let's look at how we approach broader topics, adapting to the different phases of rehearsal from the first day of music to the final rehearsal room run.

MUSIC REHEARSALS

The opera rehearsal period begins with two to three days of music with both the chorus and the principals, working separately, with the conductor. As we discussed earlier, the chorus is working on a Schedule of Services. Their first two to three days of rehearsal are music with the chorus director. This is when the members of the chorus learn their music. Unlike principal performers, the chorus is not required to know their music at the first rehearsal, so in these first few days the chorus director and/or assistant conductor work with the chorus to teach them the music. Stage management rarely attends these rehearsals, though they may set up the room. Subsequently, with the official beginning of the rehearsal period, the principal company will work with the conductor to review the music, confirming cuts and setting tempos. There will also be a day when the conductor works with the chorus to tweak what the chorus director and/or assistant conductor have taught the chorus. Again, that all occurs within the hours as listed on the chorus' Schedule of Services.

To set up the room for music rehearsals, consider the needs of the people in the space. The performers will need a chair, a sturdy music stand, and a pencil and/or highlighter. The pianist needs a tuned piano, a solid music stand on their piano as discussed in Chapter 3: Pre-production, and sufficient light to see their music. The conductor will need a stool, a sturdy music stand, and again, sufficient light to see their music on the stand. Sometimes, a company may use a special conductor's stand which may have lighting built into the stand, but those are often only seen in the orchestra pit and not in the rehearsal studio. With each of the lighting needs, be sure to consider a power source and safety tape to control renegade power cords. The cast chairs and stands should be set in a semi-circle around the conductor, approximately ten to twelve feet away from the front edge of the conductor's music stand. Think about who will be rehearsing in each rehearsal session. You do not need 20 chairs set up if you are only working with five principal singers. Likewise, if you have the entire chorus, you may need multiple rows of chairs and music stands to accommodate the size of the company. As a courtesy to the conductor, it is common to provide the chorus with name tags and a color notation for their vocal part, e.g. blue for bass, green for tenor, purple for mezzo, pink for soprano. An easy way to add the color is by creating a border of color with a highlighter. Also, as you may use these nametags for multiple rehearsals, or across several productions throughout the season, invest in reusable plastic nametags.

> Always have cool (not cold) or room temperature water, cups, tissues, hand sanitizer, and throat lozenges, such as Ricola in plentiful supply throughout the rehearsal process.

> Green Tip: Purchase reusable nametags to use across multiple rehearsals and productions and encourage performers to bring reusable water bottles for their personal use in rehearsal.

Unlike a traditional musical theatre production, it is rare for the entire company to sing through the entire opera from start to finish. You need to rely on your initial timings from the recordings mentioned in Chapter 3: Pre-Production to keep paperwork updated. Once you are into runs of acts, you can get more accurate timings for your production.

STAGING REHEARSALS

Sometimes the staging director will join the music rehearsals, but often they do not join the process until the beginning of staging rehearsals. During the pre-production period you taped out the floor and retrieved rehearsal props and costumes. Have the rehearsal room ready with these items on the first day of staging rehearsals. Additionally, have the chorus nametags on hand for use during chorus staging rehearsals. You do not need to use nametags for the principals during principal staging rehearsals, but you may want to use them when the whole company comes together for the first time.

The staging director and, if there is one, the assistant staging director will share a table at the front of the rehearsal room, to the side of the conductor whose music stand is always positioned at center. To the other side of the director's table is the stage manager's table. The assistant stage managers will usually work from the sides of the room, positioning themselves to stage right or stage left so they can cue singers and assist with props and costumes during the rehearsal.

> Since the assistant stage managers are stationed at the sides of the rehearsal hall, set up how you will be communicating with the team before rehearsals begin. For example, do you have a group chat setup on your computers or maybe you can use a group text.

Staging rehearsals are run the same as they would be for a standard theatrical production. Taking breaks according to the standards of the company or the union that is governing the rehearsal, in this case, AGMA. Note that AGMA negotiates an individual contract with each opera company under its jurisdiction; therefore, rules that govern an opera company in Pittsburgh may differ from those in Cincinnati or Houston. Always read the specific agreement for details governing the principal, chorus, super, assistant staging director, and stage management team's hours and standards of operation and safety. One major difference in opera staging rehearsals is that it is often the role of the assistant staging director to keep the official record of the blocking. However, this does not relieve you as the stage manager from knowing the blocking. Remember, the rehearsal period is preparing you for technical rehearsals, so you'll need to know the blocking to communicate with the lighting designer and call lighting and spotlight cues. Of course, it is critical to stay in good communication with the assistant staging director to ensure that you both have the same information regarding entrances, exits, and general blocking. Use this information to update the Who What Where or ask the assistant staging director to update that information directly. Having a good working relationship with the assistant staging director is crucial. As noted previously, in larger opera houses, the assistant staging director may run rehearsals while the stage manager is working with the technical team.

In addition to updating the Who What Where, the stage management team will need to know the entrance locations and timings so that they can accurately page each principal and chorus member to stage and cue their entrances during technical rehearsals and performance. Whether you have created a paper score or a digital score, for each entrance, put a translucent/colored sticky note on the page/system/measure writing the name of the character or "chorus" on the flag. This notes your cue for the performer's entrance. Likewise, two to five minutes before each entrance note a "**page to stage**" for those performer/s on a larger sticky note or flag. A sample "page to stage" sounds like this when called over the backstage paging system, "Attention *Tosca* Company. Attention *Tosca* Company. Places please for the Te Deum. Places for the Te Deum. All principals, chorus, and children, places for the Te Deum." Another sample may sound like this, "Attention *Tosca* Company. Attention *Tosca* Company. Places Tatiana Smith to stage left. Places, please, Tatiana Smith to stage left." In the stage manager's calling book, it will simply say "Page: Chorus, Te Deum" or "Page: Tatiana Smith, stage left" on the sticky note. Get these noted in your calling book sooner rather than later so that you can practice quietly saying these words during rehearsal. Learning how to call cues over the headset and page singers over the backstage paging system is akin to learning to rub your head and pat your belly at the same time so the sooner you can begin to practice, the more comfortable you'll be when you transition to the stage.

> Confirm pronoun preferences for cast members if using a formal prefix in the paging. Likewise, updated practice is to move away from gendered paging, so instead of calling the "men's chorus," rather call the "bass and baritone chorus" or "the soldier's chorus," if the chorus is easily identified by a character group, common song title such as the example of the "Te Deum," or a location title, such as "Chorus for Café Momus" in Puccini's *La Bohème*.

PAPERWORK: ADDING CREW DUTIES TO THE WHO WHAT WHERE

Staging rehearsals help prepare the stage management team for technical rehearsals. As such, the stage management team is responsible for keeping the Who What Where up to date with accurate information regarding who is entering when and

P/S/M	Time	Who	What	Where	Props	Costumes	Notes
32/2/2	27:00	Character A	EN	SR 1	Box groceries	Footman 1: Fedora, T-shirt, white, Collared Shirt, blue, Vest, brown, Bow tie, brown, Overcoat, tweed, Underwear, Trousers, tan, Socks, black, Boots, black	
32/2/2	28:00	Character A	EX	SL 1	Box groceries	**CHANGE: REMOVE** Fedora, Overcoat, tweed **ADD** Apron, white (:45 sec)	
35/1/1	28:45	Character A	EN	SL 1		Footman 1: T-shirt, white, Collared Shirt, blue, Vest, brown, Bow tie, brown, Apron, white, Underwear, Trousers, tan, Socks, black, Boots, black	

Figure 4.5 Sample Who What Where with additional entrances and exits.

where, as well as what costume each person is wearing and prop they may be carrying. This information is critical for the production crew to run the show. In addition to adding this information to the Who What Where, you can begin to add the production crew to the document as well.

Continuing from the example that was begun in Chapter 3: Pre-Production Figure 3.4, Character A may exit the stage wearing one costume but on their next entrance they will have removed some items and added others. In this example, they removed the Fedora, Overcoat, tweed and added Apron, white. In the Costume column at that exit point, a stage manager may write "CHANGE: REMOVE Fedora, Overcoat, tweed, ADD Apron, white." Then on their next entrance, their costume cell would read as: "T-shirt, white, Collared Shirt, blue, Vest, brown, Bow tie, brown, Apron, white;" of course, along with whatever was covering their legs and feet!

As the stage management team and the assistant staging director continue to build upon the Who What Where throughout the rehearsal process updating entrance and exit locations, placement, and timings, they also will begin to add information for the various crews. Let's take our example in Figure 4.5. If Character A's re-entrance was quick, following their exit you would add a row with information for the wardrobe department to "REMOVE Overcoat, tweed, ADD Apron, white from Character A." Noting location and the amount of time for the change. Perhaps Character A was carrying a box of groceries and needs to hand them off to a Props person upon their exit. That information could also be added for the props crew in a row between Character A's exit and the wardrobe change.

The Who What Where can serve as a running sheet for the wardrobe, wigs, props, and deck crew. Although many crew prefer having their information on their own individual running paperwork, a comprehensive document like the Who What Where can be indispensable to the assistant stage managers who are looking at the big picture. Check with your company to confirm company paperwork policies, while it may be common to give the Who What Where to the wardrobe department

P/S/M	Time	Who	What	Where	Props	Costumes	Notes
32/2/2	27:00	Character A	EN	SR 1	Box groceries	Footman 1: Fedora, T-shirt, white, Collared Shirt, blue, Vest, brown, Bow tie, brown, Overcoat, tweed, Underwear, Trousers, tan, Socks, black, Boots, black	
32/2/2	28:00	Character A	EX	SL 1	Box groceries	CHANGE: **REMOVE** Fedora, Overcoat, tweed ADD Apron, white (:45 sec)	
34/2/1	28:00	**PROPS**: CATCH Box groceries from Character A, SL 1, strike and store					
34/2/1	28:00	**WARDROBE**: CHANGE Character A SL1: *REMOVE Fedora, Overcoat, tweed ADD Apron, white (:45 sec)*					
35/1/1	28:45	Character A	EN	SL 1		Footman 1: T-shirt, white, Collared Shirt, blue, Vest, brown, Bow tie, brown, Apron, white, Underwear, Trousers, tan, Socks, black, Boots, black	

Figure 4.6 Sample Who What Where with props and wardrobe crew duties added.

for them to build their own running paperwork in one company, it may be up to the stage management department to build the wardrobe running paperwork in another company. Being prepared for the most complex situation is usually easier to adapt from than not being prepared and having to scramble to get the work done at the last minute.

Again, the stage management team and the assistant staging director should work together updating and ultimately finalizing this document throughout studio rehearsals and technical rehearsals. Where one assistant stage manager may be updating costume information, another may be working primarily on props, all while the assistant staging director or stage manager updates entrance placements, locations, and timings. The Who What Where is and should be a collaborative document. There is no greater way to know your show than documenting it at this level of detail. In Figure 4.7 we have an excellent example of a comprehensive Who What Where created for the Cincinnati Opera's 2023 production of *Madame Butterfly* by stage management team member, Rowan Rozzi. These two pages cover the first 14 minutes of the opera; the completed document is 11 pages long. Notice here that they used the 'costume title' option as opposed to a full list of pieces.

RUNNING THE ROOM

In addition to updating the Who What Where, the stage management team is responsible for cueing the singers onto stage for each entrance, this includes during rehearsal. It is critical to have accurate entrance notations in the stage management teams' scores.

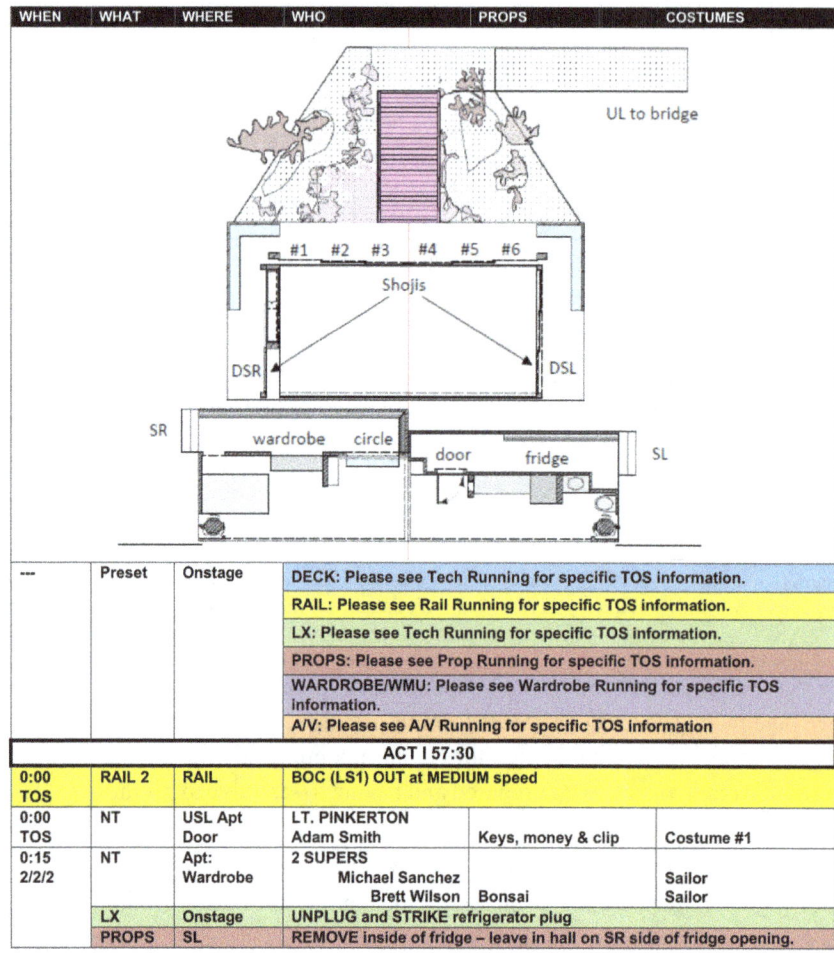

Figure 4.7 Who What Where *Madame Butterfly* at Cincinnati Opera.

Source: Created by Rowan Rozzi.

Green Tip: You can set up one digital score for the assistant stage managers to share noting all stage left entrances in one color and all stage right entrances in another color. This allows the team to know entrances on both sides of the stage giving the team flexibility for who is running which side of the stage during performance, or in case someone gets ill and must call out.

WHEN	WHAT	WHERE	WHO	PROPS	COSTUMES
0:20 3/1/1	Onstage Action	WARDROBE: Sanchez **ADD** Military jacket & boots to Pinkerton			
0:35 4/1/1	NT	Apt: Circle Screen	GORO Julius Ahn	Model	Costume #1
1:30 7/1/2	NT to Preset	SL to Apt: Hallway/ Fridge	SUZUKI Nozomi Kato 2 SUPERS Zain Mehal Anjali Alm-Basu		Costume #1 Attendant w/ hat Attendant w/ hat
2:15 10/2/2	NT	Apt: Fridge	SUZUKI Nozomi Kato 2 SUPERS Zain Mehal Anjali Alm-Basu		Costume #1 Attendant w/ hat Attendant w/ hat
2:45 11/1/2	NT to Preset	US of Shoji #4	SHARPLESS Nmon Ford	Umbrella, Hankie	Costume #1 w/ hat
4:40 17/2/1	DECK 2	SHIFT Apartment wagon A to SR on WHITE spike (Pinkerton, Goro, 2 Super Sailors riding wagon) SHIFT Apartment wagon B to SL on WHITE spike (Suzuki, 2 Super Attendants riding wagon)			
	LX	Onstage	With Deck Q2: PAGE cables on Apartment wagon A & B		
	RAIL 2.5	RAIL	#1 Black Legs (LS2) OUT at MED-FAST speed		
5:05 18/2/3	DECK 4	SHIFT Fantasy Room to DS WHITE spike (Sharpless riding)			
W/ Deck 4 COMP	DECK A/F	SHIFT Garden to DS to connect to Fantasy Room on WHITE			
W/ ASM clear	DECK 5	DECK	Apartment restore to sides of Fantasy Room		
W/ garden clear	RAIL A/F	RAIL	US Black Scrim (LS72) OUT Blue Back Drop (LS73) IN Velour for Moon Roll (LS75) IN to low Moon Roll (LS76) IN RP (LS78) IN Pagoda Bed (on motors) IN to ceiling cap		
W/ Rail COMP	LX	US ONS	ROLL US Ground Row into position		
Auto w/ shift comp	PROPS	SL	REPLACE inside of fridge after shift complete.		
5:40 20/3/1	NT	Shoji #4	SHARPLESS Nmon Ford	Umbrella, Hankie	Costume #1 w/ hat
6:35 24/3/3	Onstage Action	Alm-Basu **CLOSE** shoji #4			
9:15 31/1/1	PROPS	SL	SET Apple box for Henri		
14:20 45/1/1	Onstage Action	Alm-Basu **OPEN** Shojis #4-6 Mehal **OPEN** Shojis #1-3. Super Sailors **OPEN** DSL shoji.			
14:35 46/1/1	Onstage Action	WARDROBE: Pinkerton **ADD** Military Hat			

Figure 4.7 (Continued)

To cue an entrance, several bars before the singer's entrance get their attention, make eye contact, and raise your hand in the air. At the moment of the cue, point to the stage to indicate that the singer should start moving. Finding the right point in the score to signal the 'go' can take some adjustment and practice. The goal is that the singer is on stage when the director wants them seen by the audience. The team will get plenty of practice doing this during the rehearsal period. Don't be surprised if these cues change a bit when you transition to stage as the distance from the wings to the entrance point may be much longer than what you had in the rehearsal studio, or a heavier costume may move differently than modern clothing and slow down the performer's gait.

> When communicating the pick-up point in rehearsal to the conductor and the pianist, note where in the score you will begin. Use rehearsal numbers or rehearsal numbers plus measure numbers to give the music team the starting location. For example, "Maestro, is 3 after Rehearsal 8 a good spot for you to start?" This communicates that you would like to resume three measures after rehearsal number eight.

The stage management team arrives prior to the first cast member's call to set-up the room for the day's activities, updating sign in sheets and announcements on the callboard and laying out chorus nametags. Then, during rehearsals, the stage management team tracks changes in staging that may affect the show running paperwork, and tracks notes that are critical to the production departments. Each day, the stage management team sends out a daily production notes/rehearsal report and may also send out the daily call sheet for the next day's rehearsal. If the stage manager is not responsible for sending out the daily call, then they will be responsible for communicating the needs of the next rehearsal to the rehearsal/scheduling department by a designated time each day. Be certain to meet with your director, conductor, and if necessary, choreographer to determine each day's rehearsal's needs well before the scheduling department's deadline.

> Pro Tip: *Keep in mind that the rehearsal department is sifting through various requests from multiple departments. They can see the forest of the company, while you might only be seeing a handful of trees. And when they say they need the schedule by a certain time of day, they mean it!*
> – Connie Grubbs, Stage Manager, Metropolitan Opera

Operas are inherently expensive. There are a lot of personnel involved in most productions. It is up to the stage managers to maintain a disciplined room to keep the schedule on track and moving forward with alacrity. That is not to race the creative process, but to keep the train on the track and moving from station to station in a timely manner.

> Pro Tip: *Use technology to your advantage! Throughout the rehearsal process and especially right before you leave the rehearsal room, take photographs of furniture, prop and costume set ups and presets. Taking photographs (and even video) can be extremely helpful to visually communicate to the crew what the presets look like and how everything is being used. This practice also saves time as you no longer have to sketch presets or create a visual preset on a computer.*
> – Christy Ney, Stage Manager

FINAL ROOM RUN

Most opera singers are not performing the role in which they have been cast for the first time. This standard allows for a short rehearsal period, often only two to two and a half weeks from first music rehearsal to final rehearsal room run-through. An experienced opera staging director working with an experienced opera cast can work through an act in only a few days. Principal singers are typically rehearsed separately from the chorus and supers. Supers are typically rehearsed with the chorus. A children's chorus is typically rehearsed with the chorus, whereas a principal child would be rehearsed with the principal cast. All these groups are brought together during full act work-throughs/run-throughs. Then at the end of the rehearsal period, you'll run the entire opera, inviting the design and lead members of the production team to observe and take notes. For example, the head of wardrobe and/or wigs may attend a room run-through, but the wardrobe crew may not. The lighting designer is likely to attend the run-through, though, you're not likely to see the scenic designer if the set was pulled from the company's warehouse. Likewise, if the costumes were from a rental package, you won't see the costume designer. This all changes if this staging is an original production or if the opera itself is being newly developed and created.

During the run-throughs of the acts and then the final room run-through, the stage management team should be checking and confirming timings, entrances and exits, cueing and paging placements, as well as ensuring the stage props and costumes are all preset and moving appropriately throughout the show. You are stage managing the room and preparing for the next phase ... the technical rehearsals. Enjoy the moment!

FINAL THOUGHTS

At this point, the production has been fully staged. As your rehearsal process has resolved in final run-throughs of the show, you have noted pertinent blocking and updated your paperwork, and created the initial documents for technical teams to begin their work during stage rehearsals. The stage management team has noted entrance cues for all the performer's entrances. You may have received and written preliminary cues into your calling score or book from various designers.

You have a clear understanding of your role and responsibilities, genre-specific terminology, interaction with key collaborators, and have attended music, staging, and dance rehearsals. You and your team are well prepared for the next phase in the process: stage and technical rehearsals.

Up next, we'll look at working with the design and technical teams as we move into onstage and technical rehearsals. You'll develop strategies for noting cues in your calling book and we'll review genre-related terminology and review alternate casting considerations. Onstage and technical are an exciting time for the stage manager as we provide the glue that brings all the technical and artistic elements together into a cohesive performance.

NOTES

1 "Equity Glossary." *Actors Equity Association Membership Education*. www.actorsequity.org.
2 Ibid.
3 "Basic Agreement between Cincinnati Opera Association, Inc. and American Guild of Musical Artists." American Guild of Musical Artists. www.musicalartists.org.
4 Maria del Pilar Naranjo Rico. https://www.contemporary-dance.org/labanotation.html.
5 Sarah Lozoff, phone interview, July 31, 2023.

CHAPTER 5

Technical Rehearsals

Opera and dance performance genres handle technical rehearsals differently due to certain requirements that are only applicable to their specific fields. In the following pages we separate the disciplines to highlight processes that may be managed in ways that you may not have encountered in traditional theatre experiences. To streamline this discussion, the chapter begins with opera-specific paperwork and technical rehearsals, which will be followed by dance-specific tools and technical rehearsals. You will note that working with an orchestra is the same in both genres, so this will not be repeated. Your move to the stage follows protocols similar to general productions, and a reminder that you are a guest onstage until the safety walk and handover.

OPERA TECHNICAL AND DRESS REHEARSALS

The stage manager begins to prepare for technical rehearsals from the moment they start pre-production, familiarizing themselves with the music, performers' entrances and exits, props tracking, costume changes, and timings. Every moment in rehearsal is readying the company to move to stage, add the technical elements, and eventually to perform the opera before an audience. This is why documentation through detailed paperwork is so critical to the stage management team's success. The Who What Where, when thoroughly fleshed out provides a play-by-play of every action on the deck: a score notation and timing for every singer's entrance and exit, including what they are wearing and what props they are carrying; it also includes every scenic move done by the stage crew and every costume change made by the wardrobe crew. Prior to moving to stage, it is a good plan for the stage management team to meet to review the entire production from top to bottom so that all team members have the same information, from entrance cues for the performers to all deck moves for the crew. Assistant stage managers will typically build the crew running paperwork and the stage manager will develop the calling book.

To prepare for both final paperwork creation and the eventual move to stage, ask the director of production for a tour of the venue. You'll want to note entrances and crossover spaces on stage as well as dressing room areas, common areas, and potential office space. Knowing the limits and capabilities of the backstage space, will influence how you set up your backstage space and subsequently how you note your paperwork.

PAPERWORK, PAPERWORK, PAPERWORK!

In many companies with union crews, the stage management team is responsible for creating all running paperwork for the deck, wardrobe, and wig and makeup teams. This is not customary in all companies, so ask the director of production what the protocol is for each opera house where you are employed. As noted earlier, a thorough Who What Where will include all deck running information and all wardrobe running information; however, most crew do not want a completed Who What Where to run their track, they just want the information that is relevant to them. Show running paperwork for an opera is not different than show running paperwork for a play or musical; however, it is less common for the stage management team to create wardrobe running paperwork for a theatre company, so we'll focus on that here. From the information in Who What Where, you can quickly develop a **First Entrance Timings** (Figure 5.1). This document is critical for the wigs and makeup team to set their **chair times** for the performers. In most opera companies, there is a wig and makeup department who will do the makeup for all principal singers and specialty makeup for comprimario parts, chorus, and supers. And generally, they will also oversee not only maintaining, but also putting all wigs on and taking wigs off all performers who are wigged in the production. Unlike a theatrical play where the performers' call time is half hour prior to curtain, it is not unusual for opera singers **call times** (Figure 5.2) to begin two hours prior to curtain because of their specialized makeup needs. When performing in a sizeable opera house, makeup tends to need to be more pronounced – it takes a professional makeup artist to ensure that the performer's features can be seen by the furthest audience member, but not to look clownish to those in the front rows. Typically, a makeup artist will work on a singer for 15–30 minutes and then move on to the next performer. To make this an efficient process, the stage manager will provide the makeup team with the timing of the first entrance for each member or group in the cast, for example, the chorus may not appear until the top of Act 2, as in Puccini's *La Bohème*, whereas there are several principals who appear in Act 1.

The wig and makeup head then uses this information to assign each performer to a member of the wig and makeup team and a time for them to be in the makeup artist's chair. Be sure to include any pre-show calls that may affect the performers such as chorus vocal warm ups, fight calls, intimacy calls, onstage pre-show activity, etc. so that the wig and makeup head can plan around those. If a performer does not appear until later in the opera, they will typically receive a later call time. For your sanity, even a later call should be set at the start of the intermission so that you can check-in the performer before the second or third act begins. The wig and makeup head will then share the call time with the stage management team who will post it for all performers and the wardrobe crew.

Time of entrance	Performer	Character	Notes/Costume
07:00	Performer #1	Nurse	Act 1 costume/wig
07:00	Performer #2	Doctor	Act 1 costume/wig

Figure 5.1 Sample Opera First Entrance Timings.

	Makeup Artist #1	Makeup Artist #2	Makeup Artist #3
1:00pm/6:00pm	Performer #1	Performer #2	Performer #3
1:30pm/6:30pm	Performer #4	Performer #5	Performer #6
2:00pm/7:00pm	Performer #7	Performer #8	Chorus Wigs
2:30pm/7:30pm		Performer #9	

Figure 5.2 Sample Opera Makeup Chair Call Times.

> Typically, the performer will need to be in any costume piece that goes over their head prior to being seated in the makeup chair so remember to coordinate dressing room access with the wardrobe team to ensure that the cast is prompt to their makeup call. A late arrival to the makeup chair can back up the start time of the performance, and that error can carry significant cost to the company if it puts the performance into overtime.

While you are in rehearsal, you will need to work with the wardrobe head, or designee from the costume department, to develop the necessary wardrobe running paperwork. In addition to the First Entrance Timings and the Who What Where, the wardrobe team may need the following documents: **Costume Preset** and **Wardrobe Running Plot**; however, some wardrobe teams may prefer to simply use the Who What Where. The Pre-show/Post-show Costume Check In are not usually created by stage management, but rather by wardrobe.

The **Costume Preset** document would reflect any presets that are outside of the dressing room, for example, in a backstage quick-change booth. We don't tend to see many quick changes in operas, but in case there is, the stage management team would need to notify the wardrobe team of this. The information for what is preset would reflect the details of the costume and the location of the preset. A simple alteration to the Costume Check-in document would be to add the location of the preset, for example, "stage right changing booth." If a photo of the final costume is available, include that here as well. After all, a picture is worth a thousand words.

Stage Right Changing Booth

Performer: Performer #1, Act 1 Nurse

Tights, white

Petticoat, white

Skirt, blue striped

Corset

Blouse, white

Vest, dark blue

Cape, dark blue

Shoes, blue heels

Cap, nurse

Necklace, rosary

Performer: Performer #2, Act 1 Doctor

Overcoat, blue

Bonnet, blue

The **Wardrobe Running Plot** (Figure 5.3) will note any costume changes that are overseen by the wardrobe team, some may be quick, and some may have considerable time available for the change, but documenting all changes is critical information for the wardrobe team to do their job. Information needed in this document includes the performer's exit time, performer's name, their exit location, the location of the costume change, costume items removed, costume items added, time available for the change, the performer's next entrance time and location, and notes. In Figure 5.3, Δ means "change." Sometimes, instead of a comprehensive list of what is being removed or added during the change, the stage manager can simply note the overall title of the costume such as "Act 1 nurse" to "Act 1 pajamas," and then the wardrobe people will fill in the details that are more significant to their crew. The advantage of doing it this way is that as a costume designer makes changes during tech, the wardrobe head can usually update those changes more accurately and quickly than the stage management team. Again, all this information comes from the Who What Where which was developed through conversations with the costume department (designer, shop manager, wardrobe head, etc.) and the wigs and makeup department, in addition to the staging or blocking.

Information such as the performer's next entrance location can be helpful for the wardrobe crew member who is assisting the performer to prepare for their next entrance. In addition to the above costume specific information, you or the wardrobe head will need to assign crew members to each change. Again, who does this

EX Time	Name	EX Loc	Δ Loc	REMOVE	ADD	Δ Time	EN Time	EN Loc	Notes

Figure 5.3 Sample Wardrobe Running Plot.

is a question for both the director of production and the wardrobe head, establishing expectations ahead of time can save frustration later. Finally, this information should also be shared with the wig and makeup department as there may be wig changes with the costume changes, or they may want to touch up hair or makeup following a costume change. If wigs are also changed, then add a column to reflect that information as well.

> This document is best set up in landscape, not portrait, as there is a lot of information noted with each entry.

PAGING AND CUEING PERFORMERS

Although wardrobe running paperwork specifics are not critical to the calling stage manager, there is some costume information that is necessary to share with the calling stage manager. First, it is extremely helpful for the calling stage manager to know when a large costume change is taking place. This helps them run the dress rehearsal as smoothly as possible. For example, if the stage manager knows that several members of the cast are involved in a quick change, then they will know not to call a hold until the costume change has been confirmed to have been completed allowing both the cast and the wardrobe team an appropriate amount of time to practice their change. Second, the assistant stage manager should point out any pages to stage for the wardrobe team to the calling stage manager. In addition to calling cues, the stage manager pages each performer to stage for their entrances and calls the crew to stage for their changes. Once a change is complete, it is not necessary for any crew member to hang out backstage when they may be more comfortable waiting in a crew room. Or they may be busy in the dressing room preparing for an upcoming change and a reminder call for another change may be necessary to keep the show running smoothly. A page to stage is an announcement over the backstage paging system which presumably (or not presumably, this should be requested and checked) goes to all dressing rooms, the wig and makeup shop, and any crew and orchestra lounges or green rooms. A standard page would be something like, "Attention *Barber of Seville* Company. Attention *Barber of Seville* Company. Paging wardrobe to stage left for the soldier change. Paging wardrobe to stage left for the soldier change." It is helpful to repeat the page twice as folks may be talking and not hear the information if you rattle it off too quickly. Likewise, note the team you are paging, the location where they will be needed, and why they are receiving the page. Please be conscious of using inclusive, non-gendered, non-binary information in your pages, for example, the use of "ladies and gentlemen" has gone out of favor and more general terms such as "folks" or "members of the orchestra" are becoming more commonly heard over backstage pages. That being said, opera is steeped in tradition and often performers are paged to stage using the formal salutation of Mr. or Ms. plus their surname. Check with each performer to ask their preference on paging salutations and confirm the pronunciation of their name. Again, usage of "men's chorus" should be replaced with something more inclusive, for example, the "sailor's chorus" which represents the characters, not the gender of those performers or characters.

As noted previously, every performer is paged to stage for their entrance, likewise, they are cued onstage by a member of the stage management team. During the stage management team meeting, every stage manager should ensure that they have the same information for each performer's entrance, even those occurring on the other side of the stage from where they will be cueing. This creates a back up and allows the team to move from one position to another as needed. The calling stage manager has every entrance noted and using the timings, notes both a preliminary and a final page to stage for each performer. To determine when to page the performer to the stage consider the following: how far from the stage is their dressing room and how large of a group are you trying to get to the stage. If the dressing rooms are far away, the performer/s will need more time; likewise, if you are trying to assemble a 40-person chorus, you will need more time. In both cases, a preliminary page of five minutes is customary. The final page can be determined by how long it takes to walk at a brisk pace from the dressing room to the stage and still arrive in time for an entrance. Typically, two to three minutes is sufficient for a final page. However, if you are paging a principal performer and their dressing room is located ten feet from the backstage door, your preliminary page is probably going to be two or three minutes, and your final page will be one or two minutes. A sample page would be, "Attention *Barber of Seville* Company. Attention *Barber of Seville* Company. Paging Mr. Coconut (or Harrison Coconut if using a non-gendered approach) to stage left. Paging Mr. Coconut to stage left." Sometimes, the stage manager will include a purpose for the page, "Paging Mr. Coconut to stage left for the party scene." Keep in mind that entrances set in the rehearsal hall will likely need to be moved earlier once the company moves to the stage. Distances traveled in the rehearsal hall rarely match that of the distance from the wings to being seen onstage.

> Pro Tip: *The more prepared that you are with these announcements, the clearer and calmer you will be when speaking on the page mic. Anytime you want to address the company or crew on the page mic or over headset, it is important to remember that the tone of your voice infers a lot about you. The calmer and clearer your voice is, the more trust and confidence the company and crew have in you. The tone and clarity of your voice is extremely important and is often overlooked.*
>
> – Christy Ney

The calling stage manager writes every page to stage in the calling score. And although every entrance is noted in the calling score, they do not need to be as prominently written as would be in the scores of the assistant stage managers. The best way to mark entrances in the assistant stage manager's score is with a removable sticker, or digitally with a colored sticker. Many stage managers color code their stickers to represent principal, chorus, or supernumerary. Write the name of the character on the sticker and place it so it hovers over the staff lines in the score at the exact point where the cast member is being cued. This can be accomplished similarly whether creating a digital or analog score. When the time comes to cue the performer onstage, just as you did in rehearsal, make eye contact with the performer or you may say, "stand by, please," raise your hand so they can see it, and then at the cue time, point to the stage and say "go." If you do not have stage management team members on both sides of the stage, you can use cue lights to cue the performers. You will need to explain the protocol of "on" means standby and "off" means go to the performers as this is not a standard way of cueing opera performers. Or you could tell your performers to look to the stage manager on the opposite side of the stage for their entrance cue, or if the calling stage manager is backstage, they could throw a cue to a performer, if necessary, although this is not ideal as they have lighting, scenic, media, and sound cues as well as pages to do.

In preparation for the technical rehearsals the stage manager will meet with the design team to determine how the designers will be sharing cueing information with the stage manager. Perhaps they'll give you a list of cues and placements, or there is a calling book from the last time the company did this production, or they'll hand you a score with the cues noted in in it, or maybe, they won't give you any cues in advance, and you'll get them during cueing sessions. Whatever the means, the calling stage manager needs to "**book the cues**." Booking cues is no different for an opera than it is for a play or musical except that you will be working in a score. Cues are noted in the music by Page/System/Measure, or they may be visual cues, in that case you'll need to note the visual trigger you're looking for to call the cue. When noting cues in a score, most seasoned opera stage managers will use stickers, similar to how the entrance cues are booked for the assistant stage managers. Each department will be assigned a specific color, in Figure 5.4, for example, the stage manager used blue for lighting and pink for media, also sometimes called "Tab." Write the department and cue number on the sticker, and then place the sticker over the staff lines. Since the stickers are transparent, you can put them directly on the staff and you'll still be able to see enough of the music notations below. If cues occur simultaneously, as seen with Lx 55 and Tab 47 in Figure 5.4, stack the stickers. Regardless of whether you are calling a single light cue or lights, spots, and rail all together, it is common practice to strike through the calling point in the score with a red line. Again, this can be accomplished digitally using colored boxes instead of flags.

> Put an asterisk (*) or other marking at the point where you want to start speaking the handle for the cue so that you can then comfortably pause before you say the "go." This creates consistency for the operators and if someone else had to call out of your book, they'd know when to start speaking and not have to guess.

As you are assembling the calling book, create a corresponding **Comprehensive Cue Sheet**, sometimes referred to as a Master Cue Sheet. This documents all cues that are called by the stage manager and/or executed as an auto-follow by the crew. The Comprehensive Cue sheet should note score placement (page/system/measure) and trigger, approximate time, department (lighting, follow spots, sound, media, rail, deck, automation, and any other technical cues), number, action, and notes. See Figure 5.5 for a sample document setup.

Figure 5.4 Opera calling score, *Dialogue of the Carmelites* at University of Cincinnati's College-Conservatory of Music.

Source: Created by Rosie Burns Pavlik.

P/S/M	Time	Cue	Trigger	Action	Notes
12/2/1	07:30	Lx 15	Tosca enters	Light through door	
12/2/2	07:30	Deck 2	Tosca enters	Open door SR	Auto close after T's entrance.
12/4/1	0:8:00	Lx 16	Tosca enters	Door light out	After Deck 2 complete

Figure 5.5 Sample Comprehensive Cue Sheet.

It is important to keep both the calling score and the Comprehensive Cue Sheet up to date and accurate. Combined with a thorough Who What Where, and you have an excellent archival snapshot of the production.

> Pro Tip: *Who What Where importance: This document is massive. At the Met, it is sometimes all the stage managers get. We run the entire show off of this one document. Accuracy is important, but so is flexibility. Remember, it's not final until you close the show.*
> – Connie Grubbs

In addition to the cues that are internal to the score, it is necessary to create **Top of Show Sequence**, **Intermission Sequence**, and **Bow Order** calling documents to include in the score; however, because these points usually occur outside of the proper score, the stage manager will need to create these documents separately using a word processing program. The **Top of Show Sequence** is everything from the first backstage page until the score takes over, this includes, but is not limited to the following:

1. Courtesy pages to the company: Two hours to curtain, one hour to curtain, half hour to curtain, fifteen minutes to curtain, and five minutes to places.
2. Courtesy pages for fight, intimacy, or vocal warm ups.
3. Pages to the crew, for example, a call to headset.
4. Front of house calls or contact with house manager.
5. Places calls to the cast, orchestra, and conductor.
   a. Note: Confirm the official orchestra start time with the director of production. Often, there is a five-minute late start built into the orchestra's contract to accommodate a later start time. See Orchestra section later in this chapter.
6. Pre-show announcements (live or recorded).
7. Orchestra tuning.
8. Conductor bow (including any lighting specials or follow spot cues).
9. Light cues, including house lights.
10. Main curtain or show curtain out.

With each of these items, note a trigger, such as "@ 2 hours to curtain" or "@ end of pre-show announcement's *Thank you and enjoy the show*," and what the cue is that you're calling. Note whether the cue is called over the backstage paging system, a radio, or headset, etc. Also, don't forget to note standbys, as well as turning on or off any cue lights. Always confirm the top of show sequence with the stage director, the conductor, and the director of production. Union contracts, aesthetic, and house protocol may dictate variations in the order of operations for everything in the Top of Show call. We recommend writing out any pre-show announcements in their entirety, creating a script for the calling stage manager to follow. Additionally, if there are any live pre-show announcements, such as season-opener speeches, try to get a gist of the content so the calling stage manager can easily anticipate the end of the speech. See Figure 5.6 for a sample of the Top of Show sequence for the 2004

CARMEN
TOP OF SHOW

BLACKOUT CHECK

@ 6:45
Alan "Lx .1 GO"
Gerri: PAGE MIC On
Ameal Sound Ready
√ Maestro Cue Light OFF
√ A/V Monitors ON Pit Booms

@ 7:15
"DR Company 45 minutes"

@ 7:30
"DR Company 1/2 Hour"
"Lx 1 GO" (Preset UP)
ROGER/LARRY: Sets/Props Ready
Curtis "Confirm # of Development Titles"

@ 7:45
"CARMEN Company 15 minutes to Curtain, collecting valuables"

@ 7:50
"Crew to Headset" & "Crew to Headset"

@ 7:53
ROGER: "7 at 7 Please" (Audience bells)
Glenn "Confirming 8:05 Start"

> Headset...Radio... In person/Page
> - Carla & Connie & JAMIE
> - FLY: Carp Jon (BOC)
> - LX: Alan
> - SPOTS: Bill & Dave
> - Spots in Frames #
> - SND: Ameal, voiceover
> - Supertitles: Curtis & Laura
> - BANDA (1) Stage Right

@ 7:55
"CARMEN Company 5 minutes to Places – five, five"
JAMIE: 5 minutes to Maestro

@ 7:58
"Checking Crew on Headset"
Alan "Please give complete for Lx 6-10," Curtis, Bill & Dave, Ameal, Connie, Carla, Jamie, Carp Jon

@ 8:00
Scott: RINGS ORCHESTRA TO PIT
Jamie "Place the Maestro & let me know when you are in the pit"

"Places for Act I"
"Places ONSTAGE"
    PRINCIPALS: MR. J. KELLY
    CHORUS: SOLDIERS, VENDORS, ET AL (NO CIGARETTE GIRLS YET), SCOTT
    SUPERS:
"PLACES STAGE RIGHT"
    CHORUS: MR. AQUILINO, MS. BAKER, MR. COUCH, MS. CRIM, MR. DONG-GUEN KIM, MR. SHENKLE, MR. TRYBUS, MS. WYSZYNSKI
    SUPERS:
    CREW:
"PLACES STAGE LEFT"
    CHORUS: MS. CRIDER, MR. DEBATTISTA, MR. JEREMIAH, MR. JI-HOON KIM
    SUPERS: ADRIENNE & KATIE
    CREW:

Deneve/Robinson
Allor Scott

PSM M. Kay
revised 7/14/04, page 1 of 2

Figure 5.6 Top of Show Sequence *Carmen*.
Source: Created by Michele Kay.

production of *Carmen* at the Cincinnati Opera. This Top of Show was unusual as it included a pre-show talkback called "Insight" with the audience. Much of the information was provided to the stage manager from the director of production in a document called the "Top of Show Tango," but the format of this calling document was created by the stage manager. Additionally, as *Carmen* is a long show, pre-show timing and tight execution were critical to not go into overtime. For comparison, Figure 5.7 shows a very different Top of Show from a production of *La Bohème*

CARMEN
TOP OF SHOW

@ 8:03:00
"LX 1.5 Go" (House to ½)

@ "Voiceover" 2, 3, "Go" or "LX 1.5 Complete"
"Voice Over Go"

Good evening Ladies and Gentlemen:
Welcome to Cincinnati Opera's summer festival.
Please take this opportunity to turn off all cell phones, pagers, watch alarms, and other electronic devices.
Please note that some hearing aids emit a high-pitched tone so adjust the volume control accordingly.

The taking of photographs * and the use of recording devices are strictly prohibited.
Thank you for your cooperation and enjoy the performance.

@ Voice Over: "enjoy"
Jamie "Tune Go" ~ "Stand by the Maestro"
Curtis "Stand by Devo titles"

<< Orchestra Tune >>

@ Tune nearly complete
"Lx 1.7 GO" * (House to glow)

@ "Devo Titles" 2, 3 "Go" or "Lx 1.7 Complete"
Curtis: "Devo titles Go"

<< Slide 3 >>
<< Slide 2 >>
<< Slide1 >>

@ "Slide 1" + 2 counts
"Send the Maestro"

@ "Maestro's moving" from Jamie
"Lx 2 Go" (Maestro Bow UP)

<< Maestro BOW >>

@ Maestro faces camera
"Lx 2.5 Go" (Maestro Bow OUT)

@ Downbeat
"LX 3 & Onstage Works OUT Go" (House OUT)

GO TO SCORE...

Deneve/Robinson
40kor Score

PSM M. Kay
revised 07-01-24, page 2 of 2

Figure 5.6 (Continued)

with the Virginia Opera. Looking at the two, you can see how different companies' protocols may vary widely.

The **Intermission Sequence** is not very different from the Top of Show Sequence except that it begins with an immediate page based on the length of the intermission. Ask the director of production how long the intermission is as these are usually based on a contractual agreement with the orchestra, especially if they are a union

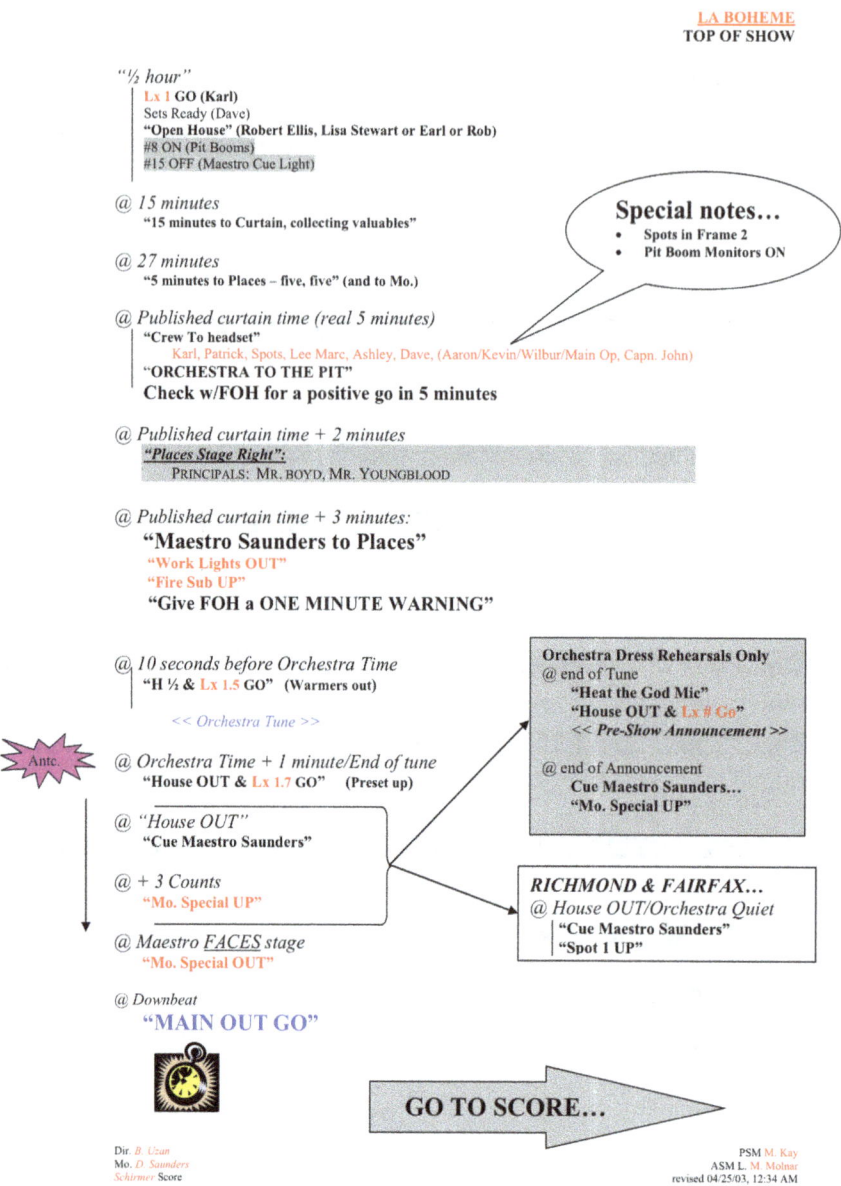

Figure 5.7 Top of Show Sequence *La Bohème*.

Source: Created by Michele Kay.

orchestra. More on orchestras later. For the purposes of both the Intermission Sequence and the Top of Show Sequence, it is important to meet with the **Concert Master** to determine the cueing of the orchestra tune. The concert master is usually the first chair in the violin section and is often found seated in the chair immediately to the left-hand side of the conductor. Think of it this way, if the conductor is standing on the podium, facing the stage, and they extend their right hand to shake that of the person on their left, whose hand will they be able to shake? That's the concert master. The tune begins at the contracted orchestra start time (see Orchestra section later in this chapter), and comes in two parts, the highs, followed by the lows. A tune doesn't take much time, maybe a minute, but sometimes the orchestra has a specific time allotted to the tune written into their contract. Get this information from the director of production and confirm it, and any variation on it, with the **Orchestra Manager**, and/or the union steward. The orchestra manager may be someone from within the orchestra but usually they are external to it. Whomever you are working with, they are the person who ensures that the rules of the collectively bargained agreement are being adhered to by the opera company. Meet with the orchestra manager or steward to confirm start times, acceptable temperatures, rules surrounding breaks, and any other matters negotiated between the orchestra and the opera company. Also, find out if there is any flexibility within these rules. For example, an orchestra may have a 23-minute break negotiated into a three-hour service. The trick comes in negotiating the orchestra's break around an opera with multiple intermissions. You do not want the very expensive orchestra sitting idle, so you may need to call the orchestra to the pit to work with the conductor while the scene change continues behind the main curtain.

> Pro Tip: *As the Top of Show sequence and Bow sequence are often not focused on nearly as much as the bulk of the show, don't be caught unprepared. Be sure to take the time as the Calling Stage Manager to practice calling these two vital pieces of the show. And be sure to familiarize yourself with the calling desk/station intimately before your first time at the calling desk as you may have just moved to that location after having spent Tech Rehearsals in the House.*
> – Christy Ney

The **Bow Order** can be a task that is orchestrated and documented by the assistant staging director. This document is exactly what it sounds like, the order of appearance of the performers in the curtain call, the bows. In opera there are three types of curtain calls: the **bounce**, the **front of curtain**, and the **onstage bow**. The **bounce** is used for a mid-show curtain call when the chorus is not involved in the final act. At the end of a preceding act, the company is quickly set on stage in a tableau upstage of the main curtain. Then the main curtain is taken out, a light cue is called to bring front light up on the performers who either remain in a freeze or maybe do a simple head bow, and then the main curtain is immediately brought back in with a light cue taking out the front light. The performers who are no longer in the remainder of the opera are then released and the intermission transition continues. An example of the bounce is often seen following Act 1 in productions of *Tosca*. The chorus, including a children's chorus, and many principal performers are onstage at the end of the *Te Deum* in Act 1. They assemble in a freeze, maybe standing up if they were previously kneeling, and then you do a bounce for their curtain call. The children are then released; the chorus sings offstage in Act 2 so may leave immediately following that song. The **front of curtain** bows are principal bows that are done in front of the main curtain at the end of an act or the end of the opera. After the main curtain is brought in, the center is parted by a stagehand and the performers

CARMEN
BOW ORDER

Curtain IN & Decked

Ms. Malfitano & Mr. Leech exit stage right doors.
CREW: Strike Madonna to Stage Right
Chorus & Supers to *tableau positions* as staged by Director.
& Mr. Venanzi ENTERS STAGE RIGHT to join chorus.

Curtain OUT & Lights up

<<<<<<< **ONE BOW WITH MR. VENANZI, CHORUS, & 5 SUPERS** >>>>>>>

3 FLAMENCO	enter **LEFT**.	Cross to center. Bow.	Clear to **LEFT**.
7 MATADORS	enter **LEFT**.	Cross to center. Bow.	Clear to **LEFT**.

*OPENING NIGHT ONLY * Ms. de Luis will bow with the Director/Designers*

MR. SCHMIDT, MR. KELLY, MR. ANDREASSEN enter **RIGHT**.
*Schmidt, Kelly then Andreassen individually step downstage BOW then step upstage.
After final bow all 3 clear to **RIGHT**

MR. PANUCCIO, MR. KREIDER, MS. BROWN, & MS. SHIN enter **LEFT**.
*Panuccio & Kreider step downstage BOW then step upstage.
*Brown & Shin step downstage BOW then step upstage.
After women bow all 4 clear to **LEFT**

MR. SCHROTT	enters **RIGHT**.	Cross to center. Bow.	Clear to **RIGHT**.
MS. VEZINA	enters **LEFT**.	Cross to center. Bow.	Cross to **LEFT**.
MR. LEECH	enters **UP RIGHT**.	Cross to center. Bow.	Step **UPSTAGE**.
MS. MALFITANO	enters **UP RIGHT**.	Cross to center. Bow.	Step **UPSTAGE**.

All principals join Ms. Malfitano & Mr. Leech in a line.

<<<<<<< **ONE PRINCIPAL, CHORUS & SUPER COMPANY BOW** >>>>>>>

MS. MALFITANO crosses **RIGHT**. Escorts **Maestro DENEVE** to center stage.
Maestro DENEVE enters **RIGHT**. **Ms. MALFITANO** returns to Principal line.

Maestro DENEVE BOWS then acknowledges **ORCHESTRA**.

* OPENING NIGHT ONLY *
Mr. Leech crosses right. Escorts **Ms. de Luis** & **DESIGNERS** to stage.
DIRECTOR and **DESIGNERS** enter stage **RIGHT**. Cross to center. <<Bow>>.
DIRECTOR & **DESIGNERS** THEN JOIN PRINCIPAL LINE.

<<<<<<< **TWO TUTTI BOWS** >>>>>>>
Led by **Maestro DENEVE**.
(All Principals step forward, bow, and then step back to original position. Repeat. Step upstage of curtain line on final bow.)

<< Additional bows at discretion of stage management. >>

Curtain IN

CINCINNATI OPERA
Deneve/Robinson

PSM: M. Kay
rev. 9/11/2023.

Figure 5.8 Bow order *Carmen*, Cincinnati Opera, 2004.
Source: Created by Michele Kay.

go downstage of the curtain one at a time for their bows. They will sometimes then all go out for a group bow. Be forewarned, since the stage manager cannot control the bow by bringing in the curtain, they can continue for quite some time. Opera is steeped in tradition and grandeur, and the front of curtain bow allows the performer to individually bask in the accolades of the audience. The **onstage**

bow, along with the bounce, is a more common bow today and is similar to what you'd see in a play or musical. The performers are brought onstage in a ranking order from smallest part to leading role. Smaller roles or comprimario parts may be brought onstage in groups, but principals are cued on individually and given their moment in the spotlight. Then the conductor is brought onstage by a principal to be recognized at the end of the principal bows. They will often make a gesture to the orchestra inviting them to stand for acknowledgment, though if the opera runs close to the scheduled service time, sometimes the orchestra members will have already left the pit.

As is tradition, on opening night only, we'll see the staging director and the designers recognized onstage following the conductor's bow. Following the acknowledgment of the orchestra, another principal singer will invite the staging director onstage for a bow, and they will in turn invite the entire design team onstage. Whether you are doing the full artistic team bow on opening night, or just the nightly principal and conductor bows, it is common practice to do two **tutti bows**, that means full company, and then bring in the main curtain. Even if your cast implores you to do more than two tutti bows, it is our recommendation to leave the audience wanting more and end with two. As noted previously, the assistant staging director often writes up the bow order. The stage management team should post this on the callboard and on every dressing room door so that everyone sees it. With permission from the assistant staging director, you can then use this document as a base to create the calling document that is added to the calling script by adding light, follow spot, and main curtain cues, remembering to note triggers for each cue, such as "after second tutti bow." Of final note, the stage management team cues on all singers for the bows. Give each performer a moment to take in the audience's appreciation but keep the moment moving forward by cueing the next performer as soon as the one onstage is starting to rise from their bow.

> Because of the expenses associated with the orchestra and to maximize time with the cast, the stage manager may never get the opportunity to tech calling the top of show sequence or the bow order in real time. Or, since the opening night bow includes designers, you may never run through that moment in real time until it is opening night. Why? Because the designers are doing their designer job during tech and may not be able to take the time to practice the bow. Or, you may have a donor who delivers flowers to the principal singers during the bow that you may not get to rehearse with them prior to running it during the performance. Writing down the plan, reviewing it with the assistant stage managers, and following the plan is the stage manager's best bet to ensure a smooth, or mostly smooth, sequence.

As the Top of Show and Bow Order segments are not a part of the musical score, it is a courtesy to create a **Maestro Cue Sheet** for the conductor. In this document, add any information that is relevant to the conductor or orchestra. In the example, (Figure 5.9), in addition to the pre-show calls and tune, the document outlines *who*

The Daughter of the Regiment

Maestro's Cue Sheet

Into ACT I

7:30	½ Hour Call
7:45	15 Minute Call
8:03	Maestro Larkin called to Places in Pit w/Jamie (Jamie is on headset w/Michele) during the preshow speeches
	Walter calls the Orchestra to the pit
	A music librarian should place your music at this time.
8:08	Cellphone voiceover
8:09	Tune
8:10	Henri Venanzi conducts National Anthem
8:11	Maestro cued to platform by Jamie
ASAP	Maestro Bows (you will be in a special for this)
ASAP	Maestro faces stage and downbeat

Into Overture

At the end of the Overture I will wait about 3 seconds then call the two cannon cues, you may begin #1 at your discretion before during or after the cannon cues.

End of ACT I

The Black Out Curtain is called in 4 measures from the cut off at the end of the act. Please hold the final note until the curtain is at deck.

Into ACT II

0 min	25 minute call
10 min	15 minute call
15 min	5 minutes to places call
18 min	Walter calls the orchestra to the pit
	A music librarian should place your music at this time.
20 min	Maestro Larkin called to Places in Pit w/Jamie (Jamie is on headset w/Michele)
23 min	House lights go to ½ and Orchestra tunes
24:30	Maestro is cued to platform
Imm.	Maestro bows
Imm.	Maestro turns to face the stage
Imm.	Black out curtain and Scrim OUT
¾ curtain	Maestro gives downbeat

End of ACT II

At cut off I will call a lighting black-out cue (it is a zero count cue). *This includes a blackout of the orchestra lights.*
During the blackout the company will adjust their positions onstage slightly.
Lights will restore in the pit after about 5 or 10 seconds.
Once lights restore (or when you feel safe) Maestro makes his way to stage right for bows.

Please see BOW order for Maestro's bow sequence.

7/23/04 Danner/Larkin   Version: A Schirmer

Figure 5.9 Maestro Cue Sheet.
Source: Created by Michele Kay.

starts each act and how each act is ended. At the top of Act 2 the conductor is instructed to begin the act when the curtain is ¾ out. Having this information in a written document is particularly important if you have an alternate conductor during some performances.

THE ORCHESTRA

In the United States, many large and mid-scale opera houses have a collectively bargained agreement with the American Federation of Musicians, or AFM. Each AFM local negotiates with the producing unit, in this case the opera company, and has rules that are reflected in that agreement. It is absolutely critical that the stage management team is aware of the rules governing the orchestra, especially those involving start times, tuning time, breaks, intermission lengths (which is based on the break schedule), length of service, and permissible room temperature for playing. Typically, there is an official clock and a temperature gauge in the theatre that both the orchestra and the stage manager must follow as the official time and temperature. Having one official clock and thermostat keeps all parties in agreement of the official readings, minimizing disputes. If the temperature goes above or below the allowable playing temperature, the orchestra may refuse to play out of safe care of their instruments. Likewise, staying within the designated service schedule is critical to not going into overtime. Since most opera orchestras are quite large, going into overtime can be quite expensive. A significant part of the stage manager's job is to start the show on time and end on time so as not to incur orchestra overtime, even if that means delivering a note to the conductor that act one ran long so to not linger in Act 2. In order to help stay within the orchestra's service, a late start time is often negotiated into the orchestra's contract. Meaning, although the audience's tickets may say the opera begins at 8:00pm, to allow for the time it takes to seat a large audience, the official orchestra service may be 8:05pm–11:05pm. Every minute of orchestra time is accounted for, and all calls revolve around the official orchestra start time. As such, the tune begins at the exact second of the orchestra's start time, 8:05pm, in our current example. The orchestra is a vital part of the composition of an opera production; ensuring that the orchestra members are comfortable, safe, and respected benefits the players and the opera company.

Setting up the orchestra is often the primary responsibility of the props department, though all technical areas will participate in some aspect of setting up the orchestra pit. Confirm this information with the director of production. Ask the conductor for a **Pit Plot** early in the process. The pit plot is a diagram indicating where each member of the orchestra needs to be setup in the orchestra pit. Stage management will need to share the pit plot with all technical areas so they can provide necessary services for the orchestra. The props department will ensure that there are enough music stands and chairs for the orchestra members. They will also provide carpeting in the pit, if requested. Carpeting helps dampen the orchestra's volume. It is necessary to confirm the need for carpeting before any elements are loaded into the pit. Once the chairs, music stands, and larger instruments have been loaded in, it is difficult and a waste of resources to unload everything to lay down carpet, and then load everything back into the pit. The lighting department will set up music stand lights and tidy all cables that run power to those lights. Sound may set up microphones and audio monitors in the pit to provide foldback to the stage, allowing the performers, stage managers, and crew to hear the orchestra clearly both onstage and off. Additionally, sound will set up a camera in the pit aimed at the conductor which feeds to a video monitor. The **Conductor Video Monitor** is an essential tool for the calling stage manager, the supertitles operator, and for any backstage singers or backstage **banda** (either individual or small groups of instrumentalists who play backstage) to remain connected with the conductor for musical cues and cutoffs. Backstage video monitors are often set up on roving units to allow them to be moved to locations visible to offstage singers or if the staging requires an onstage performer to be facing away from the conductor. In addition to roving units on either side of the backstage, there are typically video monitors set on either side of the stage on the apron, again visible to the onstage singers when they cannot look directly at the real conductor. Maintaining visual contact with the conductor is essential to ensuring that all parties are getting their cues simultaneously. Interestingly, there is some debate over whether digital video monitors distort the signal and cause a delay for those watching a digital as opposed to an analog monitor. Advances in technology have made analog monitors essentially obsolete, so this is a modern problem that has been worsened not improved by technology. Still, the delay is milliseconds long, so the debate is whether the delay is indeed noticeable.

SCHEDULING AND RUNNING TECHNICAL REHEARSALS

When discussing the orchestra, remember that like the chorus, they are working on a schedule of services, or a predetermined amount of rehearsal and performance hours occurring on specific days. An orchestra will require some number of **orchestra readings**, which are music rehearsals where the musicians work with the conductor to learn or review the music. Most operas will be scheduled with two or three orchestra readings. These generally occur outside the stage manager's oversight. The orchestra manager will oversee these rehearsals which take place in a rehearsal studio, outside of the orchestra pit. Following the final orchestra read, the orchestra's instruments and support items will be loaded into the pit. The next orchestra call will be either a **sitzprobe**, a.k.a. "**sitz**," and/or a **wandelprobe**. Sitzprobe and wandelprobe are both German terms meaning seated practice or walking practice, respectively. The sitzprobe and/or wandelprobe are scheduled for the conductor to unite the artistic forces of the orchestra and the performers. Whether you are doing a sitzprobe or a wandelprobe will be determined by the conductor. This is their rehearsal. The conductor will also let you know what they want to rehearse and the order they want to rehearse in. For example, they may want to do all the chorus numbers first so they can release the chorus and then focus on the principals for the remainder of the rehearsal. This means you will likely not work in order. The stage management team's job is to make the cast comfortable by providing chairs, music stands, water, and other amenities. Also, you may be asked to keep the break timings. Talk to the conductor about how they want you to inform them of upcoming breaks. Also, if the performers are not sitting on stage, but are warming up or waiting in their dressing rooms then the stage management team should keep on top of paging the singers to the stage in time for their rehearsal. If the conductor has requested a wandelprobe then you will not need to have chairs or stands, but rather, the cast will do their basic blocking while working with the conductor. Most companies will not do both a sitzprobe and a wandelprobe as every onstage rehearsal is very expensive. Additionally, you are not likely to have a full crew or run any technical elements during either a sitzprobe or a wandelprobe. Following the sitzprobe or wandelprobe, the next time you'll see the orchestra is the orchestra dress rehearsal. There may be one to three orchestra dress rehearsals following the **Piano Tech** and **Piano Dress**. Fun fact: singers often dress more formally for the sitzprobe.

After the production team loads in the set, lights, and other technical elements the cast will have two to three piano techs. These are not typical technical rehearsals like you'd see in a play or musical. Instead, they are more like onstage placement rehearsals for the cast to acquaint themselves with the scenic elements, and the staging director to adjust blocking to fit within the scenery. Usually, lighting and other cues are not run during this rehearsal, but rather the rehearsal is conducted under work lights with minimal crew, possibly only the house crew to allow for props to be used. As stated in the name, the rehearsal is conducted on piano. Ensure that the piano is tuned and possibly amplified so that it is audible to the cast onstage. Also, the piano will need to be set so that the conductor is visible to the pianist and the cast, and the pianist has light to see their music.

In opera, think of each workday as being divided into three segments, morning, afternoon, and evening. If the piano tech with the cast takes place during the evening segment, then the production teams will be doing other work calls or cueing sessions during the morning and afternoon segments. To maximize labor resources, end the afternoon segment by transitioning the set to that which is needed for the evening's piano tech. Another method is to plan the week so that light cueing sessions in the afternoon are in the same set as the evening's piano tech so there is less time spent shifting between sets. **Light cueing** sessions are usually attended by the staging director, assistant staging director, stage manager, the lighting designer and their team, and onstage **light walkers**. These are often volunteers or supernumeraries who are used to approximate the blocking of principal performers during light cueing sessions. This is a cost savings measure and a means of preserving the energy of the principal performers. Singing a grand opera is very challenging on the body, so we often work out the technical issues, such as light cueing, separately from the performer's calls. Again, this is very unlike traditional theatre where tech is worked out with the actors onstage in a tech rehearsal. During a light cueing session, the stage manager sits in the house with the lighting designer and staging director, and it is their job to tell the light walker where to go so the lighting designer can adequately light the scene. You can also request the assistant staging director to tell the light walkers where to go since they should be more aware of the performers' blocking. Additionally, in order to work as efficiently as possible, anticipate what is coming next and notify the props crew ahead of time when minor changes may need to be made on stage. The idea is to have the personnel ready to move the moment forward. For example, you may need to have a cart moved around during a light cueing session; props will do that for you. You are also using this time to continue booking your cues in the calling score, including adding all the pages to stage and standbys. Depending on the size of the venue, you are likely to be running the piano tech, piano dress, and calling the opera from backstage. Getting your cues booked accurately while you have the view from the house is essential as making cueing changes based on a monitor is not ideal. Many opera houses in the United States are operated by union crews. The break schedule during light cueing sessions is dictated by the collectively bargained agreement with the local IATSE and typically, the union steward or house carpenter will call for the coffee break. No work may occur during this time and often no one is allowed to be on the stage. Coffee break usually lasts for 15 minutes and although it is a good idea to know what the rules are of the local where you are working, you do not call the coffee break. Just enjoy it.

After several light cueing sessions and piano techs to set the cast on the stage, you will conduct a piano dress rehearsal. This is more akin to a technical rehearsal that you would experience in traditional theatre adding all technical elements and costumes and wigs, maybe makeup, maybe not, and all appropriate crew. Check with the director of production to determine whether you should follow the break schedule for the performers or the crew. There will likely be continued light cueing and work sessions during the day, but the piano dresses and **orchestra dresses** will usually be in the evening session. As noted earlier, when you add the orchestra to the final dress rehearsals you will need to manipulate the orchestra break with the performer's break so that you can accomplish all the things you need to work through during the final orchestra dresses. Figure 5.10 is a **Train Schedule** for *Lucia di Lammermoor* created by stage manager, Hannah Holthaus. In this you see how the stage manager was able to keep track of work time and activity, and relevant breaks for the various unions (performers, stage technicians, and orchestra) so that they could complete the orchestra dress rehearsal within the budgeted four-hour rehearsal block

The final item that is added to the technical and dress rehearsals are **supertitles**. In the United States many opera companies provide translations of the opera for the audience either over the stage or on screens on the sides of the stage, or at the Metropolitan Opera in New York, on the backs of the seats. Ask the director of

CINCINNATI OPERA — *Lucia di Lammermoor* — Orchestra Tech Train Schedule

Condemi/Balsadonna
page 1 of 1
Date edited: 6/14/2023
Score: Ricordi 41689
version: A, hlh

REHEARSAL DATE: FRIDAY, JULY 16TH   **REHEARSAL HOURS:** 2:30P-6:30P

CLOCK	START @	TIME	PAGES	WHAT
2:25-2:30p	---	5	---	Places call for Top of Rehearsal – Santiago Ballerini, Terrence Chin-Loy, Anthony Clark Evans, and Griffen Hogan Tracy to stage please Maestro Balsadonna and Orchestra to the pit
2:30-3:00p	Top of Act 1.1	30 *15' of music*	1-33	Run Act 1, Sc. 1 **Notes after running**
3:00-3:05p	---	5	---	Crew Shift to Act 1, Sc. 2 **Orchestra notes as needed during shift**
3:05-3:40p	Top of Act 1.2	35 *25' of music*	34-72	Run Act 1, Sc. 2 **Notes after running**
3:40-4:00p	---	20	---	**20' BREAK for ALL PERFORMERS MUST BREAK BY 4p** Crew SHIFT to Act 2, Sc. 1
4:00-4:35p	Top of Act 2.1	35 *25' of music*	73-112	Run Act 2, Sc. 1 **Notes after running**
4:35-4:40p	---	5	---	Crew Shift to Act 2, Sc. 2 **Orchestra notes as needed during shift**
4:40-5:05p	Top of Act 2, Sc. 2	25 *17' of music*	113-182	Run Act 2, Sc. 2 **Notes after running**
5:05-5:20p	---	15	---	**15' BREAK for ALL PERFORMERS** Crew SHIFT to Act 3, Sc. 1
5:20-5:55p	Top of Act 3, Sc. 1	35 *28' of music*	206-252	Run Act 3, Sc. 1 **Notes after running**
5:55-6:00p	---	5	---	Crew Shift to Act 3, Sc. 2 **Orchestra notes as needed during shift**
6:00p-6:30p	Top of Act 3, Sc. 2	30 *17' of music*	255-280	Run Act 3, Sc. 2 **Notes after running**
6:20p	---	10	---	**Crew Shut Down; Orchestra/Artists continue to rehearse till 6:30p**

Total break for Principals: **30min** (30min needed)
Total break for Chorus: **35min** (30min needed)
Total break for Orchestra: **35min** (35min needed)

Figure 5.10 Train Schedule from *Lucia di Lammermoor*.

Source: Created by Hannah Holthaus.

production what stage management's responsibility will be regarding supertitles. One way may be ensuring that there are audio and conductor monitors in the supertitle operator's booth. Or maybe a member of the stage management team will be calling supertitle execution to a crew member.

> Pro Tip: *Calling titles requires relentless focus and stamina. It's not uncommon to call between 700–1000 cues (including point cues) in an opera, with a cue every 5–10 seconds, and the entire audience reading every cue.*
>
> *If you get lost while calling titles, go to a blackout. Projecting the wrong text will confuse the audience, but also runs the risk of completely ruining the opera by making a serious moment comedic or by destroying the jokes in a comedy.*
>
> *The audience will forgive a late cue, but an early title is like playing the wrong note as a musician; it detracts from the desired effect of the moment.*
> – Amy C. Thompson, Assistant Stage Manager, Lyric Opera of Chicago

SUPPORTING THE PERFORMERS

As we have discussed multiple times, singing a grand opera in a grand opera hall is very challenging on the body. Many opera singers will preserve their voices by **marking**, or not singing full out during the piano techs and piano dress rehearsals; however, they will usually sing out during the orchestra dress rehearsal. Alternatively, the company may give the opportunity to sing to a **cover**, another term for an understudy. It is not uncommon for a cover to sing a role from the side stage or the pit while the primary performer does the blocking during a piano tech or dress. If a show is going to run for a long time or the role is particularly challenging, the company may **double cast** some or all the principal parts. This allows the principal singers to have more nights of **vocal rest** between performances. There are multiple ways to run a second cast through the paces of rehearsal and tech. You could, during piano tech, have each cast do the blocking for the scenes they are in. You could run each scene or act with the alternate cast. You could alternate the casts during each piano tech. Ideally, each cast gets to have a full piano dress and a full orchestra dress. If not double cast, to give their voices a rest, many American opera companies will have a **dark day**, or a day off, on the day prior to opening and most operas will not perform on consecutive nights, but rather, they will perform every other night or in repertory with another opera, again to give the singers vocal rest between performances. This is one of the greatest perks of working in opera. Following the opening, running an opera is not very different than running a play or musical. Either company management or stage management will check in daily with the principal singers to make sure that they are still healthy, especially vocally. We used to call these the "happy and healthy" calls which was literally a phone call to each performer to do a daily check in. If everyone was healthy, evening calls for performances went as planned. If not, either stage management or company management would call the cover and wardrobe and wigs to start the ball rolling for putting in the cover. You do not typically run a put-in rehearsal prior to the performance, though, depending on the production, you may want to discuss this option with the director of production, the assistant staging director, and the affected principal cast members. For example, if you had a fall in the show, you'd want to practice that prior to performance for safety purposes!

Teching operas is very similar and yet very different from teching a play, musical, or dance. Lean into the strengths that you already have from stage managing a non-opera and re-read this chapter to ensure that you understand the details of the differences. Prepare, prepare, prepare, and trust that you are ready to do this. Remember, at some point, even the most experienced opera stage manager was doing their first opera.

DANCE TECHNICAL REHEARSALS
TRANSITION TO THE STAGE

As we discussed in the last chapter, you should consider that your main task from point of contract is preparing for technical rehearsals. The transition from the rehearsal room to the stage is an important time for the dance stage manager. If you have only recently begun your contract, you will be observing final studio runs to receive as much information as possible. In this case you may hear the choreographer or rehearsal director calling out basic cues such as lights up, scene change, or curtain out. Write these timing notes lightly in your score to confirm later. If you are joining the team on a repertoire piece, you may be given a score or calling document that you can follow along with during these runs. However, if you have had the opportunity to attend throughout the studio rehearsal period, you are in a strong position to add your voice into the room by calling a few specific cues. Be sure that you check in with the rehearsal director on this first, as it may not be appropriate since the rehearsal director typically runs rehearsals until the company is onstage. Again, this is company-specific, so have a conversation with your colleagues and production manager to understand the expectations of this team. Be respectful of the company's usual protocols, and support where needed. Situate yourself near the designers to receive any cueing information during these final runs and see if any particular measurements or spike marks are needed for lighting specials. The transfer to the stage is fairly standard in comparison to other performance forms. One thing to note in dance is that you may need to assign a specific dressing room or separate space for physiotherapists and masseurs, and a space for the rehearsal director and any guest choreographers. You will do this in collaboration with the rehearsal director, production manager, and wardrobe manager. Depending on the size of the show, you will generally have one assistant stage manager. This is not assumed. There are a variety of dance company structures. If an assistant is not deemed necessary, you will be preparing the paperwork on your own, or perhaps in preparation for an assistant who will join you as you begin technical rehearsals. Throughout the chapter we refer to the 'stage management team,' but the size of the team will depend on the company and the demands of the show.

During this last week of rehearsals, you will share your time between studio runs and your stage and venue tasks once the set is loaded in. Be sure to have a full tour of the venue, including a survey of the stage, dressing room areas, common areas, and potential office space. Dance-specific tasks that must be completed prior to cast onstage include spike marking the dance floor. Once the dance floor is taped down onstage, the stage management team will mark any specific stage reference points required by the cast using spike tape and sometimes glow tape, and cover over them with a clear, non-reflective, vinyl dance floor tape. Typically, these include center and quarter marks and downstage and upstage 'T's to mark the edges of the Marley at these points (as pictured in Chapter 3: Pre-Production). Note that if the show requires multiple, colored dance floors, all layers of Marley will require center marks and any marks for specials. In this case, the floor panels are numbered to ensure they are placed in the correct order, so your spike marks should be accurate. This is not something you are responsible for, but something to be aware of. Request individual **LED center and quarter floor lights** for the downstage edge of the dance floor and a center **spotting light** at the back of house through the electrics team. If you have not worked with them before, a spotting light is a small red light placed at the rear of the house for dancers to use when performing choreography that requires turning (see Figure 5.11). This light is a center, front reference mark. Also, check your visual monitors which should include a full stage feed, an infrared feed if available, and the conductor monitor for shows with live musicians (as illustrated in the picture of the stage manager's calling desk on the cover of this book). These will either be set at the calling position side stage, or at the tech table for technical rehearsals and moved later, if possible. For cueing purposes, communication, and/or show stops, be sure that there is a **conductor cue light system** in the pit, and a conductor **handset** for direct communication via the headset

Figure 5.11 His Majesty's Theatre auditorium with spotting light and edge of stage marker lights.

Source: Photo by Hugo Aguilar Lopez.

system. If music is recorded, you should have a cue light for the sound operator if they are not planning to remain on headset once each piece begins. Other dance specific requirements include **portable ballet barres** and **rosin boxes**, if permitted on the dance floor. As the staging elements are prepared, the stage team along with stage and production management will go through the technical tracks and run a **Dry Tech** of any transitions, if required. The assistant stage manager should take on the task of updating show paperwork as you talk/walk through the tracks to ensure everyone is working off the most current running sheets. If you do not have an assistant, notate the general cues, and ask the show team to make any changes on their running sheets for you to collect and update later. Your focus will remain on preparing the calling documents.

BOOKING CUES

The calling stage manager will already have a number of cues pre-plotted from studio rehearsals, whether you arrived in the final weeks of rehearsal or have been on contract for the full rehearsal period. Discuss with the designers the most efficient method of receiving the remainder of the cue list. Cues may be given to the stage manager in list form via spread sheets, direct discussion with the designer in rehearsal, or during cueing by referencing the score or video recording, using clocked timings, and/or blocking sheets. It is not uncommon to sit with a video of a full run and place cues visually. Be prepared to receive cues through a variety of formats depending on the designer. If it's a complicated show technically, the creative/production team may opt for a paper tech to talk through all transitions prior to lighting. If the production is using in-stock or rented scenery or costumes, you may not have these designers present for technical rehearsals, as you would with a new design. However, there should be pre-existing documentation and ground plans to reference as you build your fly plot and other show running forms. Your technical director and production team will be able to answer any questions you have in this area. Wardrobe usually creates their own running sheets but may liaise with you regarding specific information such as entrances and quick changes. As with other styles of performance, you should know when and where quick changes happen for managing technical rehearsals and any paging calls for dressers, if needed.

SETTING LIGHT LEVELS

Once the show is focused, the team will begin to set lighting levels for your cues. The stage management team and specific members of the artistic team (genre/company dependent) will be in attendance. At this time, the designer and the stage manager are set up in the house at production desks or tech tables. The tables should be set up with dimmable or colored desk lamps, headsets, multiple outlet extension cords convenient for a number of computers along the table, an onstage microphone (a.k.a. '**VOG' mic**), and a computer or device with access to the rehearsal video as a reference. Performers are not called for this session. It is more likely that a light walker will be employed to move around the stage while the designer and light board operator work to create the cues. Light walkers may be asked to wear specific color clothing for this call. As a general note, neutral colors are preferred, and it is not recommended to wear white or any bright colors. The stage manager may be asked to have specific costume samples on hand, which should be requested in advance from the wardrobe team. In dance, it is recommended to request a rack with a selection of costumes that the light walker might move around the stage as needed. If specific costumes are not available, a sample of the fabric would be useful for the lighting session. A mannequin or even a make-shift hanger hook, such as a mic stand, could be used to hold a specific costume in a certain position onstage. Otherwise, the light walker may hold the costume while walking the patterns requested by the designer via the stage manager. This process shows the designer how the light levels and colors interact with the costume colors.

USING DANCE BLOCKING SHEETS FOR LIGHTING

The stage manager's dance blocking sheets provide valuable information during lighting cue sessions. Since the choreographer or rehearsal director may not be in attendance during the level setting session, it is up to the stage manager to know the blocking well enough to ensure most effective use of stage time. Remember, during this phase of the production, dedicated time onstage is considered a precious commodity as all production departments are working to deadlines and most require their own work time onstage, in specific lighting conditions. For example, the scenic departments will want work lights and grid lights on, whereas cueing lights usually require all lights off, with the exception of the backstage blue lights. The production manager will have laid out the production's technical schedule to accommodate these department-specific needs. Allocated time must be used wisely and efficiently.

A stage manager can assist by being prepared and set up in advance of the start time, and ready to answer any questions regarding blocking. They should have their cue list accessible, and cues lightly written, or placed digitally, or marked with a sticky note at the intended cue placement points in their score or cue spreadsheet (we will look at different styles of cue notation later in this chapter). During the lighting session, the stage manager will also assist in directing the light walkers by calling out the patterns the dancers move in for any specific cue, unless a member of the ballet team is present. Now it's time to take out your dance blocking sheets to share the information you have been notating. While the video may be handy as a reference, during these sessions it is faster to see the patterns on your blocking sheets. Let's look at the sample in Figure 5.12 to see how these may assist the designer in this process.

Previously, we looked at how to note the information in anticipation of what might be useful in technical rehearsals. This is your time to show how well you know this piece! In this blocking sample you see not only entrances and exits, but specific patterns of dance. This information is necessary for lighting designers adding lighting **specials** and **corridors** or **lanes** in their cues. To step through the information collected, read the following narrative paragraph, and see if you can pick out all of these moments in the sample blocking sheet provided as we move from the page to the stage.

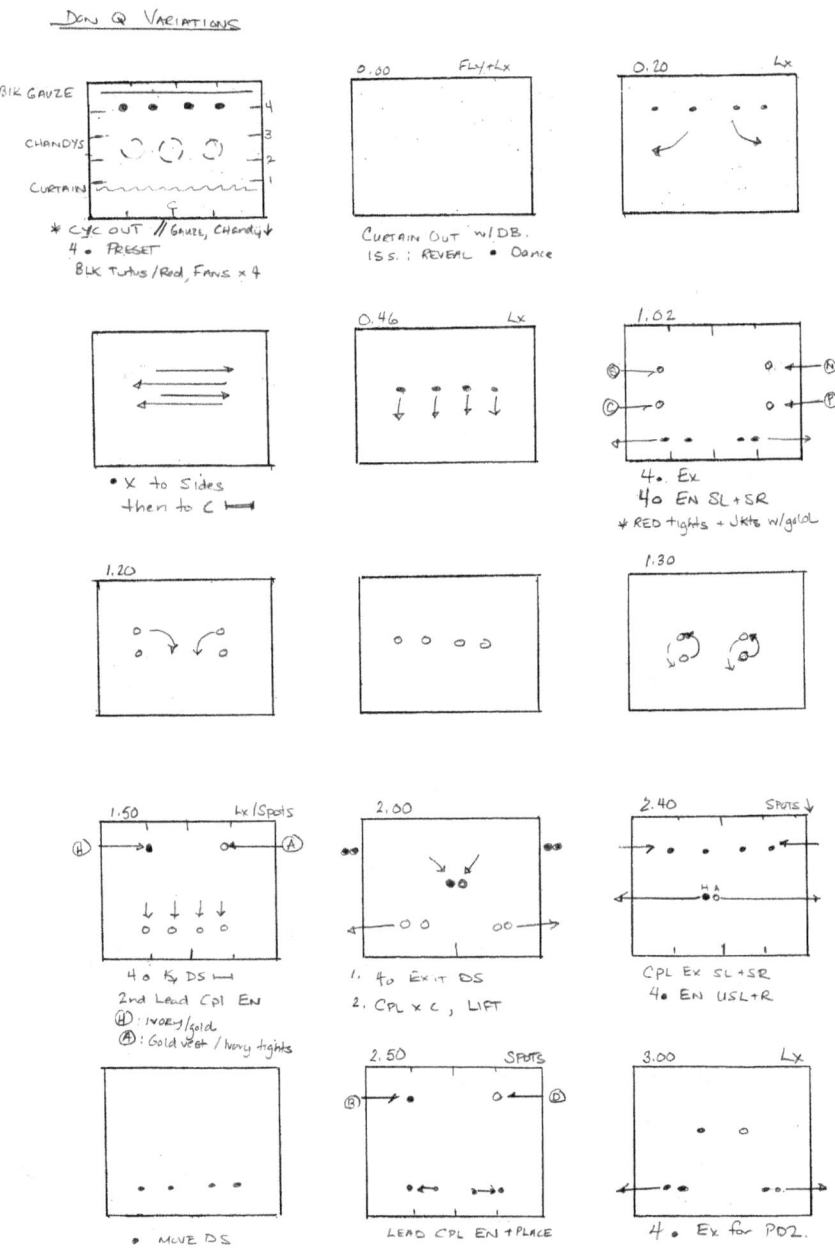

Figure 5.12 Dance blocking sample, Don Quixote.
Source: Created by Sue Fenty.

The piece begins with the house curtain in, there is a black gauze, cyclorama, and set of three chandeliers in on a midstage fly line. Four women are placed upstage behind the curtain, spaced evenly across the back. They wear black tutus with red trim and carry fans. The curtain rises over 15 seconds as the music begins, and the first variation dance begins 20 seconds into the music. A series of cross stage moves bring the dancers to midstage, and they run downstage together 46 seconds into the music and take their exit 17 seconds later, two will exit into the SR wing 1, and two will exit into SL wing 1. Exits are quick, so the wings must be clear. Four men enter from wings SR 2&3 and SL 2&3 in red tights and jackets with gold trim. Their dance begins offstage of the quarter marks, in line with their entrance wing, then they move into a midstage line. After a series of turns (1:30) they move downstage and kneel on one knee and then exit (1:50). At the same time, a principal couple enters from upstage left and right and stops at the upstage quarter marks. They are picked up in follow spot on their entrance. The female is SR, wearing an ivory tutu with gold trim and the man enters SL in gold vest and ivory tights. Once the line of men moves offstage, the couple meets at midstage center. There is a lift centre stage and the couple parts and exits into the midstage wings, exiting the sides they entered from (2:40). At the same time, four ladies re-enter from both sides into an upstage line. They travel downstage as the lead couple enters from USR (woman) and USL (man), and crosses to the upstage quarter marks. The DS women split center and exit, revealing the lead couple as follow spots fade up.

This one page of dance blocking has documented the first three minutes of the show. We've been introduced to the corps de ballet, the lead couple, and a principal couple, as well as the costume pieces, colors, and props. There are dance formations that line across the stage at DS in wing 1, at midstage, and also upstage, as well as a series of turns in the men's section. Let's look at how this information will assist when you are setting the lighting cues:

1. The costume colors will be useful for lighting palette.
2. The women are moving in lines both across stage and downstage, these might be lit in corridors or with some isolation.
3. The men use more of the stage space so they will need a larger area of light or full stage wash.
4. There are two principal couples requiring follow spots.
5. At this point, the two principal couples are not onstage at the same time, so the follow spots may double up.
6. There is a lift stage center, which might be useful to share with follow spot 1, who will likely be picking up the female lead.
7. There is a series of entrances and exits that happen fairly quickly.
8. There are chandeliers midstage.
9. There is a black gauze upstage.
10. The curtain flies out after the music starts.

Other things to note from this information:

- The stage manager notes the potential follow spot cue.
- The downstage wings must be clear for exits.
- The fly preset is noted: Chandeliers, black gauze, cyclorama, house curtain.

- The stage manager has the patterns of the dance at hand to direct the light walkers to ensure dancers will be in light as the cues are built.
- The house curtain out cue can be inserted.
- Once the cues are placed, the stage manager has timings and visuals to help place the cue standbys. For instance, after the men have finished their midstage turns, you may begin the standby to follow spots for their first pick up on the first principal couple.

> Follow spots are traditionally numbered, with spot 1 being the most experienced operator as theirs will be the hardest plot. This spot is generally reserved for the lead ballerina in dance since this operator needs to have quick reflexes to keep the dancer in the light not only on a horizontal plane, but also vertically for the lifts. Follow spotting dance is one of the more difficult tracks since you must anticipate the dancers' moves in order to keep "fingers and toes" in the light of a full body pickup without making the spot so large that it covers the stage. It should be tight to the body unless the designer specifies a smaller diameter.

During the rehearsals you have included in your blocking notation any major shifts in movement, entrances and exits, changes in music, LX cues as they are plotted, specific props, scene transitions, costume quick changes, moments of isolation on stage, solos, pas de deux, full stage coverage, and so on, all with associated timings. This information will not only help you easily place most cues that the designer requests, but also make a first attempt at adding the standbys that lead into these cues. Often dance shows are teched quickly, you are given a cue and then have to back-track for the standby. While this can be done via the score timings, the diagram method is visually faster to comprehend, particularly if you are not following the score at all times, or at all. If you have done your score pre-production work, you will be able to cross-reference the diagram timings with the score. You will now work with the lighting designer, board operator, and light walkers to build any cues that have previously been inserted, and notate any necessary additions, updating your calling copy and adding standbys as you move along. Figures 5.13 and 5.14 show two versions of shows that were blocked using the dance blocking cue sheets. As the team progresses through the tech, the stage manager places cues in the appropriate column, and then goes back to place standbys using information available such as timings, music, entrances, and dancer movements which have been recorded on the cue sheets. Figure 5.13 includes P/S/M score times, these are used to find and call specific cues in the printed score during the overture. Figure 5.14 notes LX cue descriptions alongside the cues: cue times, placement, and short descriptions.

Note that follow spot operators are typically not called for this first lighting session, they will join rehearsals when technical rehearsals with the dancers begin. The lighting designer will usually create the follow spot cue sheets or add the follow spot cue details during technical rehearsals. These generally list entrance points, character/target, cue timing details, along with any specific details for the light:

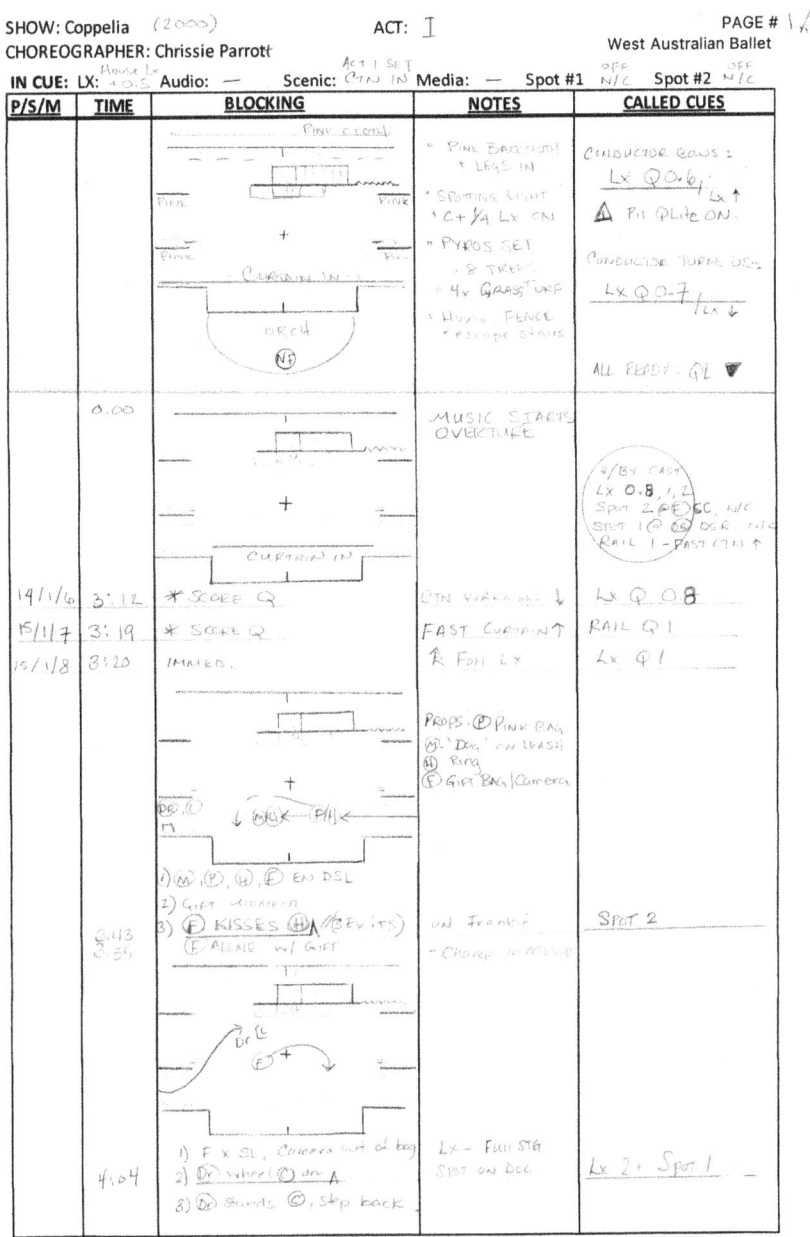

Figure 5.13 *Coppélia* Dance Blocking Cue Sheet.
Source: Created by Sue Fenty.

the gel frame number/color, size of the spotlight, and a notes section. Some of this information will be included in your standbys during the show, for example: "Standby follow spot 1 to pick up Clara's entrance downstage left in frame 1, full body." For the cue, you would merely say "Follow spot 1 GO."

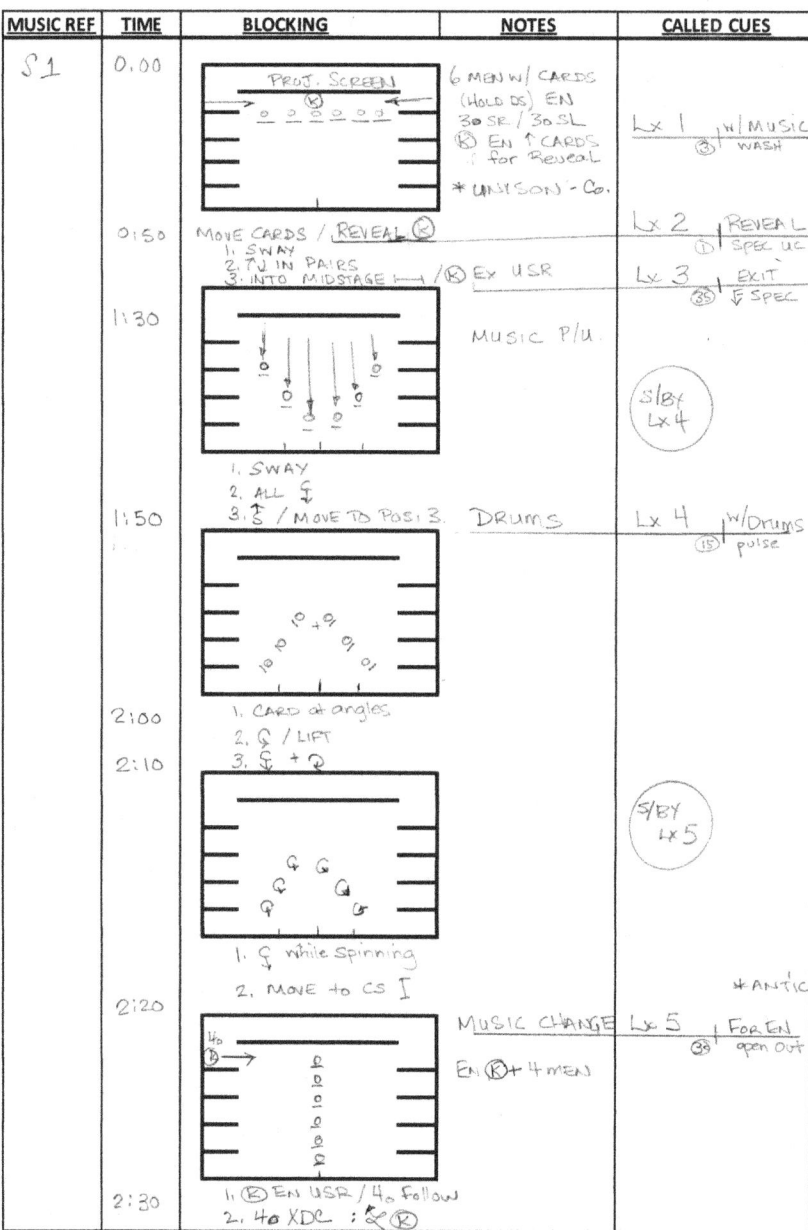

Figure 5.14 *Anniversary Gala* Dance Blocking Cue Sheet.
Source: Created by Sue Fenty.

STAGE SAFETY AND INTRODUCTIONS

Technical rehearsals will begin with introductions, a safety orientation, and walk of the stage for the performers and creatives, sharing relevant information regarding scenery, quick change logistics, exits, and crossovers. Time should be taken to introduce the cast to the technical team as they will be working together for the duration of technical rehearsals, and many will remain on for show calls. While not all companies take the time to do this, consider the impact it has. Every time a show comes together at the start of technical rehearsals, a new community of theatre-making artists is formed, each with its own particular culture. What might be a proactive way to lead this team in creating a safe, inclusive, and collaborative environment? Can your schedule afford ten minutes to introduce every member of the team? In the scheme of things, can it afford not to? Consider that you are also facilitating your first full call with the cast and technical teams, how will you present yourself, the team, and the production? Be intentional with this first meeting, remembering the tenets of creating trust within the team that were touched on in the pre-production phase of your journey of this show. With larger ballet companies it may make sense to introduce the venue team if there isn't time for full introductions.

> Pro Tip: *Do your homework: play the recorded music in your ears when you are not in rehearsal, watch the videos, chat with the cast and crew, listen to their ailments, watch the lighting focus on stage; every single bit of what happens during the day informs how you are going to call the show. When a lot of the information arrives organically (rather than trying to cram it or memorize it) the process of calling the show becomes easier.*
> – Isabel Martinez Rivera

STAGE REHEARSALS

The first onstage cast rehearsal in dance is the **Placing Call**. This term is interchangeable with '**spacing call**' and will be followed by technical rehearsals with either recorded music or a piano. If you are working with a full orchestra, they join the company for dress rehearsals and will have a limited number of calls, anywhere between one to three before the show opens (see Opera section earlier in this chapter for working with an orchestra). If you are working with recorded music for spacing or technical rehearsals, you need to ensure you know the pick up points in the music. Refer to the score reference sheet you created during pre-production. You may also want to add a column for potential pick up points in both the timecode and the score.

> If you are running the music yourself for any non-orchestra rehearsals, or supporting a ballet staff member running it, make sure that everything is set up well in advance for testing prior to the stage rehearsal. The system should be easily accessible for the staff running music cues if it is not the audio department. This will depend on the company, and whether you are in a union house.

BALLET: La Boheme ACT I			SCORE REFERENCE SHEET			Date Created: 2 May 2004	
SEASON: Spring 2004			CHOREOGRAPHER: SIMON DOW				Page: 1

P	S	M	Figure	Track	Time	Act/ Section	Cast
1	1	1	1	1	0:00	Act I Overture & Part 1	Beginners
1	5	2	25		0:17	Gauze only	None
5	3	5	148		2:27	Rudolfo & Marcello	R, Mr
6	6	4	200		3:03	Marcello's Solo	R, Mr
8	4	4	254		4:17	Spanish	R, Mr
10	4	2	323		4:50	Waltz	R, Mr
12	4	3	393		6:45	Marcello's Solo	R, Mr
13	4	4	425		7:30	Colline Enters	R, Mr, C
15	3	1	479		8:55	Schaunard Enters	R, Mr, C, S
17	6	6	558		10:25	Quartet into Chase	R, Mr, C, S
20	1	6	634		12:23	Knock/ Benoit enters	R, Mr, C, S, B
21	4	3	678			into 2nd waltz	R, Mr, C, S, B
24	3	2	753			SLAP/ Benoit's exit	R, Mr, C, S, B
26	1	1	1	2	0:00	Act I, Part 2: Rudolfo alone	Rudolfo
28	3	1	69	3	0:00	Knock/ Mimi Enters	R, M
29	2	3	97		1:14	Mimi Wakes	R, M
33	6	4	252		7.18	Rudolfo & Mimi Pd2	R, M
36	1	1	1	4	0:00	Act I, Part 3: Mimi's Story	R, M
37	5	2	48		2:34	Andante: Second Pd2	R, M
39	1	1	1	5	0:00	Act I, Part 4: Finale	R, M
39	2	1	6			Marcello enters/exits	R, M, Mr
40	5	3	56		0:40	Pd2 Resumes	R, M
41	2	2	68		1:42	Embrace (Snow)	R,M
42	1	3	82		3:02	Final lift	R,M
42	2	2	86		3:26	Kiss	R,M
42	3	3	90		4:02	Blow out candle/ exit	R,M

Figure 5.15 Score Reference Sheet.

Source: Created by Sue Fenty.

Note: In this example, the column header 'figure' refers to the score rehearsal number.

The stage manager should be aware that company class or warm up will continue to happen every day. This is for the safety of the dancers as they need to be warm to be able to perform the choreography without risking unnecessary injury. Classes may be held in a separate space or studio during technical rehearsals, and potentially move to the stage after Opening. If class is onstage, you will need to add setting and striking the portable ballet barres to the crew duties. Temperatures onstage should be set at a certain level, much like was discussed in pre-production for studio rehearsals, for both the dancers and the orchestra. Consider if there is access to temperature control, how long a temperature adjustment might take in the venue, and if there is a way to monitor the stage temperature from the stage. Your top of day checks should include checking the stage temperature.

> Pro Tip: *Pre-cut pieces of glo tape so that you can put it down quickly without having to find scissors etc. For pieces which require many dancers presetting in the dark, I pre-cut glo tape in different shapes, so that one dancer knows to find a triangle shape, and one knows to find a circle, and one knows to find a square, etc. I keep my pre-cut pieces of spike tape in an old breath mints tin.*
> – Betsy Ayer, Stage Manager, Susan Marshall & Company

Once the stage is safe for dancer access, a placing call will be scheduled. This is a rehearsal where the ballet team works with the dancers to move them through the placements of the choreography to ensure the dance is spaced onstage as the choreographer intended. Adjustments will be made throughout this call to the dance, and floor marks may be required if the dancers need them to hit a lighting special, for a specific spacing moment, or for safety reasons such as marking the floor in front of lighting booms, or to place an onstage prop or set piece if it happens during the dance. Dancers will guide off the center and quarter marks and/or lights, as well as the center spotting light at the back of the house. The Rehearsal Director will run the dancers through the shifts in movement without music, counting through the rhythm of the piece. During this call, the stage manager may be either side stage or in the house, depending on what is practical at the venue. Additionally, the stage management team must be alert for any changes to entrances and exits during this time, which may affect lighting, prop hand-offs, and costume quick changes. They should also have a keen eye out for safety, particularly in the wings around booms, making marks and adjustments such as adding white spike tape or glow tape to the floor as required. This first walk through of the pieces onstage is often conducted in work light, although the lighting designer may request to 'light over' the rehearsal, being careful never to plunge the dancers into darkness at any time. They may also add stage lights over top of work lights to see some preliminary cues.

Once a section or act has been placed, the choreographer or rehearsal director may request to see the section in the lighting states before moving on. This is something you should have discussed in either your paper tech or perhaps in a **tech expectations** meeting with the rehearsal director/choreographer and designers. If it hasn't been, then be sure to check in with the lighting designer to see if lighting is prepared to add cues before offering this option to the choreographer during the rehearsal. Remember that the placing call may be done completely in work lights, as it is purely about the spacing of the piece. Scenic elements, any floor lights or other pieces that might impact the flow of the movement should be considered and set, or at least noted (if only a **skeleton crew** is called for this session), as you move through the dance.

> Pro Tip: *Backstage for dance has two important considerations:*
>
> *1. Safety for the dancers – including essential work to keep hazardous materials off of the stage, wing space, and crossovers that can injure a dancer in bare feet. Additionally, there are often injuries! Sprained ankles, shoulder dislocations, broken toes. These are common and first aid and injury protocols need to be considered carefully and made available to dancers.*
>
> *2. Many dance pieces incorporate high-speed work backstage with quick entrances and exits that need thoughtful support. Specifically note that stagehands need to clear the wings and any space where rapidly changing traffic patterns are necessary for intense backstage choreography. Cross overs need to be well lit, free of debris and easily accessible.*
>
> – Sandra Kaufmann

TECHNICAL REHEARSALS

In dance, the order of the technical rehearsal will usually be the chronological order of the show. However, in a series of One Acts or a '**Triple Bill**,' the show may skip around depending on the most efficient use of cast time and choreographic staff. Dance will have alternate casting for shows, and you might have three alternating casts for a season. During technical rehearsals, it is generally the first cast that steps through the show. The second and third casts will either watch from side stage and/or mirror sections, or from the house. These casts will usually have the opportunity to dance their roles in one of the dress rehearsals.

During technical rehearsals you will step through the show adding all show elements. The stage manager facilitates this rehearsal at all levels. They collaborate with the creative team either directly at the **production desk or tech table** or on headset to determine cue sequences, placement, and intended cue effects. They also communicate with the company via a microphone at the tech table, to the technical team via a headset system, and to the orchestra through the conductor or orchestra management, via a headset or handset. General communications via the stage manager's microphone should be channeled into front of house and backstage speakers so everyone can hear any announcements. If there is no **'show feed'** at the venue, make sure your mic is also fed to dressing rooms and any back of house locations where the cast, orchestra, and crew might congregate. For technical rehearsals, the stage manager will be either side stage in the calling position or at the production tables in the front. In our opinion, it is preferable to run tech rehearsals from the front unless there is a specific reason to be side stage. If tech time is short or you are working on a repertoire piece that you have called before, then choose the location that is more beneficial for you. But consider that during this period, the technical elements are being worked out, and it is important that the stage manager is in direct communication with the creative team and can see the show from an audience perspective. A front view will inform you how cues and shifts or scene changes are landing. This information is important to note because once you move to the actual **calling position** for dress rehearsals, which may be either side stage or in the booth, you may not have adequate visuals through the stage monitors to see the subtleties of the cues. Having had the opportunity to view technical rehearsals from the front will give you confidence in your cue placement when you are on side stage or watching on a monitor from the calling position.

Now it's time to add costumes. The dancers may have already requested specific costume pieces in rehearsals, and/or rehearsal tutus as they impact the movement. Adding the actual costumes will give the dancers the opportunity to work through specific moves such as lifts and **partner work**. For any ensemble work that might occur in unison, how the tutu sits on the dancer could affect spacing. So, once the company is in costume, they will typically decide what moves they need to try out before a run of the piece. The rehearsal director and/or choreographer will also have specific moments they would like to space in costume. These may have already been incorporated as part of the placing rehearsal.

Don't forget to check in with the wardrobe team about management of costume quick changes. These important elements must also be included in scene change and technical rehearsals. As with any show, when you are running scene changes in time and a '**hold**' is called, the wardrobe team will also stop, so all aspects of the change are paused for accurate shift timings, unless an alternative was previously discussed. The team continues to step through the show until all sections have incorporated their specific technical elements.

SHOW PAPERWORK

Updating show paperwork will be important in this phase of production. The stage manager should concentrate on accurate cue placement and standbys in the calling script/score and keeping everyone on track in the facilitation of the rehearsal. See Figures 5.16 and 5.17 for examples of two styles of digital show calling documents.

The assistant stage managers should monitor the stage and cast, handling any company requests, checking for safety issues, monitoring entrances, and updating show paperwork throughout the process. In dance, assistant stage managers may have specific duties during scene changes and/or props hand-offs, unless you are at a union house. As you progress through the technical rehearsal period, you might also task an assistant stage manager to assist in notating curtain calls/bows if they have not yet been set. This blocking is sometimes decided during a technical or dress rehearsal (sometimes in the final dress rehearsal!). These should be documented and posted on the call board for cast and crew reference. The stage manager should also have a copy at the calling desk, see Figures 5.18a and 5.18b. Add diagrams for quick interpretation for yourself and the company if necessary.

At the end of each technical rehearsal the production team comes together for a short production meeting in the house, as is common practice with plays or musicals. At this time any urgent or pending work notes are discussed and put into the upcoming daily schedule, and call times for the next day are confirmed. Generally, the production manager or stage manager will notate these and send an email to the show teams informing them of plans for the next day, around the previously scheduled rehearsals. Check company protocol to see who is responsible for this communication.

	Dances Patrelle SM: Betsy Ayer	**Romeo and Juliet** **SM Cue Sheets Act 1**		p. 5 of 11 As of 9/11/14
Time	Run Notes		Cue	Details
	Prince & Rosaline start xt SR from plat./			
	modulation		LQ 112	15 ct
	all exit - men w/ swords (desc. Theme 2X)			
	plagues re-nt SL/			
14:13	quieter then loud duh duh **duh**		LQ 113	US out
	(plagues move arch to UC)			
14:20	**+ beat**		scrim IN	RQ 3
		(Scene Shift to bedroom)		
	Music: BB AAA C modulate			
15:13	plague (Claire) holds grapes DS			
	Huge crash then:			
	2nd loud chord in sustain		LQ 114	p/d to Plague DS
	Plagues offstage/ Ant. Music		LQ 115	
	LQ 115 est./ Scene shift complete		scrim out	RQ 4
		Bedroom		
15:40	**Nurse & Juliet at SR step**		LQ 116	12 ct.
16:12	Juliet w/ dress & Nurse dance in unison	4 MIN WARN: Shift to Ballroom Scrim		
16:23	scarf around Nurse waist; Juliet xt SL	*Wardobe: Juliet QC L.2*		
16:48	Nurse falls on steps	SBY: LQ 117 SQ A3		
	Nurse curtsey then:			12/20 pull room focus
17:04	**Juliet nt SL**		LQ 117	up
	Juliet pose, then:			
	Juliet step		SQ A3	
17:25	Nurse sits on bed			
17:49	Juliet sits on bed too - Juliet theme in music Nurse gives Juliet locket Lady Capulet nt SR up stairs, across platform, down SL			
18:40	Tybalt nt SR steps/ Juliet gives locket back to Nurse			
	Lord Cap & Paris nt SR			

Figure 5.16 Calling document *Romeo and Juliet* Act 1.

Source: Created by Betsy Ayer.

DRESS REHEARSALS

After the show has been worked through technically and, if time permits, had a **technical run**, you will prepare for **dress rehearsals**. The formal dress rehearsals run in show conditions and include all presets and pre-show duties expected for an actual performance. The stage manager runs these as they would for any other genre of live performance. You begin from at least the one-hour call giving the timings up to 'curtain.' The stage manager makes these calls in the theatre and

Ballet: Coppélia ACT III
Choreographer: Chrissie Parrott
West Australian Ballet

IN CUE: Fly/Rail: Q4   LX: 28.   AX: Q3   Spot #1. Out. / Spot #2 Out.

Score Ref.	Time	Segment	Action	Scenic	Notes	Cues
	INT.	Act III - Checks	Onstage checks	Show Cloth & Act III Backcloth IN	Props: Slide Proj. set & tested	
				Pink Legs/Borders		
				Wedding tables	props per list	
				Teddy Drop: Bags filled	Dustmops s/by	
	5 Min to Places		Headset/production checks			Page: 5 Minute Call & Technical on Headset
			LX Op & 2 Followspots		Frame 4	
			Audio, Orchestra			
			Fly/Rail (2), Deck (2)			
	Places		ASM Dancer checks		Places: Mother & Father	Page: Cast, Final Call Tech, Orchestra 1st Call
					FOH Check-In via House phone	
					Stage Preset	LX Q 29
	2 Minutes		Cast/Stage Set		Go to Blue LX	Page: Orch Final Call
						Conductor call
					On AX handset/ Fade	AX Cue 4
			House music fades out		Confirm on headset	Orchestra tune
			Conductor at pit entrance			STAND BY Conductor

Ballet: Coppélia ACT III
Choreographer: Chrissie Parrott
West Australian Ballet

IN CUE: Fly/Rail: Q4   LX: 30.   AX: Q4   Spot #1. Out. / Spot #2 Out.

Score Ref.	Time	Segment	Action	Scenic	Notes	Cues
		Conductor ENT	House LX Complete			Conductor GO
		ACT III	Conductor Enters		Pit special up	LX Q 30.5
					Standby: Conductor	Pit Q-Lite ON
			Conductor Bows, turns to stage		Pit special out	LX Q 30.7
						STAND BY House Curtain Out
			Conductor Raises Baton		On Headset	Fly Q 5: CURTAIN OUT
			Curtain 3/4 Out		Conductor Cue	Pit Q-Lite OFF
			With Conductor's Downbeat		fade curtain warmers	LX Q 31
300/1/1	0:00	En'tract	Music Begins		Stopwatch reference	
			Father sets up slideshow screen			LX Q 32
						STAND BY: LX 33, 34 & Fly Q 6 /Show Cloth Out
					RAIL QL ON	
	2:20		End En'tract		RAIL QL OFF/ Headset	Fly Q 6: SHOW CLOTH OUT & LX Q 33
342/1/1		No 2 L'Aurore	Reveal couples asleep onstage			LX Q 34
			Proposal Section		* Called Cues	STAND BY: Fly Qs 7 - 10: Teddy Bear Drops, Teddy Bear Sweepers & LX 35
342/2/1	6:35		On Music: Harp 1st triplet			LX Q 35
342/2/4	6:30		On Music: see score		SL single teddy drop	Fly Q7: Teddy Drop 1 GO
342/2/6					SR single teddy drop	Fly Q8: Teddy Drop 2 GO
343/1/3					SC 15x teddy drop	Fly Q9: Teddy Drop 3 GO
343/1/5					Lg teddy bear dump	Fly Q10: Teddy Drop 4 GO
			1 beat after full drop		2x en w/dustmops	Teddy Sweepers Go

SM: Calling Document 2000
S Fenty / Contact #####

Figure 5.17 Calling document *Coppélia* Act 3.
Source: Created by Sue Fenty.

to all dressing rooms, stage door, green room, and any designated warm up areas via a backstage microphone that is generally set in **prompt corner** or at the **calling desk** at the stage management console, for both opera and dance. The calls include 'half-hour', 15-minutes, 5-minutes and either the 'Places' (USA) or 'Beginners' call

West Australian Ballet
Ballet: **Coppelia**
Choreographer: Chrissie Parrott
Curtain Calls

End of Ballet: House Curtain in/ Dancers Clear Stage

House Curtain Out
1. **Principals enter US from opposite sides, meet center & bow, then split & exit**
   Order: Franki & Hilda
           Dr Coppelius & Coppelia
           Mr & Mrs Swan
           The Twins

2. **Ensemble bows:**
   Leanne, Holly, Nicola & Fiona enter SR, XSC & bow and stay in line
   David, Seamus, Sakis & Callum enter SL, XDS through the line & Bow
   US Line steps to join DS line: Couples bow
   All bow together and split to sides on diagonals

3. **Principals re-enter, bow center & split to sides**
   Reverse Order: The Twins (Benazir, Jayne)
                     Mr & Mrs Swan (Timothy, Edmund)
                     Dr Coppelius & Coppelia (Andrew, Melissa)
                     Franki & Hilda (Errol, Jacinta)

4. **Company form 2 lines & bow:**
   Leanne, David, Holly, Seamus, Nicola, Sakis, Fiona, Callum
   Benazir, Timothy, Melissa, Jacinta, Errol, Andrew, Edmund, Jayne

   Company takes 3 steps back, bow head
   Company move forward, full bow

5. Franki moves DSL, invites conductor Nicolette Fraillon to stage
   Nicolette Fraillon bows, acknowledges the orchestra
   Orchestra Bows
   Nicolette steps back to centre of company   (*See opening night calls)

6. **Full company steps forward & bows**
   Full company steps back & bows
House Curtain In

Extra Bows: House Curtain Out
7. **Full company steps forward & bows**
   Full company steps back & bows as curtain comes in
House Curtain In

Figure 5.18a Dance Bow Order *Coppélia*.
Source: Created by Sue Fenty.

(UK/Australia) which brings the company to the stage to begin the show. You are now working with a larger community so don't forget to include orchestra, venue, company, and technical teams in your calls. Sample one-hour call: "Good evening, Company of *The Nutcracker*, (Name of) Orchestra, and (Name of venue) technical

Opening Night Curtain Calls:

After Bow 5:
Franki & Hilda move SL, invite Chrissie Parrott to centre stage

6-A   Chrissie Parrott enters SL, XSC for solo bow
       2 flower presenters enter from SL

       Flowers are presented to Chrissie and Nicolette, each takes solo bow
       Presenters exit stage

7-A   Chrissie invites creative team to the stage
       3 flower presenters enter from SL
       Flowers are presented to Lighting, Costume and Scenic Designers
       Designers Bow / Presenters exit stage

8-A   2 flower presenters enter from SL
       Flowers are presented to principal dancers: Franki & Hilda
       Presenters exit stage

9-A   Full company steps forward & bows
       Full company steps back & bows
House Curtain In

10-A   Extra Bows: House Curtain Out
       Full company steps forward & bows
       Full company steps back & bows as curtain comes in
House Curtain In

Figure 5.18b   Dance Bow Order *Coppélia*.
Source: Created by Sue Fenty.

team, this is your one-hour call. We have one hour until curtain." (Remember to repeat the call.) At the half hour call, the assistant stage manager should collect the sign in sheet and check that everyone has arrived. If a cast member has not signed in, the assistant stage manager can then check dressing rooms and/or make an announcement for cast to sign in.

> Green Tip: There are many apps that allow you to program your pre-show and intermission calls. Many will send you a reminder or sound an alarm. One example is Show StopWatch.

Once the stage preset has begun, it is important to ensure the company is aware that they are not permitted onstage until the stage is set. Only after the Head Carpenter has confirmed that stage access for dancers is permitted, can an announcement be made: "Company of *Swan Lake*, the stage is clear if you'd like access to warm up. Company of *Swan Lake*, the stage is now clear for warm up" or you could employ a Q-light color-coded system outside of stage access entrances. For example, a red light is turned on when the stage is not accessible for cast due to safety reasons, and a green light when the company is free to use the stage for their personal pre-show warm ups. It is a good idea to give the cast at least 15 minutes of stage time after the curtain is in and house is open to test their shoes on the dance floor, and any other specific moves they might want to try before the show begins. Note: this process should be repeated at intermission if there is a set change.

> Always confirm stage access clearance with the Head Carpenter before inviting any company members to the stage!

As you count down the time to 'places' you will add additional calls to suit the orchestra and venue staff, keeping the full team on track with time management. For example: ten minutes prior to the show you might be requested to give the orchestra their first call, as well as requesting the technical team check in on headsets. During the next five minutes, go through your headset check list, marking off the team members as they put on their headset. This is the most time efficient way to ensure the full technical team is ready to begin when house clearance is given. It's also a nice way to say hello to the team if you haven't seen everyone in person! Usually, the team member will put on their **'comms'**, and check in with their name or position. You may hear a variety of responses, typically in the range of "audio on comms" or "Kyle on headset." At five minutes to show time, the stage manager will give a 'second and final call' to the orchestra, and beginners/places to cast and crew over the paging system.

> Reminder, any orchestra calls should be checked in advance and confirmed by the orchestra manager or union rep to ensure these calls consider their rules of engagement.

When these general calls are completed, it's time to check in with orchestra management for an update on the orchestra arrivals. The stage management team should be checking cast to let you know when you have the full complement for the top of show. There may be an allocated person or system to touch base with the front of house manager. This final check in will let you know if the show will start on time or if you need to hold for any reason. You are nearing the start of the show, the final page is for the conductor to enter the pit. Generally, in dance, you will call the conductor's name over the paging system: "Dobbs Franks, this is your call to the pit, Mr Franks, your call." Make sure you know their accurate title or leave it out altogether, reverting to their full name. In some instances, the conductor might prefer the title, Maestro. For instance, "Maestro Verbitsky, this is your call to the stage. Maestro Verbitsky, your call."

Once you have a system of pre-show calls that works for your production, document it at the front of your calling script and be sure to repeat it consistently with timings, verbiage, and order of calls for every rehearsal and performance to follow. You can also set an alarm on your phone or wristwatch to remind you to make the announcements. The show cast, crew, and musicians will rely on this consistency in their pre-show preparations. This also is a key point in maintaining trust in the company, you are showing yourself to be reliable in all aspects of the show on a daily basis, from the moment you arrive at the venue until post-show duties are complete.

> In recent times, the more traditional forms of addressing company members are being left behind in stage pages. Titles such as Mr, Miss, Ms will be replaced by the cast members first and last name instead.

As the calling stage manager, you will want to run your dress rehearsals as close to show conditions as possible so there are no surprises for yourself or the company when you move into previews and shows. Items that are sometimes overlooked during this phase of production should be added to your checklists and cues. These include: blackout/blue light checks, house handover/open, top of show announcements, land acknowledgments, house light cues, any specific lockout periods for the audience, bows, and any house music pre-show, post-show, and during intermission. Even if you are not running the cues in the initial dress rehearsals, it's a good idea to make sure that the process is documented so that all aspects are on everyone's radar and will not come as a surprise. It may also prompt discussions such as whether house music is necessary during intermission, or if a **lockout period** is required due to show content (see the Opera section for a comprehensive top of show sequence description).

A note regarding audience lockouts. This is a period of time when latecomers are not admitted into the theatre or, if audience members leave for any reason during the show, re-entry points may be designated. These should be clearly communicated to the front of house management via a **FOH information sheet** along with all information regarding the audience interaction with the performance: house open time, latecomer protocols, content warnings, signage, and announcements will have been decided so all of this can be conveyed on this form.

It is not unusual to skip some of the pre-show cues and checks in the first dress and move straight to the start of the company's involvement. This is because these checks will have been done at top of day before the technical notes and lighting sessions. It's also important to check in with heads of departments for any updates on adjustments to the stage, and all performance related matters before every stage rehearsal. You can then advise the company of any changes that will affect the rehearsal. Being thorough is a priority in your pre-show checks to ensure every thing is ready for each dress rehearsal, especially while you are still in the technical period of the show when work notes are happening each day. Your pre-show rhythms will fall into place as you begin final dress rehearsals. All cues, including the top of show sequence, should be called at the remaining dress rehearsals to ensure the performances will flow smoothly.

VARIATIONS TO THE PROCESS

Technical rehearsal protocols will change in response to each company, and variations in your responsibilities may occur when you are not in a union venue. For instance, you may be stage managing for a small dance company that is not union-affiliated and asked to have more of a hands-on approach to the show. In this example, you might be packing the props from the rehearsal space after the last rehearsal and loading them into the theater yourself. For this type of show the company is working with pre-recorded music that can easily be run by the stage manager on a computer-based audio system from side stage. No assistant stage manager has been hired since the dancers do not need any assistance during the show, and the limited props will be set by the crew. In this case, it might make more sense for you to be backstage for all technical rehearsals, and to ensure the sound system can be run from the calling station. Consider what is most practical for you to rehearse and run the show. Here we will reiterate our earlier advice: ensure you are aware of your role and the expectations of the company before you sign your contract, and that you have the skills to cover your show duties. If the stage management requirements of the show are too complicated for one person, speak with the producer about hiring more crew or an assistant.

FINAL THOUGHTS

Technical rehearsals in both opera and dance will ask you to use a combination of your knowledge of managing standard theatre productions alongside specific genre-related protocols for opera or dance to facilitate these time-sensitive rehearsals. Requirements will vary in dance depending on the size of the company, complexity of the show and type of music being used. Opera is more uniform in its stage management approach, based on traditional protocols.

The show has moved to the stage and now has a larger production community supporting it. You have been introduced to conversations that must happen with collaborators in different departments, with special attention to wigs and make-up, wardrobe, and the orchestra, that will keep you on point in these specialist performance styles that are steeped in history and tradition. By the time you've concluded your final dress rehearsal, all your show paperwork has been updated and you are now ready to interact with the front of house team to add the final component of your show: the audience, as we prepare for Opening Night.

CHAPTER 6

Opening and Running the Show

Your show is ready for an audience! This is an exciting time not only for the creative team, show team and performing artists, but for the venue and all associated collaborators as well. Some companies may include preview performances, but this is unusual in opera and dance. However, as it may occur, we will look at previews or performances before opening and discuss traditions, protocols, and events surrounding the much-anticipated opening of the show. Next, we'll examine the run of the production, show maintenance, alternating casts, and archiving paperwork. During this phase, protocols must be in place for potential emergency situations and show stops as you guide the production through the season.

FINAL DRESS REHEARSAL AND PREVIEWS

If a preview is scheduled, it will be handled in the same fashion as any other genre of theatre. In lieu of a preview, companies often schedule an **open** final dress rehearsal, also called an **invited dress** or **general rehearsal**. This exclusive final rehearsal can be an opportunity for companies to invite special guests, sponsors, family and friends, charity groups, and school groups. This can also be a time that the producing company engages in philanthropic work, inviting guests that might not otherwise be able to attend a ticketed performance by offering a discounted or free community night.

Because there is an audience in attendance, the rehearsal is usually ticketed and will involve a house manager and team of ushers. This type of showing will typically have a limited house capacity and the audience will be assigned to a specific seating area in the theatre, for example the front mezzanine and rear of the orchestra section, behind the designers. Production desks may remain in the house for the creative team for both practical reasons and to signify that this is a rehearsal. While the final dress is usually run per show conditions, there is often an introduction from a member of the company, typically the director. Unofficially known as the 'disclaimer speech' this is when the audience is welcomed and briefed on protocols, sharing information about the rehearsal, and letting them know there may be

DOI: 10.4324/9781003098812-6

stops or pauses. The audience is asked not to talk during any breaks as notes will be given to cast, crew, and orchestra during this time. By opening the final dress rehearsal to guests, the company still receives many benefits that a preview might bring but without the pressure of possible press attendance. The main differences are that the audience numbers will be limited, and all guests have been invited by the producing company, so there is no general public component.

Both the Open Dress Rehearsal and the Preview provide an opportunity for the creative team to gauge the audience's response to the production prior to opening, while there is still time for some revision. For the artists it can be an opportunity to engage with the energy of an audience and respond to applause within the performance. For shows that involve audience participation, it is an invaluable tool for the company. For the stage manager, they present an opportunity to run the show with the inclusion of the final elements: the audience and front of house team. Interactions with the house manager have been theory up until this moment, now you get to experience if it all goes to plan as predicted, or if adjustments are needed to your protocols to ensure the smooth running of the show. It is also an opportunity to work on timing cues around applause to variations, solos, and arias.

As with any other genre of theatre, the stage manager will create a **Preview** or **Open Dress Rehearsal Report** to be sent to the pre-established **distribution list,** keeping the producers, venue staff, creatives, and show team informed with any relevant information about the show. This will list all the information expected by the company for performances, including the time of **house handover** and/or **house open**, announcements, tuning, the show start time, duration of each segment or act, intermission, and overall **show running time** (Figure 6.1). There will also be general

	UP	DOWN	TOTAL	NOTES
FOH Handover				
Announcements				
Orch. Tune				
Act One				
Intermission				
FOH Handover				
Orch. Tune				
Act Two				
Bows				
Total Running Time:				

Figure 6.1 Example of timings section of a show report.

notes and audience response, casting, injuries, and/or replacements. Any aspect of the show that did not run as directed, designed, or choreographed will be noted in your report. The basic show report is similar to any other live performance genre, but you will add details on orchestra tuning, daily casting, and duration of individual dance pieces. And you should add a section for music or orchestra. Post-show technical meetings may continue during the preview period but will cease with the opening performance.

> Green Tip: There are several good apps you can add to your mobile device to calculate show timings. These allow you to start the show and then simply click next and the app will note the next critical timing. They also calculate the total show and running times for you, including show stops. Find one that allows you to add specific elements you need such as pre-show speeches and tunings. It's worth the small investment to save you time and effort.

PREPARING FOR THE OPENING

During the dress rehearsals or preview period, as you head towards the highly anticipated 'Opening Night' performance, you will find aspects of the show are developing into a routine. Pre-show duties will be carried out in a specific order based on practicality, and company arrivals, warm ups, and personal rituals will begin to unfold. Since the stage management team is usually one of the first teams to arrive at the venue for a show call, you will observe the habits of the company such as which company members prefer individual warm ups, and which opt for group warm ups, who waits in the green room, dressing room, or studio until they are called to the stage, which people tend to run early or late for their calls, and so on. These early shows are an opportunity to get to know the community of artists working together on this production, which ultimately increases your ability to support the artists and the production. Having an idea of what is routine and what is out-of-the-ordinary can be useful in supporting the team. *However, be aware that there is a fine line between general business and intruding on someone's privacy! Be respectful of everyone.*

The order of the technical team's pre-show activity will be determined by practicality as well as specific requests. For example, once the dance barres are removed from the stage, the dance floor will be mopped while a lighting check is conducted from side of stage or the house. This allows both tasks to be achieved without holding up the other department's checks.

An example of an unofficial task that develops through observing the company's routine is when an assistant stage manager notes that before each show a principal dancer runs a specific exit into the DSR wing. To assist with monitoring safety backstage, the assistant stage manager might decide to check the SR props around the time that the dancer's running exit tends to happen. Having an extra set of eyes DSR at this time supports the dancer as well as any unsuspecting backstage bystanders. These pre-show rhythms can develop into an ordered routine and add to the fabric of the show, creating a collaborative weave where different departments work with and around each other to effectively perform their roles within the time constraints of the production. Typically, the last task that will happen before the house is handed over to the House Manager and the stage is considered clear for cast access is the full blackout check. This is when the work lights are switched to blue running lights and a check is made to ensure no extra lights have been left on that would affect a blackout or low light cue during the show. Since many opera and dance productions are performed on a proscenium stage, you will often find that the grand drape or main curtain is in as the audience enters the house. This convenience allows the company to practice those special dance moments, or even allows you to run a fight call upstage of the curtain.

> Pro Tip: *Well-fitted dance shoes can make or break a dancer's rehearsal or performance. Stage managers can carry heel grips, inserts, gaff tape, toe pads, band aids, medical tape, foot pads and moleskin to offer dancers who may be having problems.*
>
> – Nancy Pittelman

PAPERWORK!

The initial show running duty sheets or 'tracks' were created by the stage management team in the lead up to technical rehearsals. These documents laid out pre-show duties in an order that made sense based on the team's knowledge of the show at that time. As technical rehearsals progressed, the tracks were updated to suit individual departments and compressed in a way that ensured the house would open on time, meaning that several tasks are generally happening at the same time. By the time the show opens, you should have your final version of the running plots, incorporating any performance-based edits that consider the full production team, including front of house pre-show checks, and possible cast-related requests. The stage management team will have compiled a **comprehensive run sheet**, this may be the Who What Where, ensuring they know where and when all movement happens before, during, and after the show and, also, a comprehensive cue sheet. This paperwork is essential for problem solving and for the potential replacement of show staff. Substitutions could happen at any moment in an emergency or if someone becomes ill. In our current environment, there are also company-specific protocols around Covid-19 for inclusion in the show files.

There is much to consider and take on board in this final week of rehearsals in the venue. Preparations for Opening happen concurrently with technical rehearsals and dress rehearsals. This is another reminder that so much of your work as a stage management team relies on your preparation. You began the expected paperwork for this moment back in pre-production, detailed it during the rehearsal period, and revised it in tech, so that at this juncture of the process you are not panicking to create documents, but merely putting the finishing touches on documents that are already in existence. Documents that may need adjusting for Opening include:

House Opening protocols and top of show announcements, curtain calls, and pre-show/post-show event information. If there is an announcement onstage, you might have to cue a microphone and request that someone places and strikes the microphone stand. If flowers are to be presented during curtain calls, you may need to liaise with the front of house team.

OPENING NIGHT SCHEDULE AND FORMALITIES

While you have been facilitating the stage rehearsals, various other company personnel have been planning the events surrounding the Opening Night performance. This is also their big moment, with responsibilities that might include creating the evening rundown, guest lists, catering, pre-show, intermission, post-show, sponsors and VIP receptions, flowers, and gifts. You may be asked to interface some show activities with their planned events, so be sure to meet before the technical rehearsals begin so you are aware of everything these functions entail. A sample of an opening night task list and rundown might look like this for your colleagues:

10:00AM	Pick up supplies, refreshments, flowers, and check ins with venue and caterers.
2:00PM	Meet venue team to hang opening night banners in front of theatre and main lobby.
3:00PM	Meet with executive team regarding events, liaise with Chair of Board.
4:00PM	Set up Lobby tables with VIP packs, programs, tickets, and nametags for functions.
5:00PM	Liaise with stage manager for onstage speech, post-show flowers and function.
6:00PM	Pre-show Formalities with major sponsors and company executive team/ catering required.
6:30PM	Executive team speeches.
7:00PM	Escort guests to dress circle foyer for pre-show drinks and to pick up VIP packs.
7:15PM	Seat VIPS.
7:30PM	Onstage top of show formalities: Welcome speech and land acknowledgment.

(Note: SM to run, company staff standing by backstage.)

7:40PM	Show begins/ Company staff to check in with venue for second (Intermission) function, check catering and sound system for speeches.
8:30PM	Company staff standing by in lobby to escort sponsors to function.
8:40PM	Chair of Board to deliver speech to sponsors in dress circle reception area.
8:45PM	Sponsors escorted to Lobby for second half of performance.
8:50PM	Act 2 commences/ Company staff to check on post-show function, catering, guest list, and sound system set up in main reception area.

9:25PM   Assist with flowers backstage for bows if required.

9:30PM   Move to post-show function area with guest list, Greet VIPs and sponsors.

9:45PM   Post-show speeches: Executive team, Chair of Board, and Show Director.

Supervise event throughout, liaise with venue re: last drinks and exits.

10:30PM   End of Day.

As the stage manager of the production, you will want to be included in the lines of communication for all non-performance aspects of the evening's events. To clarify, you are not responsible for these events, but you should be familiar with what has been planned and any expectations involving the performers, production team, and creatives.

> Pro Tip: *I wear a headlamp around my neck instead of using a flashlight. That way it's easy to switch it on and read my cues or a preset list.*
> – Besty Ayer

STAGE-RELATED OPENING NIGHT PROTOCOLS

Opera and dance are both genres that tend to have more traditional protocols stemming from their long history and lineage. Let's start with wishing our colleagues a successful show. "Toi toi toi" in opera and "Merde" in dance will let your artistic collaborators know that you wish them good luck for this evening's performance. Superstition prompts these old sayings, with the term toi toi toi derived from the German for devil "Teufel" (pronounced TOY-fell) and spitting over the shoulder three times to ward off evil spirits or bad luck. The dance-related word of encouragement, merde (translation: "shit" in French), is believed to have originated from the Paris Opera Ballet during the 19th century and is a wish for a full house, good ticket sales, and a well-received performance. Merde harkens to the manure piles left from horse-drawn carriages of the patrons arriving at the palace for performances, so the more merde, the bigger the audience. There are several versions of the exact reasons for these word choices, but the superstition associated with wishing bad luck to ensure good luck is also at play here, hence the tradition continues.

There are also functional protocols to be aware of regarding formalities around the performance, as well as expectations such as those related to extra bows and flowers during curtain calls. On the day of the opening performance, the stage manager should ensure they are aware of any activities that involve the stage, cast, and/or creative team. Although you may not be directly involved with activities like the VIP speeches at the intermission function, you may be asked questions regarding them. So, it makes sense to have a copy of the most current opening night rundown handy. It's also convenient to have a **face sheet** with photos of any special guests. If the Governor, Traditional Custodian of the Land, and Chair of the Board will be waiting backstage at the top of show for onstage welcome speeches, make sure you know exactly who they are. Requesting or creating a show-specific face sheet ensures that you and your team are ready to greet these official guests when they arrive backstage.

Also note that other departments' preparations may affect the smooth running of the show you are calling, so it is worth your while to check in with these colleagues to ensure everything is in hand, that you are aware of all details, and that you are listed in the communication loop for any last-minute changes to schedule. Be thorough in all aspects of this so you don't get caught not knowing important information, such as a piece of official protocol like the orchestra will be playing a short musical lead-in prior to the official introduction. This means the orchestra might need to be called to the pit and tuned earlier than a standard performance. Is everyone aware of this information, including the performers? Is this information something you could remind everyone about at the half-hour call over the dressing room paging system? Other show-related matters might include: What are the arrangements for the floral delivery for Opening Night curtain calls, who in the company will be receiving flowers onstage (you will need to cue the ushers or presenters), and who will be presenting the flowers? Where will the bouquets be located during the show, and who is responsible for taking them out of the water and drying them off before they are brought onto the stage, so they don't drip water on the costumes and dance floor? If there is a special end of night speech in front of the curtain, who has been organized to page the curtain and hand off the microphone? Are there any specific requests to how this will be cued? Will there be an archival video recording of the performance? If so, has everyone been advised?

> If opening night flowers are to be presented onstage during curtain calls, assign someone to take the flowers out of water buckets and pat the ends dry well before curtain calls so water does not drip from the bouquets onto the guest presenters, the artists, and the floor.

The personnel responsible for various extra duties will vary from company to company, and you may find that your team takes on some of these tasks on opening night. Specific opening night checklists will keep you on track when integrating the special one-show-only protocols, without impacting your calling document with too much information.

As noted in Chapter 5: Technical Rehearsals, there are a variety of bows that the company may use to ensure that all members of the company receive their accolades from the audience. Be aware that European-based traditions around curtain calls for principal artists may include downstage bows, a.k.a. front of curtain bows, particularly if a character has met their demise during the performance. This was the case in the following dance company bow list. Additionally, on opening night, the creative team traditionally joins the company onstage following the conductor's bow.

1. Curtain In / center split of curtain is paged open: Principals enter center stage, move downstage of curtain for bow, then exit center through the curtain split.
2. Curtain Out: Ensemble bows.
3. Special characters or highlighted soloists' bow.
4. Principals bow (Flowers presented to principal artists, presenters enter from side stage).
5. One of the principal artists collects the conductor from side stage.
6. Conductor bows (flowers or gift presented to the conductor), gestures to orchestra.
7. Orchestra bows or nods.
8. Full company bow.
9. Principals invite Creative Team to the stage for a bow (flowers or gift presented to creative team).
10. Full company bow (repeat as needed), Curtain In.

At the end of the night, you might feel a sense of relief that the Opening performance is completed. There seems to be a lot of pressure surrounding this specific show, and everyone wants it to go well. There is no denying that much will be riding on the reception of the show and its associated events. You may notice a mix of emotions from the various stakeholders, companies, creatives, technicians, and artists. Consider that there might be financial ramifications, such as sponsorship and potential VIP donors. Press members will be in attendance as reviews are commonly based on this one show, and it might feel like reputations are at stake. It is also the final time that the full creative team is present at one time. The show designers, choreographers, possibly the rehearsal director, and specific support staff will leave after this performance and move onto their next project. It can be bittersweet, mixing the excitement of the occasion with sadness surrounding impending departures. Remember to be empathetic with those you encounter. For you, the stage manager, it is the first official performance. It's your moment to take the reins on the production as it moves forward into its next phase: the run of the show and maintenance of the production. You will begin by composing the first performance report, sharing the progress of the show with producers, collaborating companies, creatives, and venue team.

MAINTAINING THE SHOW

Following the opening night festivities, the second performance can sometimes feel anticlimactic. This is a time to keep the company's morale in check and maintain a professional attitude. You may find the cast, orchestra, and crew more relaxed as they settle into 'show mode.'

For dance companies with alternating casts, this may be the first show that the *second cast* goes on, so there is an excitement to that and there may be a repeat of opening night flower protocols for principals during the curtain calls for this show. When we talk about alternating casts with double or even triple casting, it generally does not mean the full cast, but specific principal and solo artists. The rehearsal director/ballet master will create daily schedules that include the show casting for the specific day, as they have throughout the rehearsal period. They will also continue to attend and/or run the daily company class, which has now moved to onstage for the run of the show. The rehearsal director will attend each show since it is their responsibility to maintain the artistic integrity of the dance. Once again, we reiterate the value of having a good working relationship with this important member of the team. You will work closely with the rehearsal director throughout the season, checking in about schedules, casting, replacements, any required rehearsals, and anything that impacts the show. The stage manager does not give dancers notes during the season, that is the rehearsal director's place. If there is a technical note that involves a dancer, the stage manager should present this to the rehearsal director for discussion on how it might be addressed. In a ballet company there is a clear delineation of duties here, but these might be less obvious in smaller or independent companies. Once again, communication is key.

As noted in previous chapters, opera performance schedules are designed to protect the singers' voices so there is usually a day off between each performance of the production. In larger opera companies, they may perform other operas from the repertoire on the off night. When there is a double cast for a production, it is usually only a few performers, and you can assume then that those roles are *very* difficult to sing and therefore the performer needs more than a single night of recovery. So, the purpose of the double cast is not to be able to have performances every night, but to give the singers longer rest periods between performances. Since there are so few shows, the stage manager usually does not have to do upkeep on the singers' performances. Most operas only run for a few performances, maybe three or four, even if spread out over a longer rep season. Still, if a cover or replacement performer is to join the company, you want to run through all the technical elements of the production in which they are involved to ensure both physical and emotional safety. Whether that includes running a scene onstage with relevant technical elements or ensuring that the replacement performer has access to the intimacy director for consultation on nudity or hyper-exposed scene work or any work involving physical intimacy, the stage manager must ensure that the covers and replacements are given the same attention that was offered the main company.

> *Once, while stage managing a production of La Bohème, during our 'happy and healthy' checks we discovered that the singer performing Rudolfo was not going to be able to do the next performance. The company brought in a performer who had the role in his repertoire. When he arrived, he was taken first to costumes and then stage management was going to walk him through the staging. At this point he turned to the me and said, 'Oh darling, it's La Bohème. Just tell me where she dies.' I pointed to the bed and the stove where the manuscript gets burned and that was the end of the put-in rehearsal.*
>
> – Michele Kay

Since opera singers are performing roles from a repertoire of known roles, they often perform the role many times. The character's intentions, music, and lyrics are already known to the performer, so sometimes they just need to be told where to go *this* time. And unless the set is stylized, "darling, it's *La Bohème*," is not such an unusual concept.

> Archive as you go!

TRACKING INFORMATION AND ARCHIVING THE PRODUCTION

As noted throughout this book, we cannot stress enough how critical it is for the stage management team to maintain accurate show documentation. Every time a cue changes, blocking is updated, or a prop is cut, the stage management team must update their paperwork to reflect the changes. The team must keep track of all changes to the production and reflect those changes in the paperwork that the stage management team produces. If the team does this throughout the process, then completing the archival copy of the production book will be quick work. If, however, teammates did not update their paperwork throughout the process, then there is still work to be done once the show closes. Many stage management teams will gather for one final review of the show paperwork including the blocking and calling book/s, all performer entrance cues, Who What Where, props and scenic presets, and tracking, shift plots or run books, any costume, wardrobe, or wigs/makeup paperwork that the stage management team may have created, and any other paperwork related to running the show. The best way to do this is sit down with some snacks and assign different pieces of paperwork to each team member then start from the beginning making sure all paperwork reflects the same information from the start of the show through the end, including post-show. For example, if the Who What Where says a performer enters on 23/2/3 then that entrance cue should also be reflected in the calling book and any other paperwork that reflects entrance cues. Stage management should also include all reports, schedules, calendars, and meeting notes. Consult with the director of production or production manager to check whether it is within your job duties to collect all the archival data from other departments. If it is, begin to gather the paperwork and documentation from all production areas. This may include lighting plots and channel hookup information, sound system documentation, spot cue sheets, designer renderings, and ground plans, etc. A suggested list for a complete archive can be found in the online companion. Archival production books were once stored in large binders or folders, but now many companies are moving toward more green options and storing a digital archive. If you are storing a digital archive, make sure that it is stored on at least two forms of media, such as a hard drive as well as cloud storage. This way, you'll have a backup on a secondary media if one version is destroyed. Following the storage of the production book, there is little else for the stage manager to do other than check and restock supplies for the next production.

In some companies the stage manager may be responsible for editing an archival video recording of the production or managing the video library. Again, check with the director of production or production manager to see if this falls under stage management's jurisdiction.

SHOW STOPS

The stage manager is responsible for the flow of the performance and all technical aspects. It is in their purview to ensure safety for the company onstage, and to run the show smoothly from house to half and initiating the tuning to the final curtain calls and house lights up.

Stopping a show is not a usual occurrence. As the stage manager you should consider where there are risks of possible show stops and have a plan to run a stop (or pause) and re-start of the show seamlessly. These are generally circumstances when the show cannot continue due to technical complications, injury, or other cast-related reasons, or an emergency situation that puts the patrons and/or the company at risk.

> Pro Tip: *A show stop can be nerve wracking because you may not have all the information needed to respond to what is happening in that moment. TAKE A BREATH. Remember that what seems like a very long delay to you may actually only be a matter of seconds.*
> – Fiona Boundy

EMERGENCY STOPS

Most professional theatre venues will have standard operating procedures (SOPs) for possible emergency situations. It is their responsibility to have a plan in place that has been rehearsed with the venue team. As an employee of a producing company, you may not have been involved with any of these procedural test runs. In your orientation to the venue, you may have been given emergency evacuation paperwork. As the calling stage manager, you must make sure you understand your responsibility in an emergency. The detailed paperwork, including announcement text, should be kept at the stage manager's calling position. There will be a variety of emergencies listed that require very different responses from the venue's teams. These include weather events, (hurricanes, tornadoes, cyclones, etc.), power outage, fire, immediate threats from the audience, patron health-related situations, and so on. The venue response could range anywhere from immediate evacuation to shelter in place, with audience communication at the forefront of a calm and ordered response. Emergency responses may be mandated by the city and venue. Once your specified tasks of stopping the show are enacted, the next steps will be handled by the venue team. This typically involves the house manager, stage door keeper, venue technical manager, and other deputized team members and wardens. You may be asked to guide the company to a designated location. The sign-in sheets provide the stage door keeper with a list of all assembled company members in case attendance is required at muster points. This is one of the reasons accurate sign-in sheets are so important. One final and very important note regarding safety protocols – not all companies or venues have codified safety protocols. We recommend that you ask about safety protocols at an early meeting with the production manager and then if the company does not have protocols in place, ask that they be developed while you are there. You may use the information you've learned here to start the conversation. What you don't want is for the fire alarm to sound if you do not have a plan to evacuate 1500 patrons, a cast of 50, and an orchestra of 70 people! As always, be prepared.

PRODUCTION-RELATED PAUSES

Now consider the non-emergency show stops, these are circumstances that do not involve the immediate safety of the audience. When is it appropriate for the stage manager to stop a show and how should it be handled? When an unanticipated or undirected issue stops the forward running of the production, when an injury or illness has occurred that prohibits the immediate continuation of the show, or when a mishap occurs that interrupts or changes the storyline of the show in a way that the audience can no longer follow the narrative, a show stop (or pause) must be considered. In these types of situations, calmness, clear communication, and quick dissemination of information is imperative. Communication channels must be kept clear for the team members experiencing the show stopping issue to share information. The stage manager can then repeat the issue back over all comms channels to ensure the full team is aware of an impending show stop. When the decision is made to stop or pause the show, the stage manager should communicate that to everyone on the show channels. This should set off a chain reaction where the assistant stage manager informs cast, the front of house liaison informs the house manager who then passes the information on to ushers, and either the orchestral manager or a cue light/ emergency handset system is deployed that gets this important information to the conductor. If you are using recorded music, you will also need to notify the audio operator if they are not on headset to fade the sound and check that the SM announcement microphone is live. The more people in the loop about the show stop means fewer questions on headset, therefore the comms system is kept clear for progress updates.

As the calling stage manager, you will have considered moments that could foul the show and prompt a pause in the performance. These might include computer glitches, complicated scene or costume changes and automation-related error. In each hypothetical situation you should create your own SOP in association with the various departments to ensure you move forward in the best possible manner.

SAMPLE SCENARIOS
Situation 1

You are briefed on headset during a show that the automated fly system is showing an error, but this will not affect the show. You might take a moment post-show to ask the operator what the protocols might be to reset the system and how long it might take. Do they think the system is functioning properly for continued performances? You would note the error in the show report, noting it did not affect the show. This may serve as a warning sign to the department head or maintenance team that the fly system should be checked. For the stage manager, the discussion provides valuable information about the equipment.

In this example, two weeks later the fly operator advises during a show that the system is again showing an error. The stage manager makes a mental note of this, listening to the progress of the issue while still calling cues for the production. The SM looks ahead to see when the next automation sequence is and, if appropriate in the show, shares with the operator how much time there is before the next cue. The operator advises that the system needs to be rebooted. Based on the previous conversation, the stage manager knows this will take a minimum of two minutes and self-evaluates that there is enough time for this to happen but begins to plan for an appropriate moment to pause the performance. A few minutes later, the fly operator confirms that the computer is frozen and will not be able to run the upcoming cues. The stage manager confirms on headset to all channels that a show stop is necessary, which is confirmed by the appropriate department head.

The stage manager then communicates to all departments at what point the stop will happen, asks relevant personnel to be advised who are not on the show headset loop, and ensures there is a live mic for an announcement to the audience. In this case, since it does not affect the current scene, lighting cues for the current pas de deux continue, the dance variation concludes, dancers bow, and exit stage.

At this point the show stop goes into effect: the stage manager cues the house curtain in, which is run on a hemp counterweight system, and house lights are added to a low state as the stage manager makes an announcement that due to technical difficulties, the performance will take a short pause, please remain seated and the performance will recommence as soon as possible. The house manager is now in control of the house while updates come from the affected department.

The fly operator advises that the system is up and running again. The stage manager then cues the scene change which is executed behind the curtain in work lights. Following the scene change, the fly operator confirms that the system is working properly. The stage manager asks for blue lights backstage, and stands by the team to restart the show, with the following new cues added: house lights out, curtain out, and a cue light for the conductor.

The house manager is advised that the show will now recommence, and confirms the audience is still seated. The assistant stage manager confirms dancers are in place for the next section of the dance, and orchestral management confirms the conductor and orchestra are standing by.

The stage manager cues: dancers to stand by, work lights out and in appropriate LX cue, House Lights out, Curtain Out, LX cue, and cue lights the conductor. In this case, the restart procedure is run like the top of an act. The full pause of the performance took approximately three minutes, and the show then continued smoothly. Details of the show stop are noted in the show report for venue action.

Not all show stops will go this smoothly, but the point to take is that we are aiming for a calm and elegant stop to the show if possible. The calmer the stage manager and show team, the calmer everyone else will be in their response to the show stop. Once you've successfully executed a full show stop and restart, it is much easier to do the next time. The first time can be scary. Remember, as soon as you are in stoppage, plan and communicate the restart protocol. Restarting the train can be more challenging than stopping it, so don't forget to work through those details with your team while the people who are repairing the fault or attending to the incident are doing their part.

Your shortlist on a production related stop is:

1. The SM is advised of an issue that has the potential to stop the show.
2. Continue to call cues while the situation is being assessed.
3. Keep communication channels clear for updates.
4. When a decision is made to stop, calmly communicate this to everyone involved.
5. Facilitate the show stop in a calm manner, including the audience and back of house announcement.
6. Note the time you stopped the show and start a stopwatch to time the duration.
7. Continue to keep communication channels clear for updates.
8. Ensure everyone is aware when the show is ready to recommence.
9. Calmly recommence the show and continue with cues as usual.
10. Note the time you restart the show and duration of the show stop for the report.
11. Check in with the department to see if there are any other issues.
12. Once you have been given the news that everything is functioning, *do not* continue to ask the department if the system is still working properly.

> Turn your shortlist into a checklist and keep it with your show stop announcements at the front of your calling book or on a printed paper at the calling desk for quick and easy access. This can help you stay calm throughout the show stop and give you the confidence to lead your company through these unexpected situations.

Let's look at another situation.

Situation 2

You are running an opera and during the major scene change a fly line fouls and they cannot bring in Border #3 to mask the lighting equipment. The head of flys suggests that Border #2 can be inched into a lower trim to mask the lights for this scene. This would take the show to intermission where they can get ladders out to free Border #3. What would you do?

Regardless of whether you are working in opera, dance, or traditional theatre, form a plan. Doing some risk assessments and contingency planning, especially when you have a technically complicated show, can give you peace of mind when the risk becomes a reality and can help you keep everyone calm and the show moving forward. Anytime you need to execute a contingency plan, do a follow-up with your production team to see if anything could have been done differently to execute a better stop and restart, then add that into your future contingency plans. If we've said it a dozen times, we haven't yet said it enough, preparation is one of the most important tools in the stage manager's kit!

> If you are working with recorded music, run a back-up audio system that can be easily switched to if the main system goes down. This safety measure could eliminate a potential show stop.

FINAL THOUGHTS

Performance in any genre is challenging, but in opera and dance, the career of the performer can rest on a single point of failure. We strive to ensure that those failures won't happen on our watch, so we do everything within our power to promote a safe and healthy workspace for our company. We've also discussed the critical role of communication with the artistic and production teams throughout the technical rehearsals, into opening night, and during the run of the show. Keeping the production team apprised of any changes is critical to your success as a stage manager and increases your chances of being asked back to the company for future employment. Enjoy the run, you've earned the accolades too!

CHAPTER 7

Repertoire, Repertory Companies, Co-Productions, and Touring

In dance and opera, repertoire is vital to the performers and the general financial health of the company. The understanding of repertory systems and protocols involved is a staple of the stage manager's duties. In the last chapter we looked at archiving comprehensive paperwork and closing the show with the intention of any of the following possibilities: remount, sharing scenic elements, or touring the production. This chapter walks through how this information is essential in the context-specific circumstances as well as a general discussion of common terminology.

TERMINOLOGY

Let's begin with use of the words **repertoire** and **repertory**, as they will vary by genre and region. Both are derivatives of the Latin "repertorium" meaning list, inventory, catalogue, or repository. The selection of ballets, plays, operas that are produced by your company are their repertoire. For an individual artist, a variety of roles, solos, arias, or characters that they prepare to perform might be considered their 'repertoire.'

Repertory refers to the repeated performances of a selection of works. It can be used as a descriptor for the company itself, a particular season, or the collection. A repertory company generally schedules alternating works on a fixed schedule. In dance, you will more commonly hear the word repertoire, as dance terminology draws from the French language.

DOI: 10.4324/9781003098812-7

OPERA REPERTOIRE

As noted, an opera company may be performing opera productions in repertory with other operas; the Metropolitan Opera performs in repertory. But also, the term repertoire can refer to the productions, full or in part, that the opera company has in their scenic and/or costume storage. We discussed this in Chapter 3: Pre-production when we were building paperwork from previous productions. If the scenic and prop elements are owned by the opera company, then those productions are a part of the opera company's repertoire. If the opera company owns its own scenery, they can save considerable expense over renting or building a new set. They'll simply pull the show out of their "rep." You'll often see several shows out of the company's rep in the season alongside one or two new builds. This allows the company to budget more conservatively in leaner years, as many did during the recent pandemic. A long-time audience subscriber may see the same set for *La Traviata* several times over the course of a decade. Opera companies will typically build their seasons to parse out their rep every four to five years so as not to seem repetitive. They may also group one act operas together in different configurations. One season they may group *Cavalleria Rusticana* with *Pagliacci* colloquially known as "Cav/Pag," but the next time they do *Pagliacci*, they may group it with *Gianni Schicci*. Likewise, an opera company will often determine their season selections four to five years in advance so they can plan casting and book future productions with specific performers who have those shows in their repertoire. If you are a resident production stage manager of an opera company, you may be building paperwork for a production that occurs next season! Also, this advanced knowledge allows you lots of time to pull and brush-up the show's paperwork. Or if the company is performing a different pairing of one act operas, the stage manager may need to pull paperwork from two different archived production books.

> Since your paperwork will live with the company's repertoire, you want to do a thorough check of all paperwork to ensure it is accurate. Pulling insufficient paperwork out of the rep is incredibly frustrating. Don't let that be your paperwork!

DANCE REPERTOIRE

The repertoire is the lifeblood of a dance company. The pieces the company chooses to produce define the company in many ways. Stage management will support the repertoire in the archival process by adding information into the digital archives, documenting and/or archiving rehearsal music and props, keeping an up-to-date, accurate, and neat calling score, and archiving all documentation required to successfully reproduce any show. For dance repertoire, the archival process is also divided into pieces or ballets. For example, the components of a **'triple bill'** that is produced under a specific banner or title, for instance a show titled *American Classics* is comprised of three individual ballets that may not always be produced together. Therefore, the dance stage manager should document not only the production as a whole, but also the individual pieces for future tours, galas and re-organized shows. In the dance world, it is not uncommon for a component of a show, such as a one-act for instance, *Sheherazade*, a variation or specific section such as, *Sleeping Beauty* Act 3 Grande Pas de Deux or *The Nutcracker* Divertissements to be used in a gala or awards night as a contribution from the company. When this happens, the new documentation from the gala will be more generalized since it may not include the original scenic elements. It will be re-cued, documented, and filed separately to be accessed as and when needed as a 'stand alone' segment or piece. An extract of the document might be drawn from the original full-length production, or a new version created in linear format (Word or Excel) as a sub-file in the comprehensive show document, along with any recordings or excerpt scores that were used in performance, notes on casting, and any specifics of the event. For example: *Sleeping Beauty* Act 3 Grande Pas de Deux: dancers' names, date of performance, name of event/gala, and venue.

For stage managers on contracts that extend beyond the close of the show, additional duties within a repertory-style company may come into play during the lulls between seasons to support the upkeep of the repertoire documentation. These could include archiving music if there is not a music librarian in the company or keeping a digital list of archived videos, listing performance dates and casting as you did with the individual ballets discussed above. These duties are not part of the traditional role of the stage manager and might be considered part of the rehearsal director's domain, as dance company structures vary greatly. However, if you find yourself contracted for a permanent position with a company, be sure to ask for a documented list of duties when taking on the role so you are aware of any additional duties and can organize your time and expectations accordingly.

TOURING DANCE

One thing you can count on in most dance companies is that there will be a touring component. Touring is a fundamental part of the job. If you do not plan to tour, then perhaps individual contracted work within a specific city would be a better fit for you as a dance stage manager. However, if you want to travel, dance is a great option for career opportunities and a wonderful way to see the world. There are as many variations of tours as there are companies. Some will share their work within a state, regionally, nationally, or internationally. Some companies have a regular schedule and only work in specific theaters, others travel to festivals or create opportunities through collaborations. You will see specific tour routes repeated, so you'll get to know the venues and staff at certain theaters.

Touring staff varies with the size of the company, but it is common to see additional production team members hired during touring periods. Sometimes specific roles that are already on board in a company take on extra responsibilities during a tour, such as the duties of a company manager. A **tour manager** might be engaged, along with extra technicians and an associate lighting designer to recreate the original concept. Historically in the US, the stage manager would manage the re-light on tour. However, with the advancement of technology, we are seeing this less. Today, it is more likely that lighting personnel (head electrician, board operator, etc.) will re-light the show rather than the stage manager. Remember that every company structure is different, and companies with limited staff may look to engage a stage manager that also has expertise in lighting for this purpose.

Dance companies have a variety of structures as we discussed in Chapter 2: Organizational Structures, Personnel, and Communication. In smaller companies, you may find you have a more hands-on role across-the-board, and for the premiere companies with multiple touring companies, there will also be more staff to share the responsibilities, but below we look at duties in a medium sized company as a starting point. Repeating an important note from pre-production, it is essential that you understand what your responsibilities entail along with the expectations of the company to be successful in your role. Every contract will be different so be sure to take the time to discuss this with your direct supervisor and/or the HR team and follow up with direct communication with the company's rehearsal director.

PREPARING FOR THE TOUR

Following the closing of the original production, your company may have had a postmortem or self-reflective meeting, where the heads of department discussed the wins and challenges of the season. These may have been documented and should be available to access as you prepare for your next production or tour. There are no set rules as to when a show might tour. It may be just after the home season or two years later, so it is a good idea to review the notes from the post-mortem meeting to refresh your memory. The meeting minutes may reveal notes about scenic repairs, costume re-builds, storage of specialty items, and/or scheduling considerations for future remounts of the production moving forward. If you were not the original stage manager on the show, these notes will give you valuable insight into the production. How the company chooses to rehearse and prepare for their tour may be as unique as the company itself. Considerations that could impact rehearsals include whether the company is also performing another show during the rehearsal period, or if dancers and creatives are contracted specifically for this tour full-time. There is also the style of dance to consider; ballet is typically more regimented in its approach than other styles of dance and will have specific requirements and time expectations. If you are working with freelance artists, it is likely they will have other project commitments, so clarity within the schedule becomes critical. A certain amount of flexibility in the schedule may be required in these instances, and the rehearsal director and/or stage manager will create the schedule strategically to make the most of everyone's available time.

To make the most of the rehearsal period, the choreographer may be requested to return for a limited number of rehearsals. It is also likely that an associate choreographer or rehearsal director will take on the responsibility of teaching the dance using choreology notes or an archival video as reference. The rehearsal studio set up should be the same as any other dance rehearsal, with the stage manager using the same basic process of acquiring production information as described in Chapter 3: Pre-production. Since we will not be creating new show documentation but revising the information on file with updated dates, casting, and venues, we will concentrate our pre-production time on other paperwork, some of which may have been created in the archival period of the original production.

TOUR PAPERWORK

Ballet companies sometimes share and/or rent sets and costumes between companies. If you are working with rented elements, check the incoming props paperwork to ensure all items are accounted for and keep a log of what was unpacked from which box if thorough documentation has not been provided. If you are in a union house, this will not be your responsibility. Whether unpacking props for the current production or packing for the next, accurate paperwork from the stage manager is essential. This type of packing documentation is part of a stage manager's touring paperwork. Let's consider this fundamental task in touring.

As with any show, your first point of call is to check what paperwork is already in existence. There is no sense in recreating documentation from scratch unless you are about to embark on a complete revision of a ballet or the existing paperwork lacks clarity. If you are a contracted stage manager brought into the processes at the end of the rehearsal period, your time will be limited, and your 'pre-production paperwork' time must sit alongside the scheduled rehearsals. So, gather all pre-existing documents, paying specific attention to props since you will be creating packing check lists for these. You may also work with the technical director to create packing lists for scenic elements. This could be handled by either department depending on the size of the company and their typical work practices.

In a small company, it is not unusual for the stage manager or the production manager to take on some of the tasks and responsibilities of a company manager and/or tour manager. If your company does not have personnel creating **tour books** for the dancers, it would be beneficial for the stage manager to do so by creating a **tour pack** for the team which includes travel calls, daily schedules, emergency phone numbers and/or contact cards, directions to the venue, hours of theater operation and studio access, stage door requirements, maps, and information regarding the local area you will be touring to.

If your touring company does not include physiotherapists and masseurs, you may find it your task to locate reputable personnel in each town that you tour to. We suggest contacting or booking personnel in advance, if your budget allows, to ensure the dancers will be supported throughout the tour. Additionally, you will want medical facility information at your fingertips as well as after-hours practitioners for potential sickness or injuries while on the road. Communicate with the company touring/artistic teams to ensure you are not doubling-up on this work, since it may be considered part of someone else's purview.

> Don't forget to allocate a room at each venue for physiotherapist, medical, and massage appointments to take place, and create a sign-up sheet for the dancers.

Most venues have their technical specifications (**tech-specs**) available online. The stage management team can access these to create any anticipated signage required, as well as preliminary dressing room allocations. We use the term 'preliminary' as you will need to check the venues on arrival to ensure all rooms are accessible and there are no surprises that may require shifting the cast, management offices, or wardrobe areas. Nothing is set in stone prior to your arrival. Also ensure that you are familiar with your company's technical requirements. There is a sample at the end of this chapter for you to review (Figures 7.1a, 7.1b, 7.1c, and 7.1d). In this example, the paperwork lists the touring personnel and shows that the Production Manager is also taking on the Lighting Designer role. Look through the sample to see what other information a new stage manager might learn prior to their tour.

Tour packing lists should not only include scenic and prop elements, but any gear required to load in the show. This includes plenty of gaffer tape, specific mops and dust mops designated for the dance floor, and anything you will need to get the show up and running. While it is likely there will be cleaning supplies at the venue, we suggest including the company's preferred options in the tour pack to ensure there is no danger of residue from cleaning fluids that might make the Marley slippery, and therefore dangerous. It is a good idea to have your own touring road case with stage management supplies and first aid. Everything you might pack or unpack should be noted on your tour packing list, so nothing is left behind at a venue. Items in the refrigerator or stashed in the corner of the building are easy to leave behind. A common example of this is ice packs in the freezer. Additionally, your first aid should include quantities of items, so you know when they need to be replenished along the way.

> When touring internationally, ensure that all items in your first aid kit are permitted in the countries you are going to. Not all brands are available internationally, so if your company has a brand preference for a specific product, be sure to pack extras.

PRE-TOUR REHEARSALS

If you are hired to stage manage a specific tour, you will join the team relatively late in the process. To ensure a time-effective schedule, check in with the rehearsal director or choreographer daily to confirm the day's schedule and when they anticipate it would be most useful for you to observe, take notes or run props (depending on the company and union rules). Generally, this is during any run of the show, act, or segment. Prioritize these in your day and work to accomplish all other tour prep tasks and meetings around this. Communicate with the touring staff and designers to keep them up to date with any scheduled runs. Everyone on the team should be made aware of any changes to the original production.

FINAL CHECKS AND PACKING THE TRUCK

During the last week of rehearsals, the trucks will be packed for tour. Once again, the size and structure of each company will determine if you are responsible for any of the truck pack. You will certainly organize the stage management road cases, but props may be either packed by the SM team or the technical team. On the road, props will be re-packed by venue staff alongside the technical/SM team.

> *Early in my career while working on a non-union dance tour, I not only re-painted props and scenery prior to the tour, but also loaded the trucks, loaded-in the shows, and drove the electrics truck.*
> – Sue Fenty

We cannot stress enough that in dance obtaining a statement of duties is of utmost importance to ensure your expectations of the tour and the company's expectations of you are in alignment.

> *In later years, I would provide packing lists, but rarely participated in any of the truck pack aside from the stage manager's road case and personal equipment.*
> – Sue Fenty

Each company will have their own variation on processes, so be sure to discuss this with your direct supervisor. Include any rehearsal room audio set up, recorded music and media drives and/or computers on your check lists. In all cases, a final check of the rehearsal room, dressing rooms and dancer's areas will be part of your final sweep before the truck is closed.

> **Pro Tip:** *If I'm on an international tour where I'm going to be moving from time zone to time zone and I'm very jet-lagged, I always make a step-by-step load-in checklist which includes even the most basic items. This way I don't have to be smart while I'm jet-lagged – I only have to read down my list and I can save my brainpower for any unexpected surprises that pop-in in each venue (and they always do!).*
> – Betsy Ayer

ARRIVING AT THE VENUE

Whether your team is traveling by plane, train, bus, or automobile, hotel check-ins will occur on arrival. However, the company may not have access to the theater until the following day. Travel days are typically separated from rehearsal or load in days where possible unless it is a tight tour schedule or budget, or you are only traveling a short distance. On arrival at the venue, introduce yourselves to the local team and ask for a tour of the venue if you have not been there before. Check all **back of house areas** for safety and access, and confirm dressing room designations, including locations of restrooms which may not be inside the dressing rooms, water coolers/fountains, wardrobe, wigs/makeup, and any other assignments as you would for a non-touring show. The full touring team will need workspace, a designated office area and printing facilities. If the back of house areas can accommodate the team, all is well. If not, you may need to negotiate office space with the venue, or even use a corner of the rehearsal room or green room, if permitted. Once confirmed, the stage manager should organize signage to assist everyone with settling into the venue. The company manager or tour manager may also assist with this tour duty. Ensure that the dressing room allocation list is given to stage door personnel, wardrobe/wigs, and posted on the call board. The touring call board (either your own or the theater's) should be set up as soon as possible with the technical schedule, dancer schedule, and any physio/masseur sign-up sheets, menus, maps, etc. Essentially, the call board should be set up in a way that informs the company upon arrival what the schedule is and where they can locate places/things, such as dressing rooms, stage, studios, first aid, and tour bags. A map of the venue is also useful to post.

> Pro Tip: *Consideration of flooring for outdoor venues: In addition to making sure that the stage and backstage are free of debris, if there is rain or high humidity the day of an evening performance, condensation can develop that creates a major slip hazard for dancers. A plan to make sure that the stage stays dry should be developed and the stage conditions should be carefully monitored for moisture.*
>
> – Sandra Kaufmann

REHEARSALS ON THE ROAD

Rehearsals will be negotiated at each venue depending on the schedule, class time, pre-existing studio bookings and availability, and stage availability around technical work. The production manager will have created a touring production schedule that you will work from for any onstage calls. Similar to the technical rehearsals for the initial production, a placing call will be necessary to gauge any limitations in the space for the dance segments, and to set the spacing between dancers in relation to each other and to any scenic elements. This will happen each time you move venues and should be part of the schedule, as well as a technical walk through and/or run. If other rehearsals are required, a separate studio or appropriate area will be used. Note that a space for class and warm up is required each day the cast is working; including consideration for where ballet barres will be stored for onstage rehearsals. This is no different than a non-touring show, but the logistics around the spaces will be specific for each venue.

The class and rehearsal studio/s should be set up with everything the company needs to prepare for the show. It should have an audio system and may also have a piano. If this is a requirement, ensure that the piano has been tuned. As discussed in previous chapters, don't forget to ask the venue team how the air conditioning is managed so room temperatures may be set at the optimal level for dance when the company is onsite.

> Pro Tip: *Dancers are athletes! Aspects of their work including warm up class, studio, or warm up space to use before and after tech rehearsals, hydration, and temperature are essential for their successful performance.*
> – Sandra Kaufmann

RUNNING TECHNICAL REHEARSALS AND SHOWS

The technical schedule for your tour will be an abbreviated version of the original production schedule. Since the show is a re-mount of the production, less time is required onstage before the opening. You may find, as the tour progresses, that the technical rehearsals become condensed into a single technical rehearsal. This could look like: a dancer placing call combined with a cue-to-cue session that incorporates running quick changes, scenic shifts, and specific dance sections. It will be guided by the requirements of both the dance staff and technical teams, and generally negotiated through the technical director or production manager. At the very least, you should expect to run any complicated scenic moves, points when the dancers interact with scenic elements, and moments that are critical for safety. As with your home venue, be sure you are up to date with any specific protocols for each theatre's opening night events. The run of show routine should be based on the usual company procedures, including classes and warm ups, and ensuring stage access and stage door operating times align with your schedules.

OPERA CO-PRODUCTIONS OR TRANSFERS

While it is very unusual for an opera company to go on tour, per se, it is not unusual for an opera company to transfer a production to multiple cities in the region, or to share a production, a **co-production**, among multiple producing companies, or even to travel out of the country with one production. As with a play or musical, a co-production is when two or more companies share the expenses of the original production and the whole or parts of the production travel from company to company. Although most co-productions share all sets, costumes, and props, sometimes the whole cast may not travel with the production. For example, you may pick up the local chorus at each new venue, or a principal may have a scheduling conflict and need to be replaced at one or more venues. Likewise, you are likely to only travel with crew heads and will need to teach the local crew all the backstage tracks. Check with the director of production as to who from the original company is travelling with the transfer: principals, chorus, orchestra, children, crew, or crew heads? If you're doing an *Aida*, what about the animals (yes, there can be some very interesting animals in *Aida*).

As noted under dance touring, you'll need space in the venue for each of these groups and, of course, signage to direct the groups around their new home. Two notable differences, you're not likely to have masseurs or physical therapy on the road and while opera performers won't need a space for class, they will need spaces to warm up vocally, especially the chorus. After you've designated everyone's space and placed the directional signs, the assistant stage manager may be responsible for packing and unpacking props from road boxes, or they may not do this depending on the protocol and union affiliation of the company. They will also work with the technical director, props manager, and scenic crew to setup the backstage area including onstage spikes. Meanwhile, the calling stage manager will work with an assistant lighting designer and/or assistant staging director to review the light cues and get notes on anything that has changed from the primary venue. The stage manager will need to update their calling book with this information. As noted under the dance section, opera stage managers will work with the director of production and company manager on the tour schedule to ensure that the performers have an opportunity to test how their voices sound from the stage in the new venue and get a tour upon arrival to the venue. The stage management team will update the cast at this time with any changes that may impact their performance based on information learned during the load-in and light cueing. As with the primary venue, check in with the front of house folks to confirm their protocol, and then get ready to enjoy the show.

FINAL THOUGHTS

Whether performing at the original venue or taking the show on the road, it is imperative for the stage management team to have an accurately documented production. Making changes based on a well-built archive is much easier than sifting through messy documentation for information. As with preparing a non-touring show, the more time the stage management team spends on pre-production for the tour, the happier you'll be when on the road. Your goal is to stay well-informed and to spread that information to anyone and everyone who needs it including the production team, cast, and any creatives who may be traveling with the company. One final thought, tour can be stressful, so bring something along that will provide you comfort: maybe that's a favorite jacket or a pillow from home or packs of instant oatmeal for a quick snack. Remember, when you are both relaxed and calm, your company will be as well. A calm stage manager can help everyone perform at their best.

> Pro Tip: *Touring Stage Management is a job that gets better as time passes. It is definitely a marathon, not a sprint. It requires commitment and patience. So, make sure you love the artform you are working with, the company or project you are involved in, and that you understand what your contribution is towards the final product. Only with the repetition of certain processes or by encountering the same problems – and fixing them – over and over again will you gain the confidence required to be fair, approachable, and relaxed (or at least appear as so even if you are freaking out inside!!!)* ☺
> – Isabel Martinez Rivera

TECHNICAL ADDENDUM TO THE PERFORMANCE AGREEMENT

GENERAL INFORMATION
The touring staff of **Dance Kaleidoscope, Inc.** (hereafter called "Company") consists of an Artistic Director, a Lighting Designer/Production Manager, a Technical Director, a Wardrobe Manager and twelve (12) dancers. Company carries its own sound playback, costumes, sets, props, & gel color. The Company requires the _____ (hereafter called "Presenter"), at the Presenter's expense, to provide the equipment, services & conditions outlined below:

Company prefers to load in, focus and cue the day before the performance. Company will hold its tech rehearsal the afternoon of the first performance.

TECHNICAL REQUIREMENTS
Stage
Theatre needs to accommodate the following:
~ Minimum dancing area: 40' wide X 28' deep
~ Crossover behind stage, minimum 6 ' wide, must be indoors without steps, with blue running lights where needed

Presenter must provide the following:
~ Black legs & borders, appropriate to venue
~ 1 white cyclorama
~ 1 seamless black scrim
~ 1 grand drape
~ Quick-change booths, upstage left & right with costume rack, light, and mirror in each

Facility Floor
~ The Company requires a sprung floor and marley to cover the performance area. **A WOOD FLOOR LAID OVER CONCRETE IS NOT ACCEPTABLE.**
~ The on-stage and off-stage areas shall be made free of nails, tacks, staples, and any other protrusions or objects.
~ Company prefers all lighting and sound cables to be kept off the floor. If not possible, Company requires that the Presenter provide sufficient floor covering to cover these cables.
~ If the Company uses any other spaces or studios during its residency, all floors must be wood laid over wood sleepers, with some give. **A WOOD FLOOR LAID DIRECTLY OVER CONCRETE OR CEMENT IS NOT ACCEPTABLE.** All floors must be swept clean and ready for sock clad or bare foot dancers.

Safety
~ All of the dances in the program are performed in socks or bare feet - this is a safety priority point.
~ Prior to all technical rehearsals, warm-ups, spacing rehearsals and performances - the on-stage and off-stage areas shall be swept and made free of nails, tacks, staples and any other protrusions or objects that might cause injuries to bare foot dancers. These same areas shall be damp mopped and in general good condition for a modern dance concert.
~ Proper heat levels between 68 and 76 degrees Fahrenheit (20 and 25 degrees Celsius) must be maintained on-stage, and in off-stage areas, rehearsal rooms and dressing rooms whenever the Company is in rehearsal, class and performance.

Figure 7.1a Technical Rider for Dance Kaleidoscope.

Dance Kaleidoscope – Technical Addendum – Page 2

> ***PLEASE NOTE: If Theater's lighting inventory does not match that listed below, please have the venue's Technical Director contact Company's Lighting Designer/Production Manager Laura E. Glover at ▮▮▮▮▮▮ to discuss possible alternatives.

Lights
Presenter must provide the following:
~ All equipment and power needed to execute Company plot and hookup, including a computer light control board with a minimum of 100 channels of control
~ Plot should be completely hung, circuited and tested prior to arrival of the Lighting Designer/Production Manager - **IF NOT, PLEASE SEE NOTE BELOW**
~ Company Light Plot consists of, **at a minimum,** 110 lighting instruments of the following specifications:
  ~ 24   36 degree (750w) or similar units, LED units preferred
  ~ 8   26 degree (750w) or similar units, LED units preferred
  ~ 16   19 degree (750w) or similar units, LED units preferred
  ~ 40   Pars WFL (750w) or similar units, LED units preferred
  ~ Cyc lighting units appropriate to venue, LED units preferred or must hold gel color
  ~ 8   10' boom pipes
  ~ 32   Sidearms for hanging lighting units on booms
~ No follow spots are used
~ Appropriate cable, zetex, etc.
~ Gel frames/hanging hardware for all lighting units
~ Template holders for a minimum of 24 units
~ A red spotting lamp on center line in front of house
~ Production table set up center of house with power, 2 headsets and computer monitor
~ Blue running lights backstage left and right

Company will provide the following:
~ Necessary gel color, template patterns, and miscellaneous production supplies
~ If necessary, a basic moving light package

Props
Presenter must provide the following:
~ 2 prop tables backstage (minimum 6' long) - 1 right, 1 left with blue running lights

Sound
Presenter must provide the following:
~ Stereo amplification and loudspeakers sufficient for the house
~ QLab playback on a computer; Company can also provide a computer
~ Mixing console
~ 4 stage monitors: 2 in wing #1 left and right at bottom of the sidebooms, and 2 upstage of cyc
~ 1 microphone, wireless or with enough cable to reach from backstage to center stage in front of the grand drape; mic stand off-stage for storage
~ Headset requirements - One channel system
    ~ 2 additional headsets in the house at the production table
    ~ 2 headsets backstage: 1 DL, 1 DR
    ~ 1 headset for light board operator
    ~ 1 headset for sound board operator
    ~ 2 headsets in fly gallery for fly persons

Dance Kaleidoscope Performance Agreement and Addenda

Figure 7.1b   Technical Rider for Dance Kaleidoscope.

Dance Kaleidoscope – Technical Addendum – Page 3

> PLEASE have the venue's Technical Director contact Company's Lighting Designer/Production Manager Laura E. Glover at xxx-xxx-xxxx to discuss crew needed.

PLEASE NOTE: The Company is not a yellow card attraction.

Crew
Presenter must provide the following:
Load-in/Load-out (Strike):
- ~ 1 carpenter head
- ~ 1 electric head
- ~ 1 fly person/rigger head
- ~ 2 carpenters
- ~ 4 electricians
- ~ 1 fly person
- ~ 2 wardrobe

Focus:
- ~ 1 light board operator
- ~ 3 electricians
- ~ 1 fly person

Running Crew:
- ~ 1 light board operator
- ~ 1 sound board operator
- ~ 2 fly-persons
- ~ 2 deckhands, 1 for each side of the stage
    - ~ Deckhands are responsible for gel changes on sidelight booms; handling of props, costume pieces and clearing of stage between pieces as needed. SL deckhand will handle headset communication with Lighting Designer.
- ~ 2-4 dressers (depending upon the program)

~ PLEASE NOTE: Crew personnel must be the same for all rehearsals and performances.

Wardrobe
Presenter must provide the Company with the following:
- ~ 1 iron, 1 ironing board, and 1 industrial clothes steamer
- ~ 2 pressers for a minimum of 4 hours and a maximum of 8 hours on the day of each performance; the number of hours required will vary according to the program
- ~ Laundry facilities (washing machine, dryer, etc.) are required daily
- ~ 2 costume racks located on each side of the stage (plus the quick-change booths)

Dressing Rooms
- ~ Two separate dressing rooms with counters and mirror space for 6 men and 6 women. Rooms must have sinks or wash basins, rest room facilities and showers. Rooms should be clean, well-lighted, with chairs and 2 costume racks each
- ~ 1 room for the Artistic Director, with a desk, chair and private rest room, within a short distance of the stage
- ~ 1 room for the Lighting Designer/Production Manager, as close to the stage as possible, with a desk and chairs.
- ~ It is requested that all dressing rooms and production rooms be LOCKABLE with keys provided to Company's Production Manager. At minimum, Company requires a secure and lockable space.

Dance Kaleidoscope Performance Agreement and Addenda

Figure 7.1c Technical Rider for Dance Kaleidoscope.

Dance Kaleidoscope – Technical Addendum – Page 4

Rehearsal Space

~ The stage where the performance is to be held must be available to the Company two hours prior to each performance and must have ballet barres to accommodate 12 dancers.

~ A heated studio or large room (complying with the sections labeled FACILITY FLOOR and SAFETY) is required for a class in the afternoon on the day of the Company's arrival and prior to its first technical rehearsal. A studio or the stage area will also be needed each day that the Company is in residence at the Presenter's facility for daily class for the dancers and should have ballet barres to accommodate 12 dancers.

Hospitality

The Company respectfully asks the Presenter to try and supply the following during all rehearsals and performances:

~ Non-carbonated bottled water (e.g. Evian, Poland Springs, etc.)

~ 20 cans or bottles of assorted regular and diet sodas

~ 20 assorted juices (e.g. orange, grapefruit, etc.)

~ Hot coffee and tea to accommodate 20 people - with sugar, sugar substitute and milk

~ Appropriate utensils and cups

~ PLEASE NOTE: It is appreciated if the Hospitality is for the exclusive use of the Company.

Transportation

~ The Presenter agrees to provide, at the Presenter's expense, all local transportation for Company personnel between all performance sites and the Company's lodgings.

~ Company requires all necessary local parking permits and/or decals as required for all Company vehicles.

This Technical Addendum was revised July, 2023, and replaces all previous technical addenda. Please disregard any earlier versions. This Technical Addendum expires June 30, 2024.

These 4 pages of Dance Kaleidoscope's Technical Addendum are accepted and agreed to by the Presenter as an integral part of the attached Performance Agreement.

________________________________ ________________

Presenter **DATE**

________________________________ ________________

TECHNICAL DIRECTOR (of the performance venue) **DATE**
PRESENTER SIGNATURE IS NOT ACCEPTABLE HERE

Dance Kaleidoscope Performance Agreement and Addenda
Page 4 of 4

Figure 7.1d Technical Rider for Dance Kaleidoscope.

CHAPTER 8

Specialist Shows, Unique Companies, and Changing Landscapes

In these last chapters we have concentrated on traditional dance and opera considerations to give you a broad base with which to begin your dance and opera journey. However, it would be remiss of us not to include the voices of a larger selection of professional stage managers who are collaborating on different styles of productions. In this chapter, we hear directly from the industry, from stage managers working on iconic and innovative productions around the world. We are delighted that they have shared their unique experiences with us.

ISABEL MARTINEZ RIVERA, ASSOCIATE DIRECTOR, LES BALLETS TROCKADERO DE MONTE CARLO

> *I was born and raised in Puerto Rico and moved to the United States in my late teens, to continue dance studies in university. While I was pursuing a dance degree at Temple University in Philadelphia, I started working in dance production. I never looked back. Stage managing/production work came naturally, especially for dance. I wanted to serve the art form in the best way I could, and this was it. It was a blessing to be interested in theatre production and stage management for dance at a time where there were plenty of medium sized touring dance companies in the USA, all of which required a stage manager who was a 'jack of all trades' type of person and there was no shortage of good opportunities to go on tour.*

I am currently the Associate Director for Les Ballets Trockadero de Monte Carlo (affectionately known as *The Trocks*). I have been with the company continuously since the late 90s, as Associate Production Manager, Production Stage Manager,

Production Manager, and Associate Director and Production Manager. The title has changed based on how the company needed me to come across to the outside world, but the job description has not. Titles are a bit irrelevant when you work with dance companies of this size, to be honest. You have to be willing and capable of fulfilling a myriad of roles within the company. Resources are always limited, and the work is hard. At different times in my journey with the Trocks I have acted as an assistant stage manager, repaired props, steamed costumes and dressed dancers, called the show, organized touring logistics, negotiated tech riders, applied for visas for travel, focused the plot, ran sound, flown a curtain ... sometimes all in the same show.

The Trocks perform renditions of beloved classical ballets with a comedic twist. Incidentally, the cast is comprised of male-identifying humans, and all the artists perform under alter egos – a ballerina or danseur personae – at any given time during the show. They also happen to dance en pointe and in drag when performing ballerina roles. This may not sound too ground-breaking nowadays, but the company has been around since 1974 and has performed in six continents in 50 years of existence. When given appropriate historical context, the company is an institution!

There are two things that I find very inspiring about the company; the first one is how *hard* everyone works. Even by the standards of the world of dance, where the very definition of what is required tends to weed out lazy humans, what an artist with the Trockadero has to do on a daily basis defies comprehension. For these dancers, an average work day on tour requires a two-hour class, followed by two hours of blocking and spacing in every theater (as the casting changes daily but the same 14 dancers cover each other in all roles), one and a half hours of doing their own makeup, getting into costume, and performing a two-hour show which demands to be at the pinnacle of the art form technically, while making people laugh. I had never seen a collective of dancers that outputs that intensely day in and day out. What that does to you – a technician, a craft person working for them – is that it forces you to bring your 'A' game every single day.

The second thing that I find inspiring is that they are too busy doing the work to believe their own hype. The narrative of the company as 'groundbreaking gender-role-blurring social activist men on pointe' is the branding that has been put on the company, not by the company. We are just going around the world performing ballet that everyone in this company loves, and making people laugh, because we all need good cheer in this world. You may be doing the Swan Queen today, but you will be Prince Siegfried or the joke swan tomorrow ... this kind of approach to casting fosters positive group dynamics and a down-to-earth approach to life in general.

The Trocks are a repertory company with an unrelenting touring schedule of mostly one-offs – same-day load in and show – then travel to the next town. We have a very small team of people: An SM, a Production Assistant/Company Manager, a Lighting Supervisor, and a Wardrobe Supervisor. That is not a large Production team when you think about 150 theatres per year ...

A Stage Manager for a company like the Trockadero is responsible for the consistency of the product from a technical standpoint, but also keeps an eye on the overall well-being of everyone! They have to do so with the added pressure of a different crew every night, and just a few hours to get the show up and running, without a technical or dress rehearsal of any kind. Shy of actually dancing on stage, you have to be able to put out any fire that comes your way.

To work in companies with similar demands to the Trocks you need to do your homework. Understand the nuances and context of the crews you will be working with (geographically, culturally, socially) as it will inform how you will deliver the show over headset. Clarity and conciseness when communicating is integral to the success of the show.

You also need to spend a lot of time getting to know the dancers who are performing with the company. When the show is comedy, the jokes are intrinsically related to who is doing them. If you know the people who are getting on stage, you have a better chance of anticipating their behavior, and dance stage management is all about anticipating!

Having a solid technical theatre background will allow you to put yourself as cover for any contingencies that occur. Having trained as a dancer, although not required, will allow you to maximize the time you have to spend learning to call the pieces of a repertory dance company.

NYKOL DEDREU, STAGE MANAGER, KINETIC LIGHT

Educated as a Lighting Designer (B.S. Texas Woman's University, M.F.A Tulane University) my early career primarily focused on dance production, lots of touring and one glorious summer at Jacob's Pillow. In 2002, an unexpected turn brought me my first Equity stage management contract, and over the next 17 years I held two resident PSM positions (Phoenix Theatre, Blue Man Group), countless SM and PM freelance contracts (cruise ships, regional theatre, opera, events, Polar Express- theatre on a train!), and spent four years as Head of Stage Management at Columbia College Chicago. Currently, I teach as an adjunct professor at Columbia and DePaul, work as a Producer for special projects with Blue Man Group, and reside as the PSM for Kinetic Light, work that has taken me to amazing venues like Lincoln Center and The Shed.

When I was first introduced to Kinetic Light, it was March 2022, and the industry was still recovering from the Covid-19 pandemic. I had not worked in the performance arts in two years; to be honest, after 20 years in the business, I wasn't sure I wanted to go back. I knew that if I did, I had new expectations – primarily, the work needed to be something interesting to me, something that hadn't been done before, something that had meaning. Then I saw a job post for Kinetic Light. They were looking for a PSM for the world premiere of their aerial piece, *Wired*, at the Museum of Contemporary Art in my home base city, Chicago.

Kinetic Light is an internationally recognized disability arts ensemble. Working in the disciplines of art, technology, design, and dance, Kinetic Light creates, performs, and teaches at the nexus of access, queerness, disability, dance, and race. In *Wired*, three disabled dancers, two in wheelchairs, take flight using every form imaginable –

bungees and hard lines and a spreader bar on a winch line with two wheelchair-bound dancers. Video design is projected from all angles, creating an immersive world where dancers fly, spin, jump, and throw themselves in ways that inspire disabled audiences, and sometimes make able-bodied audiences uncomfortable.

When I first worked with the company, I thought what was unique and inspiring about them were the dancers in wheelchairs flying through the air. Not wrong, but there is so much more. I was in rehearsal during my second contract with them, working on three rep shows for tour, and I was having a conversation with the AD (Artistic Director) at the top of the day. I can't remember what she said to me, but I clearly remember thinking "the production is not the goal; we serve up accessibility and the production is merely the plate on which it is served." I had never worked with a company whose primary mission wasn't the show. I had to change the way I was thinking about access!

For audiences, Kinetic Light offers accessibility including: ASL for every performance with instrumental music interpretation, an app called Audimance for audio description that people connect to using their smartphone, multiple spaces in every house for wheelchair users and their companions (giving agency and choice), a haptics system of wire through the house that deaf audience members can hold and feel the music, a quiet space and all manner of comfort props for those who get over/under-stimulated, and radical agency – audience members are told in the curtain speech they are free to come and go as they please. Furthermore, we sometimes get requests from patrons asking for accommodation we don't normally offer, and I have never seen the company say no. For example, we were performing at Lincoln Center and a guest without a smartphone asked for an alternate way to hear the audio description; we found a way to broadcast over an FM channel to accommodate that single person.

As PSM for this company, there are many considerations and duties out of the ordinary from most of my experience. Taking care of disabled artists means making sure they have means of egress to all areas backstage and house (booth too – our Lighting Designer is in a wheelchair); large dressing rooms with roll-in showers; scheduling rehearsals in a way that is kind to their bodies; being vigilant about potential injury – a paraplegic human does not necessarily feel pain when they get injured; helping train new flight operators (landing a human is hard enough, imagine landing a human on wheels!); in-air rescue rehearsal for dancers in wheelchairs; and this very big idea – when to offer help and when to step back. When you see a performer struggling, it is instinctual for a stage manager to offer help. I have learned working with disabled artists, they more often than not prefer the agency to help themselves.

In addition to all the performer care of the PSM role, I also have gained working knowledge of all our accessibility technology, and as I said earlier, learned to prioritize access over production. From the company's website: "In our work disability is not a deficit, it is a powerful, intersectional creative force that is essential to our artistry. Access is integral to our art and creative process." We were about to begin a final dress run at a touring venue, the words of the opening call sequence had just come out of my mouth, when the presenter showed up at my backstage calling station. The AD called her at home about a problem involving not enough space in the house for motorized wheelchairs. I held the call, alerted the AD, also backstage as she is one of our dancers and was standing by for her entrance. The presenter and

AD proceeded to have a conversation in the wings for roughly the next 30 minutes while the rest of the company remained standing by for the start of dress. This is what it means to prioritize access. I was so accustomed to access being the layer put on top of the production, almost an afterthought in most companies, but with Kinetic Light, it's access that is driving the ship.

NANCY PITTELMAN, STAGE MANAGER, RADIO CITY MUSIC HALL, 2005–2023

> Since 2005 I have been a part of the stage management team at Radio City Music Hall. During those 18 years I had the honor to serve as the Production Stage Manager of the Christmas Spectacular starring the Rockettes. In addition, I was the Production Stage Manager for three non-Christmas Productions, Heart and Lights, The New York Spring Spectacular, and the New York Spectacular, all starring the world-famous Radio City Rockettes.

The Radio City Rockettes are a world-renowned dance company known for their athleticism and iconic precision style combining elements of ballet, jazz, and tap, as well as techniques of modern and contemporary dance. For nearly a century, the Rockettes have been American icons. Not only have they appeared at Radio City Music Hall in thousands of stage spectaculars, but they have also performed at the center of many memorable moments in history – like joining the USO and entertaining troops, performing at a Presidential inauguration, the Tony Awards, the MTV VMAs and the Life Ball in Vienna, Austria. It has been a tremendous journey to work alongside these talented dancers and a privilege to support their, always SPECTACULAR, performances.

When picturing New York City at Christmas, one of the most iconic images is Radio City Music Hall and the Rockettes. Since 1933, this dance troupe has been dazzling audiences with their precision dance routines that feature their signature eye-high kicks. In between the Rockette numbers, Santa, Mrs. Claus, their helpers, and a complement of singers and dancers tell a story of Christmas, sharing, magic, and family. The culmination of the performance is a live depiction of the Nativity, where the entire cast, along with camels, sheep, and a donkey transport the 6,000-seat audience to Bethlehem for a memorable re-telling of the Christmas story.

The 90-minute show is a non-stop celebration of dance; and technical elements are skillfully woven in to enhance the storytelling and audience experience. Behind the scenes, the show is equally exciting; with a group of over 200 cast members, crew, orchestra, and a myriad of other show personnel. The stage management team, with a clear vision and plan, sits at the center of the success of this operation.

Unlike a Broadway show, the Christmas Spectacular runs multiple shows a day, up to five shows a day, seven days a week, for a total of up to 31 shows per week. There are two full casts to allow for adequate rest and recovery time of the performers. The companies are split into a morning and evening schedule, with each cast getting a day off a week, and the opposite cast performing up to four shows on that day. The companies rehearse and tech the show together to ensure that both casts are executing the same choreography. On occasion, for coverage purposes, a performer from the morning cast may cover a role in the evening cast, the shows are similar enough to allow for that type of lateral move.

Each company has 36 performing Rockettes who are 'on the line.' In addition, there are six Rockette Swings per line, these dancers are given specific tracks to focus on coverage-wise, however, often swing for other tracks when necessary.

The Rockettes choreography is taught and maintained using a series of dance lines and numbers spanning the 100' wide by 66' deep stage. Several flush number lines and multiple colors and patterns of dance lines provide landmarks for the dancers. The key behind the precision of the Rockettes is each woman using these guides to ensure they are always in the proper space. Being a Rockette requires a great amount of technical skill, typically rooted in ballet technique. In addition, spatial awareness, and the ability to move as a group, and blend as a group of dancers is equally important. That is what creates the impact of the Rockettes; a group of 36 women who appear to be effortlessly dancing in unison, arms, legs, heads, and focus all precisely the same. That, in-itself, creates a spectacle.

All of the technical elements contribute to enhancing this precise effect, and they are approached with the same attention to detail. Opened in 1932, the Radio City Stage, was, technically very advanced, and to this day, remains a stand-out due to its automation and capability. The stage is comprised of four hydraulic lifts, spanning 70' each. The stage lifts have a capacity of 81 tons, they can travel 13' above stage and 27' below stage allowing for, even large scenery, or a full line of Rockettes, to have a spectacular reveal, rising out of the floor. In addition to the scenic elements and capabilities, the Christmas Spectacular also features a large video and projection package including the world's largest indoor flying 8K LED wall, and 32 projectors that allow for video content to appear on all eight of Radio City's iconic arches, allowing the audience, even those seated in the third mezzanine, to look up see the immersive content. The Rockettes, with the assistance of a wardrobe crew of over 25 individuals, change costumes eight times during the 90-minute show, with the fastest change clocking in at 87 seconds. Rounding out the spectacular, a live orchestra of 34 musicians provides a heartwarming score of original music and arrangements of every Christmas favorite. Peppered with pyrotechnics and a menagerie of camels, sheep, and even a donkey, the Christmas Show brings Christmas joy to over 1 million people annually.

The operations of this spectacular depend on very careful planning in the pre-production and creation process. Adding in a new element, such as a new Rockette number, takes months of planning, and the stage management team is central to ensuring the new elements can blend in with the existing elements. The entire show runs on a **show control system**, which keeps all elements, music, video, lighting, and sometimes automation, in sync. Once music is created and a tempo is mapped out for a new number, the stage manager works with each department to insert this material into the show. The stage manager lays out the show control system map, and assigns beds of time code for each number, and demo track is created with a timecode embedded so that all designers are working off of a quantitative file. The timecode frames become the language to cue the shows as lighting and video content is created to match the new music and choreography. While those elements (commonly referred to as **assets**) are being developed, on the scenic side of things items are being designed and sent out to bid. Prior to designs being finalized, the stage managers work with the scenic designer and technical director to figure out how each scenic piece plays on stage, but more importantly, how it stores in the wings or below the stage. The stage management team develops 'paper dolls,' moveable scaled pieces of the new and existing scenic assets and develops a plan for movement and storage. Out of this work, stage management can determine if pieces need to be built in a specific way to fit in available storage, but also can ascertain necessary transition timings, stage crew staffing, and details what backstage real estate will be available to wardrobe.

Because of the enormous scope and scale of the venue and the show, the manufacturing of these items must be planned well in advance. For instance, when a new Rockette costume is designed, a shop cannot simply go out and purchase enough fabric to make 84 costumes. Typically, this fabric must be specifically created for the Rockettes. There are the common dancer needs to consider, breathability and stretchability of the fabric, and on such a large-scale, production often takes months. Because there is a desire for a uniform look across dancers with a variety of body types, torso lengths, and arm lengths, the design process can be lengthy, typically involving several prototype reviews.

Unlike traditional theatrical processes, by the time the Rockettes begin the rehearsal phase, the entire show has been fully flushed in terms of design, development, and production. The rehearsal process serves as a time for the choreographers to teach the material to the dancers. There is no time allocated in this process to make a chorographic, musical, or staging change. Because the entire show control system has already been mapped out, and designers are working on asset development based on the aforementioned demo track with time code, there is not time to make adjustments across all departments.

Operationally, once in the run of the show, it takes five stage managers to run each performance. There is a calling stage manager, who is in communication with the operators of the show control system, lighting, video, audio, fly rail, automation, stage control board (running the hydraulic system, stage lifts), follow spots, projectionists, and stage managers and crew. There is a stage manager on either side of the stage assisting talent and crew, and managing the safety when the 70' stage lifts are down, and a fourth stage manager who manages the levels underneath the stage, assists talent and crew when the stage lifts are down in those areas, and oversees the loading, offloading, and movement of the orchestra on the bandcar (which is yet another scenic element that is automated and appears in different positions throughout the performance). The fifth position is a '**floater**.' This stage management track is the most unpredictable, as the floater attends to any issues that come up that are out of the ordinary. For instance, it is common that during a production a performer may become unwell or injured. The floater would assist with getting that person out of the show, and getting a swing in, make sure that wardrobe, wigs, audio, and all others affected are aware of the change in the line-up, so the show continues without issues. The members of the nine-person stage management team rotate through these five positions, so that everyone gets perspective on all aspects of the show, and, because the show is performed so many times a week, it keeps the run of show from becoming repetitive.

Central to the success of creating and maintaining this complex show is communication. The stage management team provides clear and efficient communication during all phases of production. In the development process, frequent communication with the design team is a must. For example, often there will be several artists working on one single video asset in a number. Ongoing design reviews ensure that the creative is all moving in the correct and same direction, and that the entire team is aware of what is being developed. A missed step in communication can cause a lot of work to be created in the wrong direction. In rehearsal, communication is key to the efficient running of the room, when there is a finite amount of time to get all the show material taught, while also balancing costume and shoe fittings, and publicity requests, there has to be a clear and concise plan, and it must be well communicated so that none of these important moments are missed. In tech, all of those elements remain crucially important, while layering in the elements of onstage and backstage safety, and in show, having a clear and concise plan for management when problems arise is of the utmost importance. With a show that contains this many moving parts, people, and technology, stage managers know to expect the unexpected and prepare our cast and crew on how we will manage these situations. We rehearse our known 'plan B' and technical failovers (backup machinery or equipment going active when the primary system fails), but in the moment when an issue is happening, it's not always precisely as it is written on paper. The stage managers must stay calm, keep safety as the top priory, and communicate effectively to right the ship and get the show back on course. When a production involves over 200 individuals behind the curtain, the stage management team has the responsibility to keep everyone apprised of the current information; the team also has the incredible opportunity to set the tone for the production. While running a tight, clean show is important, I maintain that successful stage managers are those who lead with kindness and empathy, give space for people to feel heard, recognize and value all contributions, and keep the dialogue open to making corrections and changes. The world, the show, and our industry is ever-evolving. If we can see the best in people and continue to change and adapt, we will thrive in our jobs as managers of people.

LILLIAN HANNAH U, STAGE MANAGER, BANGARRA DANCE THEATRE (AUSTRALIA), 2018–2020

I am a first-generation Hong Kong Chinese-Australian stage manager from Gadigal, Eora (Sydney, Australia). From 2018 to 2020, I was resident stage manager at Bangarra Dance Theatre, touring extensively abroad and around Australia. In 2021, I moved to Dubai to join the stage management team for EXPO2020 delivering headline talent events in EXPO's premier venue: Al Wasl. Following EXPO, I have been the Stage Manager for Phantom of the Opera (AUS tour), Deputy Stage Manager for Hamilton (Brisbane/ New Zealand) and Death of a Salesman and I am currently with the Australia/ Asia tour of Miss Saigon. Recently, I was the Show Caller for the Opening Ceremony of Red Sea International Film Festival in Jeddah, Saudi Arabia. My practice has always been rooted in inclusive, collaborative, and culturally considered stage management practices.

I worked for Bangarra Dance Theatre from the years 2018–2020 as the resident Stage Manager. Bangarra Dance Theatre is Australia's premier professional Indigenous contemporary dance company based on Gadigal Land (Sydney) comprised of only Aboriginal and Torres Strait Islander dancers and performers. They create work inspired by traditional stories from the vast diaspora of Aboriginal and Torres Strait Island (TSI) communities around Australia. The company generally comprises of 15 to 20 full-time professional dancers, resident creative team, and a small touring production team of eight (Company Manager, Stage Manager, Assistant Stage Manager (production only), Production Manager, Production Assistant, Head Electrician, Head Mechanist, Sound Technician (production only)). The company standardly completes a national, regional, and international tour annually as well as a 'Return to Country' – a dedicated tour which returns a past Bangarra show's story back to their community it came from.

Bangarra's work is unlike any work you will see in the world. Every work is richly textured, viscerally grounded, and deeply connected to culture. A new work begins with community engagement and the researching, trading, and gifting of stories and knowledge by community Elders. For me personally, Bangarra's work always struck a chord within me because it touched a part that longed for a deeper connection to culture. In the Australian dance and theatre landscape in particular, its impact is twofold: the company brings an awareness and sharing of 65,000 years of Aboriginal and TSI culture to Australian audiences, but also gives the Indigenous performers and staff within the company the space to stay connected with their own culture.

While it is easy to say that Bangarra's mission statement and purpose is the most inspiring thing about the company, what inspired me about the company lives within the subtleties of how they make performance. As a practitioner, I am incredibly interested in how culture lives inherently in every physical body and how that manifests in our practices as artists, stage managers, and people. How the physical body (with all its cultural, socio-economic implications) we bring into a space can shift and influence the 'vibe' of a room and thus the art being made.

Every Bangarra show is built in collaboration with the dancers in the company. The dancers and creatives interface with cultural consultants and Elders, are told stories (sometimes with no particular structure or haste), listen to recordings, watch videos of Country they may never have visited before, and if time and community allows, visit the Country where the story is from. As a stage manager, I then had the privilege of seeing how their bodies become imbued with these stories, these gifts from community and Country, and subsequently how they enter a structured, creative space to build a performance inspired by what they have experienced. Of course, in any context, performance building is somewhat less romantic than what I have painted above, and these observations are incredibly subtle but present nonetheless.

As a stage manager in this context, my role required me to be attuned to the shifting sensitivities of culture on a daily basis and shift my practice as a stage manager accordingly. In such a context, I had to learn what knowledge could or should be shared, what questions I could ask and when, and when I had permission to participate or to just observe. I also learned that, in my particular instance, as a non-Indigenous POC in an Aboriginal company, I could code switch in subtle ways – firstly, so I could integrate more into the company but also to create comfort and trust.

I do have to note here that as an Indigenous contemporary dance company existing within a western theatrical context, many of the hard-skill practices remained the same as you would if you were stage managing a theatre show. I generated prompt copies, delivered schedules, props lists, and running orders. However, how I acquired this knowledge was a little less straightforward than in the usual theatre or musical theatre context. I have to admit, I didn't always nail it, but learning to read the moment became incredibly important as well as not letting the urgency of the western theatre building practices overwhelm you.

Around this time and outside of Bangarra, I also worked on cultural events with a multitude of different cultural groups. From this I also learned that every community is different – each coming with their own expectations, understanding of how a stage manager relates to them, and rules around what cultural items can be handled by whom.

Upon reflection, the greatest learning for me as a young stage manager in this context, having been trained in a western institution, was to let go of my expectations and urgencies. The expectation to be told everything, the expectation that you, as the stage manager, are the most trusted role in performance building, and the expectation that things will occur in a timely manner (and I mean this one without offense).

For me it was such a privilege to cut my teeth in such an unusual theatrical context and a learning experience that I wish I had the groundedness to have sat in more patiently when I was younger.

I was privy to so many beautiful and important cultural stories and to parts of Australia inaccessible without community permission. I would encourage any young stage manager to seek a theatrical experience outside of the western performance context.

BETSY AYER, STAGE MANAGER, SUSAN MARSHALL & COMPANY

> *I stage manage dance, opera, and theatre, and have over 25 years' experience in New York, the US, and internationally. Favorite dance credits include: New York City Ballet, Pam Tanowitz Dance, Trisha Brown Dance Company, and Susan Marshall & Company. I have stage-managed premieres of new work by choreographers including Justin Peck, Michelle Dorrance, Lauren Lovette, Jessica Lang. I specialize in coordinating multidisciplinary projects such as Anthony Roth Costanzo's Glass Handel for Opera Philadelphia. Opera stage management credits include New York City Opera, plus 20 different works and counting with director Peter Sellars. I served as an Interim Production Manager at Carnegie Hall. I am a graduate of Smith College and a member of Actors' Equity Association (AEA) and the American Guild of Musical Artists (AGMA).*

As in many contemporary American dance companies, the stage manager is not a full-time position, but is hired in for specific projects or tours. I first started working with the Susan Marshall & Company in 2006 with their piece *Cloudless*, which toured throughout much of 2006–2007. While the piece was in development, I had to coordinate the movement of various pieces of scenery and props to the correct rehearsal studio. The piece involved projectors on little wheeled dollies which were manipulated entirely by the dancers, so a lot of practice with those items was necessary! We had a wonderful residency at Montclair University where we had plenty of time to tech the piece with a full crew. The piece required four deck crew members who had very specific tracks as they made their shifts a vista on stage – the deck crew were really a part of the piece as they manipulated the scenery, props, and video elements. However, we did not tour with these four people, so we had to train a new local crew in each venue. I would run a 90-minute scene shift rehearsal to walk them through the specifics and teaching them the dancer traffic patterns and interactions as well. *Cloudless* also involved dancers doing some aerial work, which was designed by a rigger with experience working with aerial dance work. However, this rigger did not tour with the company, so I was the designated person to reproduce the exact rigging setup in each venue for safety reasons. The sound design for *Cloudless* was also very much dependent on the timing and movement of the choreography, and the choreography was designed with a certain amount of freedom for each dancer to explore timing, so it was a very sound cue-heavy piece. While there were composite music tracks that the sound designer put together for rehearsal, I would often have to come to rehearsal and run the sound for the final studio rehearsals.

After *Cloudless*, I continued working with the company for several other projects: *PlayPause* (2013), *Chromatic* (2015), and *Construction* (2019). Most of these pieces had developmental phases of workshops and artistic residencies at least a year prior to the premiere and toured over the course of at least two years after their premieres. I was generally involved in the workshop processes because of the sheer amount of production needs, and continued through the final performances on tour.

When the company performs shorter works on mixed-bill programs such as *Kiss*, *Arms*, or excerpts from *Cloudless*, *Sawdust Palace*, or *Frame Dances,* I often have to pull and pack or ship props for specific segments from that piece, and often travel with the dancers to execute the pieces from a technical perspective.

For *Rhythm Bath*, the needs are a little different. The floor surface has to be durable enough to also accommodate an audience in shoes, so the dancers are dancing in sneakers and the floor is a laminated hardboard instead of a Marley floor. As stage manager, I have to coordinate with costumes and wardrobe to make special modifications to the sneakers such as moleskin on part of the sneaker soles so that the dancers can turn. I have to coordinate a different cleaning routine with the stage crew – we don't want to use any water on the laminated hardboard because if it seeps into any seams or cracks, then the hardboard will warp. So, we sweep, dust-mop, vacuum, and rub away any marks from people's shoes with a tennis ball. The props that are used – chairs, cushions, and fans with balls and very large confetti – are used by both performers and audience members. So, audience members don't necessarily put things back where they found them, and I find I need to check things more frequently to make sure items don't get lost. The music that the audience hears is much more minimal. However, the dancers listen to a more complex track with more audible cues and beats in it so that they can maintain unison choreography even if they can't see each other. The dancers wear a wireless radio receiver with a mono earbud in one ear, and we transmit the dancers' music track through a wireless radio transmitter at the exact same time that the audience music is cued (we learned that radio transmission was more accurate time-wise for music than WiFi was).

Susan Marshall is a post-modern choreographer who mostly deals with the interactions and relationships between different people and between people and objects. More information here: http://studiosusanmarshall.org/susan. For a stage manager, that means more props and scenery than is normal for most contemporary dance companies. Because the dancers interact with the props and scenery, there's also a steady stream of repairs as the items are handled. My theatre background comes in handy here with tracking and organizing all of this.

Susan Marshall & Company is a very collaborative company where the dancers have a lot of input on the choreographic content (hence the "& Company" part of the name!). This also means that everyone in the room gets a voice, although ultimately the major creative decisions rest with Susan Marshall. It's a very lovely company culture to work in. For a stage manager, this can be particularly difficult on tour when schedules are tight – you have to remind people that while it's great to discuss everything as a group, there's only x hours of rehearsal on stage before the performance and that the crew needs to learn the entire show by then.

The current piece, *Rhythm Bath*, is part of Susan Marshall's refocus on co-creating contemporary performance-installations with neurodiverse audiences. More information here: http://studiosusanmarshall.org/rhythm-bath. Because this is a piece where the audience and the dancers share the same space, we always have to consider where the audience might be sitting, standing, moving, or vocalizing during the piece. The choreographic content itself is quite rhythmic and repetitive to create a soothing pattern. Susan and Mimi Lien, the set designer, are always considering how to make the space welcoming to neurodiverse individuals – such as creating a small 'dark room' which is quieter, has cushions to sit on, and is freer of external stimulus, so that if audience participants find the main space too overwhelming, they can retreat to the dark room. The large performance space also has a variety of surfaces and items for audience participants to sit on or lean against, and the shape of the space is curved and soft. The dancers always have to be prepared for unexpected audience movements and must be able to adapt and re-space their choreography in the moment. The performance space is open before and after the dancers' performance as an installation work which the audience can explore on their own time.

Generally speaking, I am inspired by the ethos that everyone involved in the project gets a voice and that everyone's opinion is asked for and considered. For *Rhythm Bath* in particular, I am inspired by the fact that we are trying to create a work of art for an underserved audience – a neurodiverse audience.

There is no one position in the space where the stage manager can see the cue for every scenic, lighting, and sound cue. So, I call the show by being in the space and moving the way an audience member would, trying to find positions that are out of the sightlines of the majority of the audience while still being able to see the things I need to see. I call from a cue list on a clipboard, but this would also be a great project on which to call from an iPad. As we continue to develop the piece, I expect that I'll be able to condense my cue list greatly, but at the moment Susan still makes changes to cueing for nearly every run, so having a framework where I can easily change the order and placement of cues is very helpful. I also have to speak very, very quietly over headset so that I don't disturb audience members.

Because the space for *Rhythm Bath* is not a traditional dance space, but is performed in the round, we don't have a 'stage left' or 'stage right,' or standard center or quarter marks. Instead, we all refer to directions in the space as in the face of a clock – we choose one direction to be 12:00 and base everything else off of that. This carries through from the dancers/choreography to all designers. Luckily, I had quite a bit of experience with non-traditional spaces working for Trisha Brown Dance Company with their Early Works, which are pieces that are designed for everyday locations rather than theatres.

The biggest challenge during performances is not letting yourself get distracted by unexpected audience behavior – we have trained ushers to assist with audience members in distress. There's a lot of front of house work to prepare audience participants for the work – a document with photos which describes what the experience will be like so that they can take the time to think about the experience and get comfortable with it before they come to see the installation and performance.

ERIN JOY SWANK, STAGE MANAGER, FREELANCE

> *I've enjoyed a widely varied stage management career in theatre, opera, dance, circus, and other events. Through it all, my favorite cast members ever were likely the three adorable camels that toured with me (and the Rockettes) during the Radio City Christmas Spectacular. I love sharing experiences with stage managers of all levels, including as a guest lecturer. My personal website hosts a popular blog geeking out about stage management, and I collaborated on Off Headset: Essays on Stage Management Work, Life, and Career. I actively volunteer for the Stage Managers' Association, the United States Institute for Theatre Technology, and Actors' Equity Association, and belong to the American Guild of Musical Artists as well. During warmer months, you'll also find me paddling any waterway possible.*

I work in multiple genres and have a bit of a reputation for "sure I'll try that." Several years ago, I saw a job posting looking for a local stage manager for a circus/cirque-style production. Had I done circus before? No, but I'd shadowed a friend calling one and had also observed the aerial sequences backstage during *Peter Pan*'s tour. I had definitely worked on shows with large cast sizes (from 57 to 200+ performers), automation with performers in air, and short tech periods. The real truth? I didn't know anyone in town with an appropriate skill set who was available for the show. I took my chance and ultimately landed the job.

What a learning experience and a big leap! I pulled from my resources, especially close friends with circus experience. Someone connected me with a past stage manager for the same company to learn *their* style. She helped me set up a musical theatre-ish script that made sense to my brain (and hers). The company manager had also been a stage manager for them and provided insight. By the time the show closed, I wished I had known more going in, but it was a huge opportunity and more experience for my toolkit.

Several years passed and suddenly my multi-genre worlds collided again. I had flown home Monday, anticipating a relaxing month before heading to my next job. On Thursday, my phone rang unexpectedly from a stage manager I'd known 20+ years. Early in my career, it was he who had recommended a theatre hire me for my first Equity contract. After a few pleasantries and asking about the job I had just finished, he commented, "So you *are* free this weekend?"

An opera company was doing a production in tandem with circus artists, and the contracted stage manager had to pull out due to an emergency. Circus artists were arriving for Sunday's rehearsal, and opera artists would work with them starting Monday. At the time, the Venn diagram intersection of immediately available stage managers who had both opera and circus experience appeared to be … me (I've learned now of another and I'm sure there were more, but I was the one found quickly). Additionally, it was performing within the national park system in a newly erected circus tent. This would not be my first time doing opera in a tent, plus I have "past river guide" in my list of experiences you wouldn't immediately think could relate to stage management. The gig would be a total of nine days, including travel, rehearsal, tech, and four performances. I ultimately said yes, packed my National Parks Passport book, bug repellent clothing, and travel-sized stage management kit for my personal use (especially in a temporary venue), and went for it.

Both opera and circus/cirque may rehearse in short timeframes. Each set of performers arrive with a lot of prep compared to what you might have in theatre. Opera singers are expected to know their music solidly before rehearsals. Circus artists have compiled a whole range of skills to input into another production. However, the length of rehearsal each day is very different between the two genres. Opera singers are generally not amplified; a rehearsal day is scheduled around how much their voices can handle, and they will mark without full voice on 'less important' rehearsals. They may sing full out the first time with the orchestra, for instance, but not for other dress rehearsals. These opera artists were rehearsing a separate opera during the day as well, so hours were very limited. Meanwhile, the circus performers had to learn how to adapt their routines into this new performance space. In addition to fitting in time with new music, think about what they need for rehearsal physically. You can't practice an aerial act in housing. You can't juggle large pink umbrellas in a hotel either. As a result, most of my rehearsals were with the circus artists, with the director scheduling a couple hours each day per act. I was given leeway to not be present for the entire day (long for rehearsal staff, but not each performing act), but the opera people were more used to having a stage manager there the whole time. The pace and atmosphere would shift when the opera singers were brought in, usually at night, and we'd focus on group numbers first, then smaller combos, and finally transitions.

When it came to tech, both groups were a bit used to stitching together various acts into sequence. In opera, you may not get every performer together until the final room run. Stage managers are the ones gathering all the puzzle pieces together and getting everyone on the same page. This was a bit tricky with the logistics of the outdoor tent and lack of audio communication, but we made do. My job also became interpreter/translator between the two genres and the third entity of being outdoors.

The end product was one of the most beautiful things I've worked on, and I'm so proud and honored to have been involved. I will never listen to "Dance of the Hours" from *La Gioconda* again – known familiarly as "Hello Muddah, Hello Fadduh! (A Letter from Camp)" – without picturing lovely cascading pink umbrellas, or the *Pearl Fishers* duet without memories of a hoop diving act. I'm glad my worlds collided for that brief week or so. I can't wait to see where my experiences take me next.

CHAPTER 9

Employment in Dance and Opera

The final chapter, Employment in Dance and Opera, sums up the critical skills required as a stage manager in these art forms and how to market them when job-seeking. We look at applying for work, networking, resume creation, and interviews.

Throughout this book, we've shared specificities of working in dance and opera performance. By creating an awareness of the genre-specific differences in these specialist fields, and sharing tools, tips, and practical considerations, we hope that you have begun to *think* like a stage manager who might thrive in these disciplines. Your foundational knowledge from prior learning, college classes, and lived experience will be your grounding as you incorporate the new knowledge shared in this volume to set you up for success in dance and opera stage management. Opportunities can be limitless if you are open to diverse performance platforms. Your foundational skills along with a shift in your perspective inspired by these chapters could take you to any number of companies, venues, festivals, and opportunities, if you are prepared to trust your instincts and say 'yes' to roles you might not have considered previously.

NETWORKING

Now we look to finding gainful employment. This process includes networking, creating a great first impression, landing a show, and completing your contract in a way that inspires companies to invite you back again and again. So, what is the secret to this type of success? Some might say it's *who* you know as much as *what* you know. That's where networking enters the discussion. Every time you engage in a show, meet someone in the industry, shadow on a production, or send out a resume, you are building a network of people that you might have the opportunity to collaborate with in the future. So, it makes sense to keep colleagues and acquaintances apprised of what you are doing, when you are free for work, and what your aims and goals are.

> Pro Tip: *Networking is more about who knows you than who you know. For example, everyone may know the president, but if they don't know you, they're not in your network.*
>
> – Stacy Taylor, Stage Manager

To help others get to know you, bear in mind all the ways in which you build your network. Of course, each person you meet on a job adds to your network but consider adding other opportunities to engage with folks outside of the work setting. Conferences and industry gatherings such as those offered by USITT (United States Institute for Theatre Technology), SMA (Stage Managers Association), and the Broadway Stage Management Symposium are all places where you can meet new colleagues outside of shows. Now that you are interested in opera and dance, consider including the Opera America or Dance/USA annual conference to your networking opportunities. Additionally, look into shadowing or observing stage managers when dance or opera productions are in your area. Stage managers are, in our opinions, very generous humans; if the company policies allow it, they are often welcoming to an observation. And if company policy does not allow guests backstage, you could ask the stage manager out to coffee to engage in a low-pressure conversation about their work.

If you are actively looking for work, you will no doubt engage in social media groups that highlight such work, like the Facebook groups: Dance Stage Management and Stage Management jobs in Opera. This is also networking. You can use social media to keep up to date with both the *who* and the *what* of each discipline putting you in a great position for industry discussions. Follow tips on best practices and take an opportunity to introduce yourself to the group. Always present yourself in a professional way and be judicial about what you share online or in a group forum. In the end, for better or worse, every online comment or interaction tells this industry network something about you.

RESUMES

So, up until now, you've been checking online posts and social media and perhaps have found an interesting position or opportunity to apply for. What now? First, review the critical skills required in the role of a stage manager in dance or opera, then reimagine how you will present yourself to the hiring team, reframe your resume to suit the role, and, finally, interview for the position and negotiate your contract. This is a critical time for you to show your competency, professionalism, collaborative skills, approachability, and empathy. Don't forget to ask about your duties and responsibilities so there are no surprises.

> *After I took a position as resident stage manager at the Virginia Opera, I found myself casting supers because that task had been done by the previous stage manager. Although that is not a typical stage managerial duty, it was the practice at that company. So, I did it.*
>
> – Michele Kay

If you are reading this book, chances are you already have a standard, one-page resume showcasing your recent credits and sharing details about the creative teams you've worked with. That's great! Keep that resume as a base tool. Now we will craft this into a genre-specific showcase of who you are as an individual and unique stage manager. With many employment options and opportunities out there, you will want to have several versions of the document that showcases the best 'you' in every circumstance. Theatre makers approach this aspect of industry in a variety of ways. Some stage managers update resumes regularly and keep them on-hand, digitally at their fingertips. If this is you, it means that when you are scrolling through online content and happen upon the perfect *next step* in your career, you are ready! Create a company-specific or show-specific cover letter and send out your 'calling card' with confidence.

To make a genre-specific resume, you'll want to highlight relevant credits to show your experience in the discipline. If you have little or no professional experience in opera or dance, then list shows that speak to your understanding of the important competencies associated with these genres. For example, list a musical theatre production to demonstrate that you have called something that relies on musicality, or something that involves vocalists, musicians, bands, or physical theatre, circus, and so on, which may demonstrate size, scale, and adaptability. If you want the project to catch the employer's eye, put it in the top third of your resume; this ensures that they'll see what you think is most important. Research tells us that many reviewers do not move past the first third of the resume if they do not see what they are looking for in a new hire.

In addition to specific productions, you want to highlight skills and competencies that are relevant to the art form. For example, reading music or music comprehension is a critical skill for calling out of score. Working with children is also a skill that comes in handy when working on many operas. Likewise, if you have experience with animals in a production, that can be useful when stage managing a production of Verdi's *Aida*. If you have proficiency or a conversational level skill with a language other than your native language, add that. Both opera and dance often have a mix of performers from a variety of countries. If you can communicate effectively because you spent a year in high school in a study abroad program, then share that important skill. If you don't already have a passport, get one. You want to be prepared if the company announces it is taking the production on an international tour. Likewise, you don't want a passport delay to prevent you from applying for a job. Add "Valid (insert country) passport" to your resume. Also, the company may require a valid driver's license for various reasons, so include that as well. Although not necessary, CPR and first aid certifications are an added bonus for a stage manager, as is mental health first aid training. You can now update your CPR certification for relatively little expense online through the American Red Cross! Many dance companies require that the stage manager knows video recording and simple editing techniques. If you are one of those stage managers, put this under the "Skills" section of your resume. If you are not one of those people, then you may want to consider investing some time in learning the basics through either formal or informal instruction. Uploading videos to an online cloud service is also often a requirement of stage management; familiarize yourself with how to use Vimeo, Dropbox, YouTube, etc. At this point in history, we can assume people know how to use basic document editing software such as word processing and spreadsheets. If you're strapped for space on your resume, you can probably remove these. Finally, we believe that if you have any specialized training in Diversity, Equity, Inclusion, and Belonging, or Intimacy Training from an accredited program, you should highlight that. Again, being able to demonstrate empathy and understanding is critical to successful collaboration in a multicultural environment.

Skills really need to be skills that you will be comfortable performing in service of the production. Be intentional about what you decide to list under special skills. If you have personally taken dance lessons, perhaps include this in your cover letter, but unless you are being hired for this skill, leave it off the resume itself. If it is not a skill you are comfortable demonstrating, then don't add it to your resume until you've had some more practice with it. A piece of advice a production manager friend passed along, "if it is on your resume, and I hire you because of that, you better be able to do it well." Never, ever lie or exaggerate your skill level on a resume. You can always make a note in your cover letter that you are learning a new skill. There is no shame in admitting that you are learning, there is shame in lying on a resume.

> Keep your references current and remember to ask first before listing them on your resume. Also, as a courtesy, apprise them of when you've sent your resume to a company so they know a phone call or email may be coming.

COVER LETTERS AND INTERVIEWS

After you've added opera and/or dance genre specific details to your resume, you want to tailor your cover letter to suit the needs of the position. Look for details in the competencies listed in the advertisement to help you showcase yourself to the employer and add context to what your potential employer will be seeing on the resume. For example, if you're making a move from circus to classical dance, you may want to explain how you believe your experience in one genre will be applicable to the other. Perhaps here you can highlight your role in assuring performers' safety. Or, if you worked with a director on a musical who is now directing an opera with the company, you may want to highlight that, assuming, of course, that you had a great working relationship with that director. Remember, although the cover letter is a great way to provide context for what is presented on your resume, it is also only an introduction. You don't have to explain your life story in the cover letter – keep it brief. Finally, it goes without saying to research the company, the director and designers, and the production before you apply for the position. That research will help you prepare for the interview and may also add focus to what you include in your cover letter.

In our experience, opera and dance interviews are quite similar to what you have probably found when seeking work in other art forms. However, we advise taking some time to reflect upon *why* you would like to add opera and/or dance to your repertoire. Your company research along with your self-reflection will be great resources for you to tap into during the hiring process. Don't be surprised if the director of production asks you about your favorite opera, or why you are transitioning to dance. Your preparation will help you address that question with confidence. Finally, if you do not know something, be candid about that gap and share what you are doing to fill that knowledge gap. Just like on the resume, you *must* be absolutely honest when presenting your skills and abilities.

FINAL THOUGHTS

Dance and opera are steeped in history and tradition, and it is important to recognize that you are becoming a part of that history and tradition. Your input into the documentation and maintenance of a living repertoire will be the legacy you leave with each company you work with. So, make this decision to move into these genres a meaningful one beyond just looking for 'another job.' It will change your attitude in both how you interview and how you approach the work, and maybe even change your career path. We hope this new perspective gives you the confidence to step into these industries. While you are there, be sure to acknowledge the moments of privilege, joy, and satisfaction as you work towards a better understanding and appreciation of these art forms, and your role within them.

Merde & Toi Toi Toi!

Glossary

American Federation of Musicians (AFM)   Union representing more than 80,000 musicians in the United States and Canada.

Assistant staging director   The person who assists the staging director. Often they are a member of the stage management team.

Bel canto   Italian for "beautiful singing" or "beautiful song." Refers to a style of opera that demands vocal dexterity, technique, and beauty.

Bounce, curtain call   Refers to a quick curtain out for an end-of-act company bow.

Bow order   List of the order of curtain calls, end of show.

Castrato / castrati   A male singer who was castrated before their voice changed to maintain the vocal range of a soprano or other higher ranges. Although this vocal demand was popular in the early 1700s, the practice was cruel and became illegal in Italy in 1861, though some castrati still sang in the Sistine Chapel choir in Rome as late as 1903. Hormonal or other non-surgical means such as endocrinological diseases, can also reproduce this vocal quality.

Chair times   Schedule of cast call times for the wig and make-up artists' chair prior to a performance.

Choreographie   A 19th-century publication developed by Raoul Auger Feuillet noting dance execution and notation.

Choreologist   The person whose primary job is to record dance moves or teach a ballet from recorded choreology notes.

Chorus director   The person who teaches the chorus their music, and then maintains the integrity of the choral work throughout the production process.

Classical tutu   A short skirt of layered tulle that flares out to reveal the leg and allow for jumps (pictured in Figure 1.2).

Coda   The final part of a ballet, dance section, or piece of music, commonly used to conclude a pas de deux.

Coloratura   Ornamental vocal music that runs up and down the musical scale. Often includes trills and very rapid progression of notes. *O zittre nicht, mein Lieber Sohn* from Mozart's *The Magic Flute* is among the most famous demonstrations of coloratura.

Company class   The daily physical warm up led by a rehearsal director or coach for dancers prior to a rehearsal or performance.

Comprehensive Cue Sheets   Full list of all cues in the show with the cue placement.

Comprimario role   A role in an opera that is smaller in scope than a principal. They are often named or have a title, like "messenger."

Concert master or concertmaster   This musician is the lead, first violin player in the orchestra.

Corps de ballet   These dancers are members of the ballet company who dance together as a group. This is the entry or first level of dancer in the company.

Coryphee In dance, these dancers are often young artists whose talent is showcased in the corps de ballet. Also known as **second soloists**.

Corridor A stage lighting state that includes a specific lane or pathway, such as a 'downstage corridor' implying that there is isolated light across a downstage path between the left and right wings.

Cover Understudy

Da capo aria Comes from the Italian musical term meaning "from the top" or "from the head." A Da Capo Aria is constructed in three parts, with the first part being repeated as the third part, as in ABA. The third part is often largely embellished by the singer. Da capo arias are found in Baroque opera.

Director of production Commonly used in opera; this is an alternative title for a production manager.

Diva From the Italian meaning "female deity," this term refers to a woman who is celebrated for extraordinary talent. Also, sometimes called the "prima donna" which translates to "first lady."

Divertissement A short dance within a ballet that showcases specific dancers. The section can be a solo or group piece that is not critical to the storyline or plot of the show, but mainly for entertainment.

Double cast Two alternating casts.

Face sheet A document that is a visual who's who in the cast or creative team.

First entrance timings A document containing timings for each character's first entrance point in a show or act.

Front of curtain, curtain call A bow that is taken downstage of the curtain, principal cast members will enter and exit through a paged split in the center of the curtain.

Gesamtkuntswerk From German meaning "total work of art." Often associated with Richard Wagner who elaborated on the idea of unifying all arts, music, design, poetry, and artistic process.

Grand opera Birthed in the 19th century, this form of opera is often performed in four to five acts and is notable for having large casts, orchestras, and opulent design.

IATSE (International Alliance of Theatrical Stage Employees, Motion Picture Technicians, Artists and Allied Crafts) Union representing stagehands in the United States, its Territories, and Canada.

Labanotation or Laban A record of movement for documentation of dance using a series of signs and symbols concentrating on movement in relation to space.

LED center and quarter floor lights Small LED lights that can be set on the floor at the center and quarter tape marks to highlight these positions for dancers' reference, not obvious to the audience.

Leitmotiv From the German meaning "leading motif," this is a short, evocative musical thread often associated with a particular character, place, or theme. Although usually associated with Richard Wagner, a modern version of the leitmotiv is Darth Vader's *Imperial March* composed by John Williams for the film Star Wars.

Light walkers Personnel who walk the stage during lighting sessions so the designer can see what the cues look like as they are created or revised. The cast are not called for this session.

Maestro / maestro Although this term means a virtuoso, or artistic genius, for our purposes, this is the term we use for the conductor of the orchestra for opera or dance.

Marley A vinyl dance flooring that provides a shock-resistant, consistent and non-slip dance surface.

Music librarian This person is responsible for storing and coordinating the music parts for the orchestra.

Onstage bows, curtain call A full stage bow with house curtain out.

Opera buffa Comic opera from the 18th century written to depict everyday people experiencing everyday problems.

Opera seria Italian opera written in the 18th century, these operas depicted tales of heroes and gods and appealed to the nobility.

Operetta A style of storytelling that falls between an opera and a musical. Operettas are often light in tone and humorous.

Oratorio From the Latin for "to pray," an oratorio is a grand musical piece usually performed as a concert, including orchestra, chorus, and principal singers. There may be minimal staging and the plots are sacred or religious in nature, e.g. Handel's *Messiah*.

Orchestra manager This person is responsible for managing and coordinating all aspects of orchestral operations.

Pages to stage/Paging Stage Managers' back of house announcements calling cast, crew, or musicians to the stage.

Partner work Choreography that is created for two dancers who interact.

Pas de deux Is a dance for two people.

Piano technician The person who maintains and tunes the pianos used by the company. They may be employed by the organization or hired as needed.

Pit plot The layout or plan of the orchestra in the orchestra pit. This is usually determined by the conductor.

Place When dancers set onstage in preparation for the start of the music. The term is commonly used for the beginning of a variation.

Pointe shoe Specially designed ballet shoe that was developed to give the dancer the appearance of ethereal weightlessness or flight by enabling the dancer to stand on their toe tips. The shoe has a toe box to encase and provide support for the dancer's toes. The shank, which runs along the bottom of the shoe, serves as a support for the dancer's arch (pictured in Figure 1.2).

Pointe work Classical ballet that is performed on the tips of the toes with feet fully extended while wearing pointe shoes.

Portable ballet barres Dance barres that may be easily set and dismantled or moved.

Principal (in opera) A singer with a titled, main character in the opera.

Principal conductor Term more common to dance companies than maestro.

Principal dancer These are the highest level of dancer in a dance company.

Recitative / 'recit' Is a form of sing-talking, often a monologue or dialogue that is used to further the plot. A recit is not fully sung like an aria or duet. The performer is usually accompanied by a single instrument, such as a harpsichord.

Rehearsal department or Scheduling department Used by many opera companies to coordinate rehearsal schedules, including fittings.

Rehearsal director The person responsible for organizing and running dance rehearsals. They work closely with the choreographic team, coaching dancers and maintaining the integrity of the dance work. Also known as the ballet master or ballet mistress, though this language is being phased out by many companies.

Rehearsal pianist This person plays the piano for all rehearsals. Often, there are several rehearsal pianists employed for one production to be used throughout the rehearsal period.

Release, also known as a Leave of Absence Scheduled time off that is often negotiated as part of an employee's contract.

Repertoire From the Latin "repertorium" meaning list, inventory, catalogue, or repository. A) The roles that a singer has learned and is able to perform, and B) The dances or operas that are regularly performed by an organization.

Repertory From the Latin "repertorium" meaning list, inventory, catalogue, or repository. This refers to the repeated performances of a selection of works or the rotation of the catalogue of being produced by the company.

Repetiteur The person who runs through sections of the dance or music with the performers as they learn the piece.

Romantic tutu Is a longer, softer style of skirt that is bell-shaped and hangs down to the dancer's calf or ankle (Pictured in Figure 1.2).

Rosin Used by dancers to increase friction between their shoe or parts of their shoe such as the tip or heel, and the floor to prevent slipping. It can be in solid form: Rock Rosin to be crushed by the dancers to the preferred consistency, or in powdered form, often called resin.

Rosin box A wooden box containing powdered rosin or rock rosin that can be crushed or ground easily in the box, for dancers' use on pointe shoes.

Schedule of services The contractual schedule for the chorus or orchestra

Score The full sheet music for an opera or ballet.

Sinfonia / symphony Introduced in the 17th century, this is an orchestral piece used as an opener to the opera.

Singspiel German light opera that includes spoken dialogue between songs.

Spotting light A small red light placed at the rear of the house for dancers to use when performing choreography that requires turning. This light is a center, front reference mark.

Staging director "An individual engaged to create and direct the staging for productions according to the design concept as agreed by the EMPLOYER" (language drawn from the Basic Agreement between The American Guild of Musical Artists and The Dallas Opera.)

Supernumeraries or super Cast members in an opera who do not sing and usually do not speak.

Supernumerary captain or Super captain This person is the liaison to the supernumeraries. They may oversee scheduling, staging, or be a repetiteur for the supernumeraries.

Supertitles Either a literal or representative translation of each line of the opera that is broadcast as they are sung for the audience as during the performance.

Tech-specs The onstage and offstage technical specifications of a venue that are sent to a touring production company in advance of them arriving at the venue.

Tempi The pace of the music for the opera or dance as set by the conductor in conjunction with the staging director (opera) or choreographer (dance).

Triple bill   A dance show featuring three separate pieces.

Triple cast   Three alternating casts.

Tristan chord   Opening Richard Wagner's *Tristan und Isolde*, this chord (F, B, D sharp, G sharp), became famous for creating tension without resolution.

Trouser role or pants role   These are male characters performed by a female singer, often from the mezzo-soprano vocal range. These roles were originally written for the castrati singers in the 17th/18th centuries, though some were written to be performed by female singers.

Tutu   The skirt portion of a ballet dancer's costume. Often worn with a bodice. Classical tutus are short and stiff, projecting horizontally from the hip, like a plate. There are variations of the short stiff tutu including the pancake which is flat and with few ruffles, and the platter which sits at the waist and has more ruffles than the pancake. Romantic tutus, on the other hand, are softer and longer ending between the calf and ankle.

Union steward   This is a union member who is responsible for monitoring compliance with the rules from the collectively bargained agreement between the union and the organization. You will often find a union steward when working with IATSE and American Federation of Musicians.

Variation   A choreographed section of dance that includes a change or adaptation, usually derived from the first part, repeating some of the phrases. For example, in a grand pas de deux, the couple will dance together, then there will be a variation for a female solo, and a variation for a male solo, the couple then comes together again for the coda, completing the pas de deux. The term variation is synonymous with solo in this context.

Verisimo   Italian for "realism," depicting operas not of kings and gods, but of average people addressing their problems

Vide   Latin for "see or refer to." Used to designate a cut in the music.

Vocal coach   A person who works privately with a singer as they learn the music for an opera. Often an opera company will employ a vocal coach to work with singers from young artist programs, covers, or others at the request of the conductor.

Appendices

PRODUCTION AND ARCHIVAL CREDITS

COVER PHOTO

The Nutcracker
November 17–December 10, 2023
West Australian Ballet with West Australian Philharmonic Orchestra
Venue: His Majesty's Theatre, Perth, Western Australia
Choreographers: Jayne Smeulders, Sandy Delasalle-Scannella, Aurélien Scannella
Set Designer: Phil R. Daniels
Costume Designer: Charles Cusick Smith
Lighting Designer: Jon Buswell
Associate Lighting Designer: Mick Rippon
Production Stage Manager: Hugo Aguilar Lopez
Composer: Pyotr Ilyich Tchaikovsky
Musical Arranger: Michael Brett
Principal Conductor: Jessica Gethin

DANCE PRODUCTIONS

Coppélia
1998, 1999, 2000
West Australian Ballet with West Australian Symphony Orchestra
Venue: His Majesty's Theatre, Perth, Western Australia
Choreographer: Chrissie Parrott AO
Costume Designer: Deborah McKendrick
Lighting Designer: Kenneth Rayner
Set Designer: Andrew Carter
Stage Manager: Sue Fenty (1999, 2000)
Stage Manager: Terasa Staltari (1998)
Music: Leo Delibes
Conductor: Nicolette Fraillon

Goldberg Variations
September 09–24, 2022
West Australian Ballet with West Australian Symphony Orchestra
Venue: His Majesty's Theatre, Perth, Western Australia
Choreographer: Natalie Weir
Set and Costume Designer: Bruce McKinven
Lighting Designer: Matthew Marshall
Stage Manager: Hugo Aguilar Lopez
Music: Johann Sebastian Bach
Music Arranger: Bernard Labadie

The Helix Project
2014
The Heath Ledger Theatre at the State Theatre Centre of Western Australia
Choreographic Team: Barry Moreland and Darryl Brandwood
Lighting Designer: Jon Buswell
Film/Cinematography: Ian Batt
Stage Manager: Sue Fenty

La Bohème
May 21–June 5, 2004
West Australian Ballet with West Australian Symphony Orchestra
Venue: His Majesty's Theatre, Perth, Western Australia
Choreographer: Simon Dow
Costume Designer: Anna French
Lighting Designer: John Buswell
Set Designer: Andrew Carter
Stage Manager: Sue Fenty
Music: Giacomo Puccini
Music Arranger: Kevin Hocking
Musical Director: Dobbs Franks

Romeo and Juliet
September, 2014
Dances Patrelle
Choreographer: Francis Patrelle
Lighting Design: David Grill
Stage Manager: Betsy Ayer

Sanggar Paripurna: Anniversary Gala Event

2023

Sanggar Paripurna

Segment Director: I Made Sidia

Choreographic team: I Made Sidia, I Wayan Budiarsa, Ari Sidiastini

Stage Manager: Sue Fenty

OPERA PRODUCTIONS

Carmen

July 17–25, 2004

Music: Georges Bizet

Libretto: Ludovic Halévy and Henri Meihac

Venue: Cincinnati Opera

Conductor: Stéphane Denève

Staging Director: James Robinson

Stage Manager: Michele Kay

Costume Designer: James Schuette

Lighting Designer: Mimi Jordan Sherin

Set Designer: Allen Moyer

Wig Master: James Geier

Daughter of the Regiment

June 17–19, 2024

Music: Gaetano Donizetti

Libretto: Jules-Henri Vernoi de Saint-Georges and Jean-François Bayard

Venue: Cincinnati Opera

Conductor: Christopher Larkin

Staging Director: Dorothy Danner

Stage Manager: Michele Kay

Costume Coordinator: Reba Senske

Lighting Designer: Thomas C. Hase

Set Designer: Boyd Ostroff

Wig Master: James Geier

Dialogue of the Carmelites
November 18–20, 2022
Music and Libretto: Francis Poulenc
Venue: University of Cincinnati, College-Conservatory of Music
Conductor: Christopher Larkin
Staging Director: Robin Guarino
Stage Manager: Rosie Burns Pavlik
Costume Coordinator: Iris Harmon
Lighting Designer: Alaina Pizzoferrato
Media Designer: Jessica Drayton
Set Designer: Mark Halpin

La Bohème
April 25–May 20, 2003
Music: Giacomo Puccini
Libretto: Giuseppe Giacosa and Luigi Illica
Venue: Virginia Opera
Conductor: Dan Saunders
Staging Director: Bernard Uzan
Stage Manager: Michele Kay
Costume Coordinator: Pat Seyller
Lighting Designer: John Hoey
Set Designer: Charles Allen Klein
Wig and Makeup Designer: Steven Bryant

Lucia di Lammermoor
June 22–24, 2023
Music: Gaetano Donizetti
Libretto: Salvadore Cammarano
Venue: Cincinnati Opera
Conductor: Renato Balsadonna
Staging Director: Jose Maria Condemi
Stage Manager: Hannah Holthaus
Costume and Scenic Designer: Philip Witcomb
Lighting Designer: Thomas C. Hase
Wig and Makeup Designer: James Geier

Madame Butterfly
July 22–29, 2023
Music: Giacomo Puccini
Libretto: Giuseppe Giacosa and Luigi Illica
Venue: Cincinnati Opera
Conductor: Keitaro Harada
Staging Director: Matthew Ozawa
Stage Manager: Hannah Holthaus
Costume Designer: Maiko Matsushimi
Lighting Designer: Yuki Nakase Link
Set Designer: dots
Wig Master: James Geier

MUSEUM OF PERFORMING ARTS ARCHIVAL COSTUME PIECES AND CREDITS

FIGURES 1.2 AND 1.3

Costume selection: Ivan King AO, Historian and Curator and Neil Sheriff, Collections and Engagement Officer

Set up, display and object handling: Neil Sheriff, Collections and Engagement Officer

Venue: His Majesty's Theatre, Perth, Western Australia

FIGURE 1.2

Left:

Borovansky Ballet

1953 – Corps de Ballet costume for *Coppélia* (Léo Delibes)

It was the last commission for Borovansky Ballet prior to becoming The Australian Ballet

This is an appropriate reproduction of what could be classed as a Romantic tutu

Right:

The Australian Ballet

Classical tutu created for the role of Aurora in *The Sleeping Beauty*, Act I (Pyotr Ilyich Tchaikovsky)

Designer: Kenneth Rowell

1973 – worn by Lucette Aldous AO, at the Sydney Opera House

Right, Front:

Pointe shoes (signed) worn by Dame Margot Fonteyn in Australia, 1974

FIGURE 1.3

Ballets Russes

Costumes from *The Firebird Suite* (Igor Stravinsky)

Designer: Natalia Goncharova

Produced in Covent Garden (1929) for the Australian tour

Index

Academie Royale de Danse 8
accessing production documents 51–52
actors 26
Adamo, Mark 7
Adams, John 7
administration 22, 28–29
AGMA *see* American Guild of Musical Artists
AGVA *see* American Guild of Variety Artists
Aida 161
Aida (1871) 5
Ailey, Alvin 13
Akhnaten (1983) 7
Alcina 4
Aldous, Lucette 10
Alfano, Franco 6
American dance history 8
American Federation of Musicians (AFM) 30, 110–111
American Guild of Musical Artists (AGMA) 24, 27, 29–30; contracts 67; opera rehearsals (in studio) 86–87
American Guild of Variety Artists (AGVA) 30
American opera 7
Anthony, Mary 12
Appia, Adolphe 13
archival videos 40–41, 51–52
archiving productions 146–147
arias, Da capo aria 3
Ariodante 4
arriving at the venue, touring dance 159–160
artists, dancers 27
Arvey, Verna 6
assistant conductors 24
assistant stage managers 116
assistant staging directors 24
audio playback programs 74
Ayer, Betsy 127, 142, 159, 176–179

back of house areas 160
Balanchine, George 12
ballet 8–10; costumes 10
ballet d'action 9
ballet master/mistress 23
Ballet Russes 9–12

banda 111
Bangarra Dance Theatre 175–176
Barber of Seville 26
Baroque period 3–4
barres 62; portable ballet barres 118
bass 25
bass-baritone 25
Beginners 131
Bel canto 4
bel canto style 5
Bellini, Vincenzo 4
Benesh, Joan 15–16
Benesh, Rudolf 15–16
Benesh system 15–15
Benoit, Alexandre 11
Binder, Christine A. 14
Binkley, Howell 15
Bizet, George 5
Blanchard, Terence 7
block and blade 17
blocking, birds-eye view 16
blocking notation 16; dance blocking cue sheets 56; dance movements 75–77; football blocking sheets 54–55; longhand/spreadsheet blocking 57–58; opera blocking 58–60; score backing pages 55–56
Bolcom, William 7
Bologne, Joseph 4
booking cues 101; dance technical rehearsals 118
Borovansky Ballet, *Coppelia* (1953) 10
bounce 107
Boundy, Fiona 58, 147
Bow Order 103, 107–110; *Coppelia* 132–133
Britten, Benjamin 6

Caccini, Francesca 3
Cage, John 13
call sheets 51
call times, opera 96
Callas, Maria 26
calling 36, 129
calling book 37
calling desk 131
calling document: *Coppélia* 131; *Romeo and Juliet* 130; *see also* SM Score

calling position 128–129
calling score, opera technical rehearsals 101–102
calling titles 115
Carmen 197; Bow Order 109; Top of Show Sequence 104–106
Carmen (1875) 5
Casa Ricordi publishing house 6
castrato singers 3
cast-related items, opera-specific paperwork 48
Cavalleria Rusticana 6, 154
"Cav/Pag" 154
CBA *see* collectively bargained agreement
center mark 117; LED center floor lights 118
Cernovitch, Nicola 15
chair times, opera 96–97
Champion (2013) 7
character artists 27
children 26–27
choreographers 22–23, 73; Modern Dance 12–13
Choreographie 9
choreologist 23
choreology 15–16
chorus 26–27; Schedule of Services 65, 85
chorus directors 23–24
Christmas Spectacular, Radio City Music Hall 171–174
Christofer, Michael 7
Cincinnati Opera 7
Classical period 4; ballet 10
classical tutu 10
Cloudless 177
codas 56
Cold Mountain (2015) 7
collaborating in dance rehearsals (in studio) 77–79
collectively bargained agreement (CBA) 30
color schemes, taping floors 63
coloratura 4
coloratura mezzo 26
coloratura soprano 26
coloratura tenors 25
combining information from SM score and videos 43–44
comic opera 4
comms 134
communication: dance-specific communication channels 31–32; external communication channels 32; internal communication channels 30–31; production-related pauses 148–151
community engagement 28
company class 73, 145

company manager 28
Comprehensive Cue Sheet 101–102
comprehensive run sheet 80, 140
comprimario role 26
concert masters 25, 106
conductor cue light system 117
Conductor Video Monitor 111
conductors 22
conferences, networking 184
consent-based work, dance rehearsals (in studio) 81–84
contemporary American Opera 7
Contemporary Dance, lighting 13–15
contralto 26
Copland, Aaron 6
Coppélia 195; Bow Order 132–133; calling document 131; dance blocking cue sheets 123
Coppélia (1953) 10, 57
Coppélia (Leo Delibes, 1870) 9
co-productions, operas 161–162
corps de ballet 27
corridors 76, 119
coryphee 27
Cosi fan tutte (1789) 4
Costume Check-in document 97–98
costume paperwork 44–46
Costume Preset 97
costumes: ballet 9–10; Ballet Russes 10–11
countertenors 25
court dances 8–9
Covent Garden Theatre 4
cover letters 186–187
creative teams 22–24
crew duties, adding to Who What Where 87–89
cueing performers, opera technical rehearsals 99–110
cueing singers onto stage 89–92
cues: booking 101; dance 17; *see also* booking cues
Cunningham, Merce 13
Cuomo, Douglas 7

Dafne (1598) 3
daily schedules 51
dance 8; ballet 8–12; Contemporary Dance 13–15; intimacy 81–84; Modern Dance 12–13; notation 15–17; repertoire 154–155; stage managing, 17–18; *see also* touring dance
dance blocking 16; cue sheets 56; for lighting 119–123; sample 121; sheets 53–58; symbols sheet 78
Dance Kaleidoscope, technical rider 163–166
dance lighting plot 14
dance movements, notating 75–77
The Dance of the Hours 27

dance production analysis 53
dance rehearsal spaces, preparing 61–62
dance rehearsals (in studio) 71–72; attending 72–75; collaborating in 77–79; consent-based work 81–84; notating dance movements 75–77; show documentation 79–80
dance technical rehearsals: booking cues 118; dance blocking cue sheets for lighting 119–123; dress rehearsals 130–136; introductions 123–125; paperwork 129; setting light levels 118–119; stage rehearsals 125–127; stage safety 123–125; technical rehearsals 128–129; transitioning to the stage 116–118
dancers 161; levels of 27; in opera 27; unions 27
dance-specific documents 49; accessing production documents 51–52; archival videos and analysis 52–53; dance blocking sheets 53–58; scheduling your workday and gathering information 50
Dance/USA annual conference 184
dark day 115
Das Rheingold (1869) 5
Daughter of the Regiment 197
Da capo aria 3
de Saint-George, Chevalier 4
de Toulouse, Michel 17
Dead Man Walking (2000) 7
The Death of Klinghoffer (1991) 7
Debussy, Clause 6
Dedreu, Nykol 169–171
Delibes, Leo 5
De'Medici, Ferdinando 3
DeMilles, Agnes 12
Denishawn school (Los Angeles) 12
Der Ring des Nibelungen (1848) 5
development/philanthropy 28
Diaghilev, Serge 9–12
Dialogue of the Carmelites 198
Die Fledermaus 27
Die Walküre (1870) 5
Die Zauberflöte / The Magic Flute (1786) 4
director of production 25, 29
disclaimer speech 137
divas 3
divertissements 56
document design, creating stage manager's score 42
Don Quixote 121
Donizetti, Gaetano 4
double cast 115, 145
Doubt (2013) 7
Dr. Atomic (2005) 7
dramatic vocal parts: baritone 25; mezzo 26; soprano 26; tenors 25

dress rehearsals 95–96, 137–139; dance technical rehearsals 130–136; for opera 112; *see also* opera technical rehearsals
dressing rooms 62, 116; show feed 128
Dry Tech 118
Dudley, Jane 12
Duncan, Isadora 12
Dunham, Katherine 13

education departments 28
Einstein on the Beach (1975) 7
emergency stops 147–148
employment: cover letters 186–187; interviews 186–187; networking 183–184; resumes 184–186

face sheet 48, 142
Facebook groups 184
Falstaff (1893) 5
Fellow Travelers (2013) 7
Fenty, Sue 14, 157
Feuillet, Raoul Auger 9, 17
Fillion, Carl 5
final dress rehearsal 137–139
Fire Dance 12
The Firebird Suite 11
first aid: for rehearsal spaces 64–65; touring dance 158
First Entrance Timings 44, 96–97
first soloists 27
flooring 61–62; orchestra carpeting 111; taping 62–64; touring dance 160; *see also* taping floors
flowers, opening-night protocols 143
Floyd, Carlyle 7
Fluty, Kristina 81, 83
FOH information sheet 135
follow spots 122–123
Fonteyn, Margot 10
football blocking sheets 54–55
Franko, Mark 16
French Revolution 4
front of curtain bows 107
Fuller, Loie 12

Galileo Galilei (2002) 7
general rehearsal 137
Gershwin, George 6
"Gesamtkuntswerk" 5
Gianni Schicchi 154
Gianni Schicchi (1918) 6
Girl of the Golden West (2017) 7
Giselle (Adolphe Adam 1842) 9
Glass, Philip 7
Goldberg Variations 196
Gordon, Ricky Ian 7
Götterdämmerung (1874) 5
Graham, Martha 12, 14
grand opera 5

The Great Gatsby (1999) 7
Grubbs, Connie 92

Handel Frederick 4
Hansel and Gretel 26
happy and healthy calls 115, 145
harpsichords 61
Hawkins, Erick 13
health and wellness 28
Heggie, Jack 7
heldentenors 25
The Helix Project 196
Higdon, Jennifer 7
history of opera 2–6
Hoffman, William 7
Holm, Hanya 13
Horton, Lester 12
house handover/open 138
house opening protocols 141
Hughes, Langston 6
Humphrey, Doris 12

IATSE *see* International Alliance of Theatrical Stage Employees
IC *see* intimacy coordinators
Idomeneo (1781) 4
Il Barbiere di Siviglia/ The Barber of Seville (1815) 4
Il Pagliacci 6
Il Tabarro (1918) 6
Il Trovatore (1853) 5
Ingalls, James F. 15
Intermission Sequence 103, 105–107
International Alliance of Theatrical Stage Employees (IATSE) 30
interviews for employment 186–187
intimacy: facilitator 81; Professional, coordinator (IC) 81; rehearsals 81–84
Intimate Apparel (2016) 7
invited dress rehearsal 137
Italian opera 5
Italian overture 3
Italian Renaissance, ballet 8–9

Janacek, Léon 6
Joplin, Scott 6

Katz, Natasha 15
Kaufmann, Sandra 12, 75–76, 128, 160–161
Kay, Michele 22, 46, 59, 145, 184
Kinetic Light 169–171
Kinetography Laban 15, 75

La Bohème 6, 45, 96, 104–105, 145–146, 196, 198; Top of Show Sequence 107; dance score with backing page 55
La Clemenza di Tito (1791) 4
La Fanciulla del West (1910) 6
La Gionconda 27

La liberazione di Ruggiero dall'isola d'Alcina (1625) 3
La Rondine (1917) 6
La Sylphide 9
La Traviata 154
La Traviata (1853) 5
Laban, Rudolf 15
Labanotation 15, 75
Lakmè (1883) 5
L'amant anonyme (1780) 4
Laron, Libby 7
Larson, Jonathan 6
Le Nozze di Figaro / The Marriage of Figaro (1786) 4
Leitmotiv 5
Leoncavallo, Ruggero 6
Lepage, Robert 5
Lien, Mimi 178
light cueing sessions 113–114
light walkers 113, 118–119
lighting: conductor cue light system 117; Contemporary Dance 13–15; with dance blocking sheets 119–123; dance rehearsals (in studio) 79; LED center and quarter floor lights 117; opera rehearsals 85; opera technical rehearsals 112; setting light levels 118–119; spotting light 117
Lily 12
Limon, José 13
Little Women (1998) 7
lockout period 135
Lohengrin (1848) 5
longhand/spreadsheet blocking, dance 57–58
Lopez, Hugo Aguilar 80
Lord-Sole, Craig 51, 75–76
Lozoff, Sarah 81–83
Lucia di Lammermoor 114, 198
Lully, Jean-Baptiste 8–9
lyric vocal parts: baritone 25; mezzo 26; soprano 26; tenor 25

"The Machine" 5
Madame Butterfly (1904) 6
Madame Butterfly (2023) 199
Maestro Cue Sheet 110–111
maestro/maestra 22
maintaining shows 144–146
Manon (1884) 5
Manon Lescaut (1893) 6
marking, performer 115
Marley 61, 64, 117, 158, 177
Marshall, Susan 178
Mascagni, Pietro 6
Maslow, Sophie 12
massage 62; masseur 116, 157, 160, 162; physical therapy 162; therapist 28, 62
Massenet, Jules 5
Matisse, Henri 11

McCandless, Stanley 13–14
meeting the team, pre-production 33–34
Messiah (1742) 4
Metropolitan Opera 5, 115, 154
Meyerbeer, Giacomo 5
mezzo-soprano 26
MGM movies, ballet 12
Micich, Danielle 81, 83
Mignon (1866) 5
mirrors 61–62
Moby Dick (2010) 7
Modern Dance 12–13
Monteverdi, Claudio 3
Morning Star (2015) 7
Mozart, Wolfgang Amadeus 4
Murray, Samantha 81, 84
Musgrave, Thea 6
music: dance technical rehearsals 125; pre-production 35–36; for rehearsals 74
music director 22
music librarians 24
music rehearsals, opera 85–86

Nabucco (1841) 5
nametags 48, 85–86
narrative ballet *see* story ballet
Neoclassical era, Ballet Russes 11
networking to find employment 183–184
neutral body 82
New Dance Group (New York City) 12
New York City Ballet 12
New York City Opera 6
Ney, Christy 92, 100, 107
Nijinsky, Vaslav 9
Nixon in China (1987) 7
notating blocking: dance blocking cue sheets 56; football blocking sheets 54–55; longhand/spreadsheet blocking 57–58; opera blocking 58–60; score backing pages 55–56
notating dance movements 75–77
Nottage, Lynn 7
Noverre, Jean Georges 9
The Nutcracker 9, 155, 195

Of Mice and Men (1969) 7
on road rehearsals, touring dance 160–161
onstage bow 107
open final dress rehearsal 137, 138
openings: paperwork 140–141; preparing for 139–140; schedules and formalities 141–142; stage-related opening night protocols 142–144
opera: co-productions 161–162; history of 2–6
Opera America 184
opera blocking 58–60
opera buffa 4

opera casting 25–27
opera daily call 68–69
Opera Fusion: New Works 7
opera publishers 36
opera rehearsal spaces, preparing 60–61
opera rehearsals (in studio) 84–92; final room run 93; music rehearsals 85–86; paperwork 87–89; running the room 89–92; staging rehearsals 86–87
opera repertoire 154
opera scheduling 65–66; opera daily call 68–69; Show Calendar 66–68
opera seria 4–5
opera singers 145–146
opera technical rehearsals 95–96; orchestra 110–112; paging and cueing performers 99–110; paperwork 96–99; scheduling 112–115; supporting performers 115–116
opera-specific paperwork: cast-related items 48; costume paperwork 44–46; props and scenic paperwork 46–47; Who What Where 42–44
operetta style operas 37
oratorios 4
orchestra: bows 109; opera readings sitzprobe, wandleprobe, and dress rehearsals 113; setting up 110–112
orchestra dresses 114
orchestra managers 25, 107
Orfeo (1607) 3
organizational structures 22; administration 28–29; creative teams 22–24; opera casting 25–27; performers 24–25; production personnel 28–29
Otello (1887) 5

packing the truck, touring dance 159
page to stage 87
paging performers: gendered 87, 100; opera technical rehearsals 99–110
Pagliacci 154
pants roles 26
paperwork: dance technical rehearsals 129; openings 140–141; opera technical rehearsals 96–99; touring dance 157–158
Parade 11
Paris Opéra Ballet 8–10
Paris Opera 5
partner work 129
pas de deux 76
Pavlova, Anna 9
Peri, Jacopo 3
pianists 24
piano dresses 112, 114
piano score 35
piano tech 24, 112–114, 115
pianos 60–61, 85

Picasso, Pablo 11
Pierce, Greg 7
Pit Plot 111
Pittelman, Nancy 60, 140, 171–174
'Places' 131
placing call 125, 127
pointe shoes 8–10
pointe work 9
Ponchelli, Amilcare 27
Porgy and Bess (1935) 6
portable ballet barres 118
post-Romantic period 6
pre-production 33; building a working score 36–40; creating stage manager's score 40–41; dance-specific documents 49–58; getting started 35; meeting the team 33–34; music 35–36; opera blocking 58–60; opera scheduling 65–69; opera-specific paperwork 42–48; preparing the rehearsal venue 60–65; watching archival videos 40–41
pre-show activity 139–140
pre-tour rehearsals 158
previews 137–139
Primus, Pearl 13
principal conductor 22
principal dancers 27
principals 26
production desk 128
production manager 29, 31
production personnel 28–29
production team 28–29
production-related pauses 148–151
prompt corner 131
pronoun preferences 87
props and scenic paperwork 46–47
Puccini, Giacomo 6

QR codes 48–49
quarter marks 63; LED quarter floor lights 118
Queen's Theatre at Haymarket 4

Radio City Music Hall 14, 30, 171
Radio City Rockettes 171–174
Realism 6
recitative 4
reel-to-reel audio media 17–18
rehearsal, creative team 23
rehearsal director 23, 116
rehearsal music 74
rehearsal pianist 24
rehearsal reports 81
rehearsal schedules 71
rehearsal venues: dance rehearsal spaces 61–62; opera rehearsal spaces 60–61; preparing 60–65; taping floors 62–64
rehearsal/scheduling department 29
rehearsal directors 127

rehearsals *see* dance rehearsals (in studio); dance technical rehearsals; pre-tour rehearsals; opera rehearsals (in studio); opera technical rehearsals
release 34
Renaissance tablature 16
Rent (1996) 6
repertoire 25–26, 146, 153–155
repertory 153
repetiteurs 23
resumes 184–186
Rhythm Bath 177–179
Ricordi, Giulio 6
Rigoletto (1851) 5
Rimsky-Korsakov, Nicolai 11
"Ring Cycle" 5
Rinuccini, Ottavio 3
Rivera, Isabel Martinez 30, 162, 167–169
Rockettes 30, 171–174
Romantic period 5; ballet 8–10
Romantic tutu 9–10
Romanticism 4
Romeo and Juliet 130, 197
Rosenthal, Jean 14
rosin boxes 118
Rossini, Gioacchino 4
Rossini tenors 25
The Royal Ballet 4
Royal Opera House 4
The Royal Opera 4
running the room, opera technical rehearsals 112–115

Satyagraha (1979) 7
Scarlatti, Alessandro 3
Scène Éthique in Montreal 5
Schedule of Services 65, 68, 85
scheduling 29; dance-specific documents 50; opera technical rehearsals 112–115
Scheherazade 11
School of American Ballet 12
score 35; building 36–40; creating stage manager's score 40–41; reading 36; *see also* music
score backing pages 55–56
score reference cheat sheet 50, 126
second casts 144
second company 27
second soloists 27
Sellars, Peter 7
senior artists 27
setting light levels, dance technical rehearsals 118–119
Shanley, John Patrick 7
Shawn, Ted 12
Sheherazade 155
Show Calendar, opera scheduling 66–68
show control system 172

show documentation, dance rehearsals (in studio) 79–80
show feed 128
show report 130–139
show running time 138
show stops 149; emergency stops 147–148; production-related pauses 148–151
show timings 139
side lighting 14–15
Siegfried (1871) 5
sign-in sheets 48–49, 147–148
sinfonia 3
singspiel 4
sitzprobe 112
Skelton, Thomas R. 15
Sleeping Beauty 155
The Sleeping Beauty (Tchaikovsky 1889) 9
The Sleeping Beauty (Sydney Opera House, 1973) 10
SM Digital Call sample 58
SM digital cue sheets 34
SM Score 34–36; opera blocking 59–60; timings 41
SMA *see* Stage Managers Association
Smyth, Ethel 6
Sokolow, Anna 12
soloists 27
soprano 26
SOPs *see* standard operating procedures
spacing calls 125
Spears, Gregory 7
spotting light 117
St Denis, Ruth 12
stage hands, unions 67
Stage Management Jobs in Opera 184
Stage Managers Association (SMA) 184
stage rehearsals, dance technical rehearsals 125–127
stage safety, dance technical rehearsals 123–125
stage-related opening night protocols 142–144
staging directors 22–23
staging rehearsals, opera 86–87
standard operating procedures (SOPs) emergency stops 147
Still, William Grant 6
stopping a show *see* show stops
story ballet 36
Strauss, Johann 27
Strauss, Richard 6
Stravinsky, Igor 6, 11
studio floors, dance 61
studio rehearsals: dance rehearsals 71–84; opera rehearsals 84–92
Suor Angelica (1918) 6
super captains 24
supernumeraries (supers) 26

supertitles/surtitles operator or team 29, 114–115
support team for performers 28
supporting performers: opening-night protocols 142–144; opera technical rehearsals 115–116
Susan Marshall & Company 177–178
Swan Lake (Tchikovsky 1876) 9
Swank, Erin Joy 179–181
symphony 3

Tannhäuser (1845) 5
taping floors 62–64, 116–117; glo tape 127
Taylor, Paul 13
Taylor, Stacy 184
Tchaikovsky 9
tech table 128
technical rehearsals: dance *see* dance technical rehearsals; opera technical rehearsals *see* opera technical rehearsals; touring dance 161
technical rider, for Dance Kaleidoscope 163–166
technical specifications (tech-specs) 158
temperature of stage 126–127
tempi 24
The Tenderland (1954) 6
tenors 25
Tharp, Twyla 13
Thomas, Ambroise 5
timings, creating stage manager's score 41
Tipping, Molly 81, 82
Tipton, Jennifer 15
titles, calling 115
Top of Show Sequence 103–108, 110
Top of Show Tango 104
Tosca (1900) 6
tour books 157
tour managers 155
tour pack 157
tour packing lists 158
touring dance 155–156; arriving at the venue 159–160; final checks 159; flooring 160; packing the truck 159; paperwork 157–158; preparing for 156–157; pre-tour rehearsals 158; on road rehearsals 160–161; technical rehearsals 161
touring paperwork 157–158
touring staff 155
touring stage management 162
Train Schedule 114
transfers, operas 161–162
transitioning to the stage, dance technical rehearsals 116–118
Treemonisha (1911) 6
triple bill 128, 154
Tristan and Isolde (1859) 5

Tristan Chord 5
The Trocks 168
Troubled Island 6
trouser roles 26
Turandot (1926) 6
The Turn of the Screw 27
tutus 9–10

U, Lillian Hannah 174–176
Un Ballo in Maschera (1859) 5
union stewards 24–25
unions 29–30; American Federation of Musicians (AFM) 30, 110–111; American Guild of Musical Artists (AGMA) 24, 27, 29–30; contracts 67; dancers 27; International Alliance of Theatrical Stage Employees 30; United Federation of Musicians union 24
United Federation of Musicians union 24
United States Institute for Theatre Technology (USITT) 184
University of Cincinnati, College-Conservatory of Music 7
USITT *see* United States Institute for Theatre Technology

Verdi, Giuseppe 5
verismo 6
vide 37
A View from the Bridge (1999) 7
vocal coaches 23
vocal ranges 25–26
vocal rest 115
VOG mic 118

Wagner, Richard 5
wandelprobe 112
Wardrobe Running Plot 97–98
water, for dance rehearsal spaces 64
Weidman, Charles 12
Werther (1892) 5
Western opera 3–5
Whitlock, Evangeline Rose 36, 76
Who What Where 42–43, 95, 102, 103, 140; combining information from SM score and videos 43–44; costume paperwork 44–46; dance 53; First Entrance Timings 44; opera rehearsals (in studio) 87–89; props and scenic paperwork 47
Wigman, Mary 12
Wilson, Robert 7
work visas 28
A Wrinkle in Time (1962, 1991) 7

young artists programs 27

Zimmerman, Mary 7

For Product Safety Concerns and Information please contact our EU representative GPSR@taylorandfrancis.com
Taylor & Francis Verlag GmbH, Kaufingerstraße 24, 80331 München, Germany

www.ingramcontent.com/pod-product-compliance
Lightning Source LLC
Chambersburg PA
CBHW081809300426
44116CB00014B/2295